iMac™
fast&easy™

Jan L. Harrington
with
Bryan Walls

PRIMA TECH

A DIVISION OF PRIMA PUBLISHING

A Division of Prima Publishing

Prima Publishing and colophon are registered trademarks of Prima Communications, Inc. PRIMA TECH and Fast & Easy are trademarks of Prima Communications, Inc., Rocklin, California 95677.

Publisher: Stacy L. Hiquet
Associate Publisher: Nancy Stevenson
Marketing Manager: Judi Taylor
Managing Editor: Dan J. Foster
Senior Acquisitions Editor: Deborah F. Abshier
Project Editor: Rebecca I. Fong
Assistant Project Editor: Estelle Manticas
Editorial Assistant: Brian Thomasson
Technical Reviewer: Mark E. Loper
Copy Editor: Judy Ohm
Interior Design and Layout: Marian Hartsough Associates
Cover Design: Prima Design Team
Indexer: Katherine Stimson

ISBN: 0-7615-1985-8
Library of Congress Catalog Card Number: 98-68770
Printed in the United States of America

99 00 01 02 03 DD 10 9 8 7 6 5 4 3 2

To my pets
(from oldest to youngest)
Max, Casper, Timothy, Katie, Lillith, and Sam.
I know it's silly, but they've kept me sane
through a lot and I owe them one.

Acknowledgments

Many thanks to the people at Prima Tech who worked on this book. Thank you for all the time you gave and for your assistance.

To Dan Foster and Debbie Abshier for the opportunity to write this book and for supporting the Mac platform. Special thanks to Mark Loper for his technical expertise and for making sure this book stayed true to the Mac. Thanks to Judy Ohm for her attention to detail and to Marian Hartsough for an excellent layout design plus the added contribution of her own iMac knowledge. And finally, thank you to Rebecca Fong for managing this book through the entire editorial process.

About the Author

Jan L. Harrington, Ph.D., has been working with and writing about the Macintosh since March, 1984. The author of more than 25 computer-related books, she is also a full-time faculty member of the Department of Computer Science and Information Systems at Marist College. Dr. Harrington is committed to helping Macintosh users get the most from their investment in hardware and software.

Contents at a Glance

Contents

Introduction

Prima Publishing's *Fast & Easy* guides are a highly visual way to get started quickly with computer-related subjects. Using clear directions with illustrations of each step, this series makes it clear how to do tasks without the confusion of long text descriptions or the frustration of trying to "make do" with online documentation. *iMac Fast & Easy* is an introduction to Apple Computer's new personal computer, the iMac.

Who Should Read This Book?

This book is intended for first-time computer users and for converts to the Macintosh from the Windows world. Those moving up to the iMac from an older Macintosh will also enjoy new features and find the step-by-step approach helpful.

This book has been designed specifically for the iMac. The illustrations in this guide will accurately represent what you see on the screen, and all software that is discussed is already included in the iMac package.

Special Features of This Book

Besides the detailed descriptions of useful tasks, this book also includes:

- **Tips**. These shortcuts, features, and hints help make your iMac experience even more productive and fun.

- **Notes**. These give background, additional information, or further ideas on how to use various features.

Remember, as the Apple slogan says, "Think different." Have fun with this book and with your iMac!

PART I

iMac Basics

1

Anatomy of an iMac

If this is your first new computer, you'll probably want to get it set up and running as fast as you can, and this chapter will help you do exactly that. In this chapter, you'll learn how to:

- Unpack your iMac and plug in the parts
- Understand the parts of the computer
- Identify the two major types of software used on a computer
- Understand the Desktop and how it represents parts of the computer

Unpacking Your iMac

Besides being stylish, very fast, and quite reasonably priced, the iMac is one of the easiest computers to set up. In fact, the Welcome to Your iMac trifold packed in the iMac's box has very few steps.

1. **Lift out** the **cardboard accessory box** including the piece of Styrofoam, and set it aside.

2. Carefully **lift** the **iMac** out of its box and take off the protective wrap.

3. **Open** the **cardboard accessory box** and find the bright orange Welcome to Your iMac trifold. This trifold shows you Apple's easy setup steps. You can either follow the directions in the trifold or follow the directions in this book. Either set of directions will get you set up in no time.

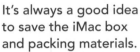

TIP

It's always a good idea to save the iMac box and packing materials. If something is wrong with the computer, something is missing, or something breaks, you'll need to be able to pack up the computer so it can be repaired.

4. **Unpack** the **keyboard** and **mouse** from the accessory box and remove the plastic outer wrappings.

5. **Place** the **computer** on a desk.

6. **Swing** the **foot** forward.

7. **Plug in** the **power cord** that's found in the accessory box.

8. **Open** the **panel** on the right side of the iMac. It will pop open if you stick your finger in the hole and tug.

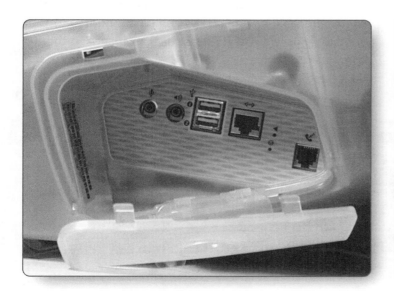

> ### TIP
> Be sure to thread each cord through a hole *before* you plug in the cord. Otherwise, you won't be able to close the panel! You will learn more about the ports later in this chapter.

9. Plug the **keyboard** into a USB (Universal Serial Bus) port. USB ports are discussed later in this chapter.

10. Plug the **mouse** into one of the USB ports on the keyboard. If you are left handed, you may want to put the mouse on the left side instead of the right.

11. Plug a **phone cord** into the RJ-11 port (a standard modular phone jack) if you are going to be using the Internet.

Keyboard

The iMac keyboard contains some special keys that will help you work with your iMac more effectively.

- **Command ⌘ key**. The *command key* is a *modifier key*. You use it in combination with another key on the keyboard to generate an alternate meaning. ⌘ plus another key will not produce any marks you'll see on the screen. Instead, command key combinations are most commonly used to send "shortcut" commands to the computer. With practice, you may find these shortcuts faster and easier to use.

> **TIP**
> The ⌘ key also has the outline of an apple (🍎) on it. This is a holdover from the old Apple II series of computers and was placed there to make the transition to the Macintosh easy for those users. You will almost never find Macintosh software that refers to the "Apple" key.

- **Escape (Esc) key**. The *escape key* does exactly what its name implies. It allows you to escape from some action. The uses of the escape key will vary from one program to another.

- **Control key**. The *control key* is yet another modifier key. Like the ⌘ key, when used with another key, it produces nonprinting characters.

- **Option key**. The *option key* is another modifier key that, when pressed along with a letter, number, or symbol key, produces an alternative character.

- **Arrow keys**. The *arrow keys* are used to move around a document, usually moving over one space, character, or item at a time.

- **Function keys**. *Function keys* allow you to execute a program command by pressing a single key. The tasks that each key performs vary from one program to another.

- **Navigation keys**. There are three *navigation keys*: Home, Page Up (pg up), and Page Down (pg dn). Pressing Home moves you to the beginning of the document on which you are working. Pressing Page Up moves you one page backward; pressing Page Down moves you one page forward.

- **Caps Lock key**. The *Caps Lock key* only locks the caps for the letter keys; the number and symbol keys are not affected. For example, if you press the Caps Lock key and type a number, you will see that number. But to get a dollar sign, you must hold down the Shift key and then press the symbol key.

Ports

When you set up your iMac, you plugged the keyboard cable into a port on the side of the computer. Ports provide places to connect peripherals to a computer. You can find more information about connecting peripherals in Appendix B, "Adding Peripherals." Your iMac comes with a number of different types of ports.

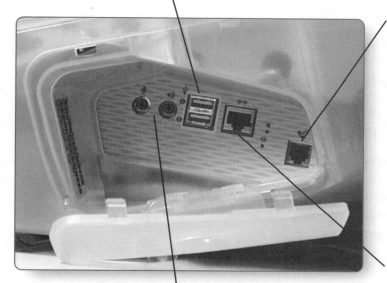

- **Universal Serial Bus (USB).** The *Universal Serial Bus* ports allow you to connect multiple devices designed to work with that type of port. Such devices include keyboards, mice, scanners, trackballs, disk drives, and printers. This is the iMac's primary interface to outside equipment.

- **Modem.** The *modem* port is where you can connect a telephone line so that your iMac can communicate with the Internet or other data communications services. Connection to the modem port requires a standard telephone cord with an RJ-11 modular connector. Read more about the modem in Chapter 14, "Setting Up a Connection."

- **Ethernet.** The word *Ethernet* describes a way that computers can share data over a network. The iMac's Ethernet port is designed for networks. Unless you will be connecting your iMac to a local area network or intranet, you don't need to worry about the Ethernet port.

- **Audio.** The iMac has both audio input and output ports. You can attach a microphone to the audio input port to record sounds or other equipment such as a CD player or tape deck.

- **Headphones.** There are two headphone ports on the front of the iMac, located at the left edge of the right speaker.

Types of Software

The term *software* refers to the programs that your iMac uses. A program contains instructions that a computer follows. Without software, a computer is nothing more than an expensive doorstop.

There are two major types of software that you will use with your iMac: application software and system software. Each has its own specific job.

Application Software

Application software (or more commonly referred to as a "program") is specialized software that performs useful work for you—the reason you bought your iMac. Once you have started up your iMac, you can run one or more programs of your choice.

Applications generate *documents*, places where created items are stored. You run an application, but you store the result of your work in a document. You usually have only one copy of an application on your hard disk, but any number of documents. As you will see later in this chapter, the iMac makes it easy to tell the difference between an application and a document.

Application software includes the following:

● **Word processor**. A *word processor* is a program that allows you to enter, edit, and format text. Many of today's word processors also can handle graphics.

● **Spreadsheet**. A *spreadsheet* is the electronic equivalent of an accountant's journal. You use a spreadsheet to manage numeric data, such as analyzing a budget. Most spreadsheet programs can also draw graphs from stored data.

- **Graphics**. Graphics programs allow you to create and edit pictorial images.

- **Data management**. Data management software allows you to store, organize, and retrieve data. You may hear the terms *database management* or *file management* applied to data management application software.

- **Communications**. Communications software lets you connect your computer to other computers or the Internet so you can exchange messages.

- **Games**. Game software lets you have fun with your computer.

You will also encounter a great deal of specialized software, such as Intuit's Quicken, that accompanies your iMac. Quicken is designed to help you manage your finances.

System Software

System software is software that manages the computer. The most commonly used example of system software is a collection of programs known together as an *operating system*. The iMac's operating system, known as the Macintosh Operation System or Mac OS, is on your Desktop. The Desktop is a visual metaphor for how the parts of the computer are presented on your screen. The parts are supposed to resemble items on a desk. When you manipulate items on the Desktop, you are working with the Mac OS.

NOTE

Programs and documents are stored in *files*. A file is a named, self-contained element on a computer. You will learn much more about files in Chapter 5, "Manipulating Folders and Files."

Introduction to the Desktop

Today, the Desktop is generally accepted as the easiest way for people to interact with their computer. The pictures on the Desktop that represent elements of the computer are known as *icons*. Icons represent disks (hard disks, CD-ROMs, and any other disks you may have attached to your computer), programs, and documents. Icons also represent containers known as *folders* that help you organize the storage on your disks.

The basic elements of the iMac Desktop are

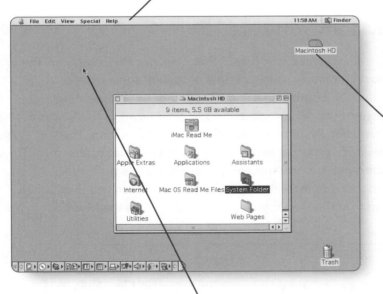

- **Menu bar**. A *menu* is a list of options from which you can choose. The Mac OS uses one *main menu bar* that always appears at the top of the screen, and other menus appear depending on the specific program you are using. You will learn about pull-down menus and making menu choices in Chapter 4, "Using Menus."

- **Hard disk**. A hard disk is a device that provides permanent storage for programs and documents. You will learn a great deal about viewing and manipulating the contents of a disk in Chapter 5, "Manipulating Folders and Files."

- **Mouse pointer**. The *mouse pointer* lets you point to items on the Desktop and manipulate elements such as icons and menus. The mouse pointer moves on the screen as you move your mouse.

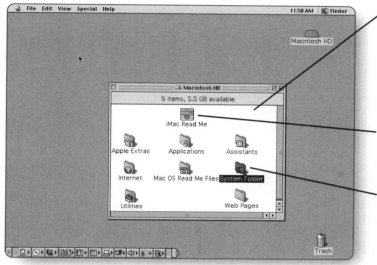

- **Window**. A *window* is a container that allows you to view the contents of an item. As you will see throughout this book, windows also show the contents of documents.

- **Document icon**. A *document icon* represents a document that is stored on a disk.

- **Folder icon**. A *folder* is a container for documents, programs, and other folders. You will learn more about folders in Chapter 5, "Manipulating Folders and Files."

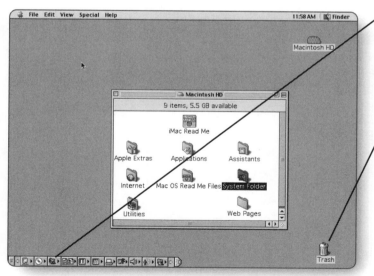

- **Control bar (or Control strip)**. The Control bar provides easy access to change various settings that you'll use frequently, such as speaker volume.

- **Trash**. The Trash icon is used to delete items. Any item in the Trash folder will be deleted when you empty the trash.

2

Getting Started

In this chapter you'll learn how to get your iMac up and running. The instructions will take you through the first steps in turning your iMac into a personal tool. In this chapter, you'll learn how to:

- Start up and shut down your iMac
- Work with your mouse
- Set up your working environment with Mac OS Setup Assistant

Turning on Your iMac

Turning on the iMac is as easy as pressing a single button.

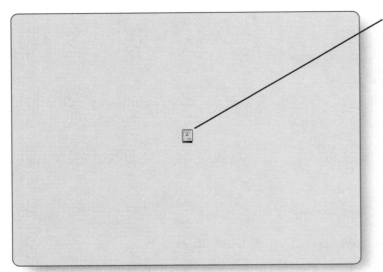

1. Press the **Power button**
($\circlearrowleft$). The first image you will see
is the "happy Mac."

TIP

The Power button ($\circlearrowleft$) is
a round button located
just to the right of the CD
Player on the main unit.
There is also a Power
button at the top of the
keyboard, between the
F12 and Help keys.

NOTE

Along the bottom of the
screen, you'll see several
icons appearing one after
the other. These icons are
called system extensions
and they indicate
additions to the Mac OS
that are being loaded into
main memory.

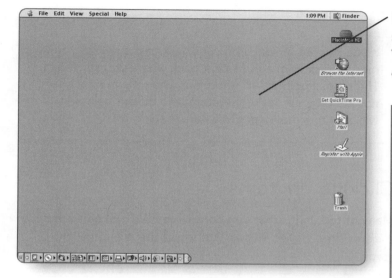

Once everything is loaded, the screen changes to the Desktop. Your computer has now *booted*, or started up.

> **NOTE**
>
> The term *boot* comes from the idea of "pulling yourself up by your boot-straps." In fact, in the early days of computing, starting up a computer was called *bootstrapping* and the program that managed the self-startup was known as a *bootstrap loader*.

Using the Mouse

At this point it is a good time to learn about using your mouse. You use the iMac's mouse to interact with items on the Desktop and to work with programs. As you read this book and software documentation, you will find references to several basic mouse skills.

Moving the Mouse Pointer

1. **Place** the **mouse** on a firm, dry surface such as a mouse pad.

2. **Push or pull** the **mouse** in the direction you want the mouse to go. The mouse will move in that direction.

> **TIP**
>
> If you run out of space on your desk to move the mouse, pick it up and place it back where you started. The mouse pointer will not move when the mouse is not flat on your desk. Therefore, the mouse pointer will continue moving right where you left off.

Clicking on Items

Many of the things that you do with the iMac involve a *mouse click*, or simply *click*. To perform a click use the following steps:

1. Move the **mouse pointer** on top of the item you want to click.

2. Press and release the **mouse button** once. You will hear the mouse make a soft clicking sound, and the item you clicked will be highlighted, or *selected*. The result of selecting something depends on the type of item, and you will learn more about specific results throughout this book.

Double-clicking

You can sometimes simplify interactions with windows, folders, and files by performing a *double-click*.

To double-click, press and release the mouse button twice in rapid succession. The mouse button will make two quiet clicking sounds. As with a click, the result of a double-click depends on exactly what was double-clicked. The results will be discussed throughout this book.

TIP

You'll find that clicking too slowly or moving the mouse accidentally while clicking may not give you the desired result. You can learn how to adjust the mouse settings later (see Control Panels in Chapter 6, "Customizing Your iMac.")

Dragging

Dragging lets you move something from one place to another.

1. Move the **mouse pointer** on top of what you want to move.

2. Press and hold the **mouse button**. The item will be selected.

3. Move the **mouse pointer** to the new location for the item. The item will move along with the mouse pointer to the new location.

4. Release the **mouse button**. The item will appear in its new location.

Setting Up with Mac OS Setup Assistant

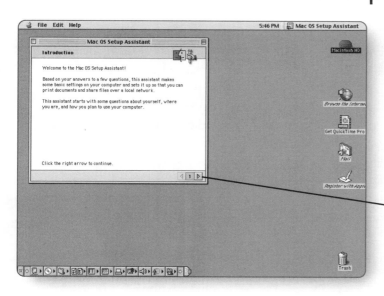

The first time you boot your iMac, you'll be greeted by the Mac OS Setup Assistant. This assistant will help you enter some of the information needed to use your machine.

1. Read the **Mac OS Setup Assistant Introduction**.

2. Click on the **right arrow** at the bottom of the Setup Assistant screen. The setup process will continue.

Regional Preferences

People around the world use different formats for things like dates and currency. Fortunately, the iMac offers several choices.

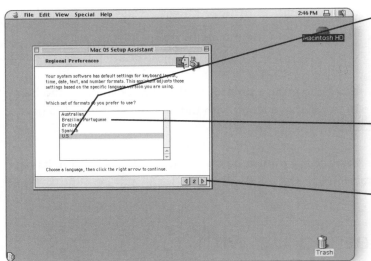

1a. **Click** on **U.S.** if you live in the United States. It will be selected (or *highlighted.*)

OR

1b. **Click** on a **country**. The country you choose will be highlighted.

2. **Click** on the **right arrow.** You will move to the next screen.

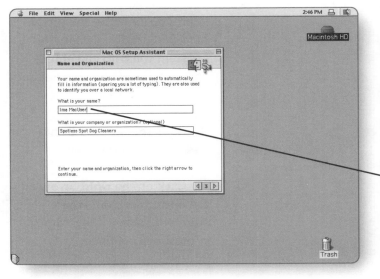

Your Information

A flashing line, the *I-bar*, appears in the What is your name? text box. The I-bar indicates where your text will appear. It is known as the *insertion point*.

1. **Type** your **name**. Your name will appear in the text box.

2. **Press** the **Tab key**. The insertion point will move to the next text box.

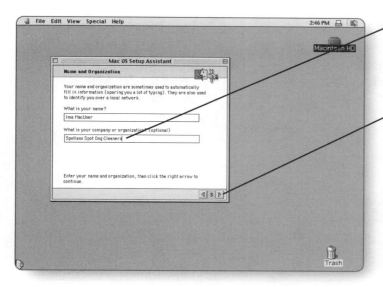

3. Optionally, **type** a **company or organization name**. This information will appear in the text box.

4. Click on the **right arrow.** You will move to the next screen.

After you type in your name and organization, iMac will automatically insert it for you, for example, when you set up your Internet account.

Setting the Clock

A computer should be set with the correct time, date, and time zone. This allows the computer to keep track of when files are created or changed. The date and time are also important when you start exchanging e-mail with people around the world.

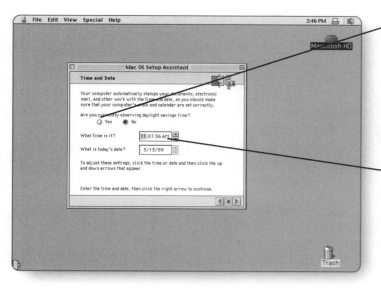

1. Click on **Yes or No** to indicate whether or not your area is currently observing Daylight Savings Time. The round button (called a *radio button*) will be highlighted with a black dot in its center.

2. Click on the **hour area**. It will be highlighted.

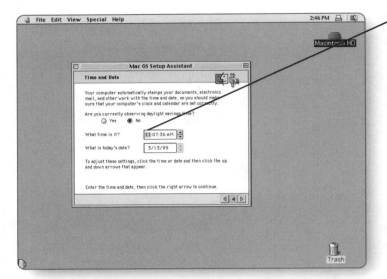

3. Type the correct **hour**. The hour will appear in the text box.

4. Press the **Tab key**. The Minutes display will be highlighted.

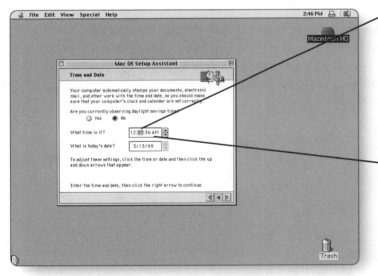

5. Type the correct **minutes**. The minutes will appear in the text box.

6. Press the **Tab key**. The Seconds display will be highlighted.

7. Type the correct **seconds**. The seconds will appear in the text box.

8. Press the **Tab key**. You will be taken to the next option area.

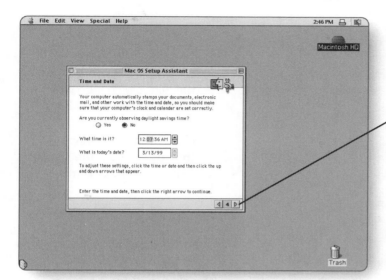

9. Follow this same **procedure** to select and set AM or PM and the current month, day, and year.

10. Click on the **right arrow**. You will continue to the next screen.

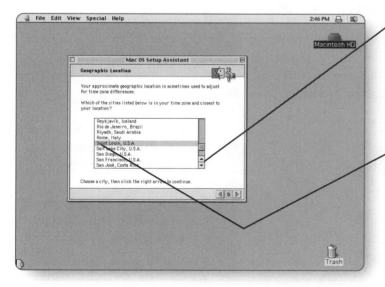

11. Click on the **up or down arrows** to find a city that is in your time zone. As you press the arrow key, the highlight will move in the direction of the arrow.

12. Click on the **city** you want to use. It will be highlighted.

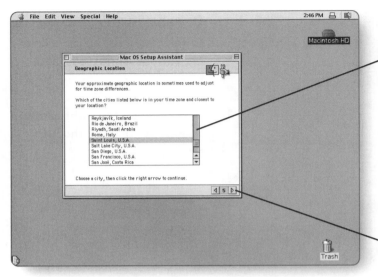

TIP

You are *scrolling* the window if the contents of the window change when you press the arrow keys. Another way to scroll is to click on the box shape in the vertical bar, (the *scroll bar*,) at the right of the screen.

13. **Click** on the **right arrow** to continue. You have completed the clock-setting sequence.

Simple Finder

The Finder is the program that launches when you start your computer and gives you access to the computer's files, folders, and other programs. In short, its job is to manage the Desktop. The *Simple* Finder preference simplifies the commands available in the Finder to make it easier to use but is too limiting to allow you to follow along in this book.

1. **Click** on **No**. The Finder will fully load without the Simple Finder preference.

2. **Click** on the **right arrow**. The Local Network Introduction page will appear.

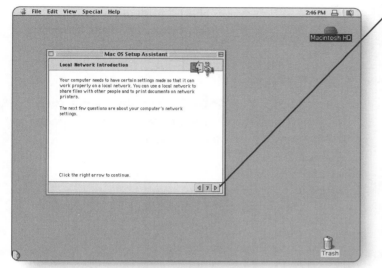

3. Click on the **right arrow**. The Computer Name and Password page will appear. The insertion point will be flashing in the first text box.

Giving Your iMac a Name

Setting up the local network information is most useful if your iMac will be attached to a network with other Macintosh computers. If not, you are still required to fill in the name and password to proceed.

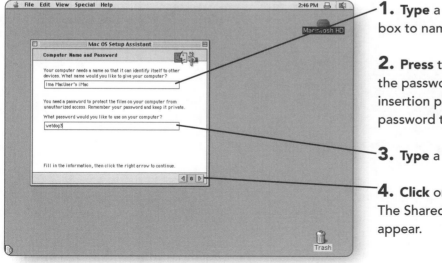

1. Type a **name** in the first text box to name your iMac

2. Press the **Tab key** to go to the password text box. The insertion point will appear in the password text box.

3. Type a **password**.

4. Click on the **right arrow**. The Shared Folder page will appear.

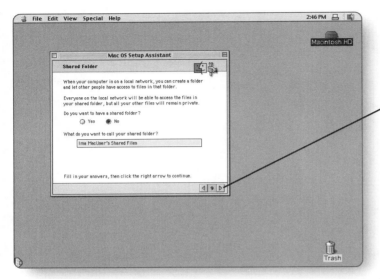

Shared folders are only useful if another computer is accessing yours, which is not covered in this book.

5. **Click** on the **right arrow**. The Printer Connection page will appear.

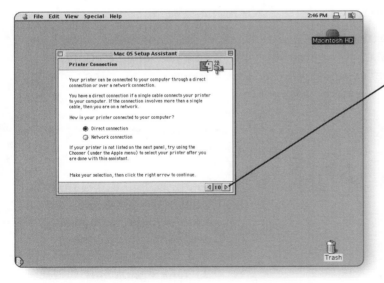

Hooking up printers will be covered in Appendix B, "Adding Peripherals."

6. **Click** on the **right arrow**. The Printer Type page will appear.

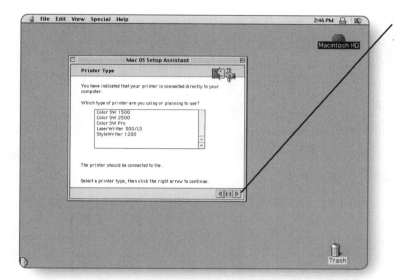

7. Click on the **right arrow.** You will move to the next page.

Finishing with the Assistant

Once you have selected your options, you need to save them with the Assistant.

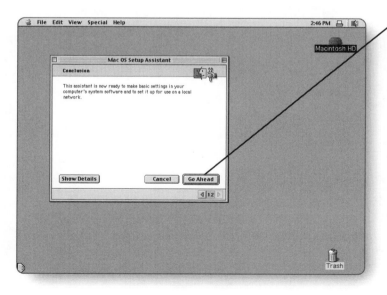

1. Click on the **Go Ahead button**. The computer will tell you what it is doing as it sets up all the options you've chosen.

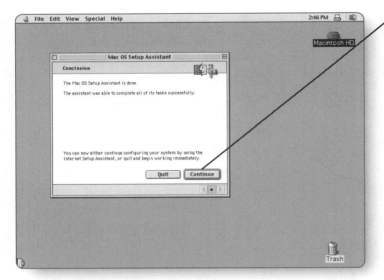

2. Click on the **Continue button**. The Internet Setup Assistant welcome screen will appear.

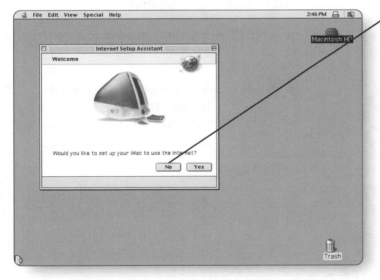

3. Click on the **No button** for right now. The assistant will quit, and you will return to the Desktop. You'll learn how to get on the Internet in Chapter 14, "Setting Up a Connection."

Turning Off Your iMac

Your iMac needs to be shut down in an orderly way to prevent possible data loss.

1. Press the **Power button** (⏻) on the keyboard or on the computer. A small window known as an *alert* will appear.

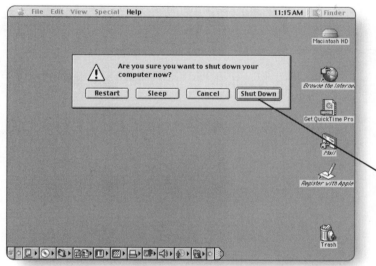

NOTE

An alert is different from other windows because you must take some action regarding it before you can proceed.

2. Click on the **Shut Down button**. The computer will turn itself off.

NOTE

The shut down process is a bit more involved when you have programs running. If you have data that hasn't been saved on a disk, the computer will give you a chance to save that data before shutting down those programs and turning off.

NOTE

If you let your computer sit for about 30 minutes without touching it, the screen will go dark and the Power button (⏻) will turn orange. Your computer has gone into Energy Saver mode, or to "sleep," which uses only a little power to keep the electronics warm. The screen actually turns itself off and the hard disk stops spinning. You reactivate the computer by pressing the Power button or any key other than a modifier key on the keyboard.

3

Working with Windows

Almost everything you do with your iMac—with the exception of interacting directly with the Desktop—occurs within a *window*. A *Finder window* displays the contents of a disk or folder; a *document window* displays the contents of the document. In this chapter, you'll learn how to:

- Identify the parts of a window
- Open, close, move, and resize a window
- Scroll the contents of a window
- Change the way in which the contents of a Finder window are viewed
- Understand the difference between Finder windows, documents windows, dialog boxes, and alerts

The Parts of a Window

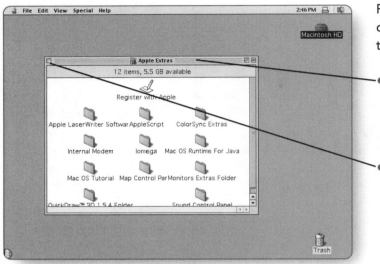

Finder windows and standard document windows have many things in common.

- **Title bar**. The *title bar* is the strip along the top of the window that contains the name of the window.

- **Close box**. The *Close box* can be found at the far-left edge of the title bar. You click on the Close box to close the window.

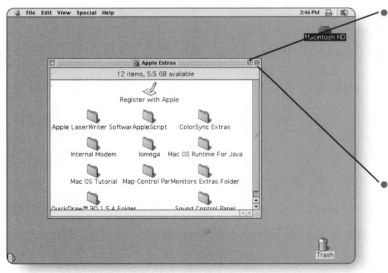

- **Zoom box**. The *Zoom box* is the leftmost square at the right edge of the title bar. You click on the Zoom box to expand the window to fill the entire screen or just to view all of its contenst. Click on it again to return the window to its original size.

- **Windowshade (or Rollup box)**. The *Windowshade* is found at the right edge of the title bar. You click on the Windowshade to hide the entire window except its title bar. Click on it again to show the window.

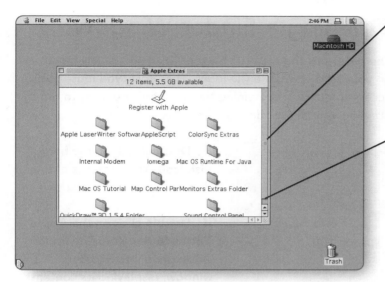

- **Scroll bars**. A window can have a *vertical scroll bar* and a *horizontal scroll bar*, both of which are used to bring hidden portions of the window's contents into view.

- **Scroll box**. The *scroll box* (or *thumb*) is found in a scroll bar. It is used to help you bring parts of a window's contents into view.

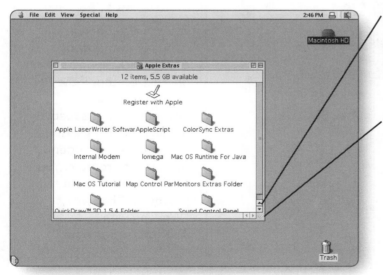

- **Up and down arrows**. The up and down arrows found in a scroll bar also help bring parts of a window's contents into view.

- **Size box.** The *size box* is the lower right corner of the window. You drag it to resize the window. As you drag, the top left corner of the window is fixed in place.

Opening a Finder Window

The programs that you run on your iMac will usually be stored on your hard drive or a CD-ROM. Therefore, you must gain access to the disk containing the program you want to run by opening a Finder window on the Desktop.

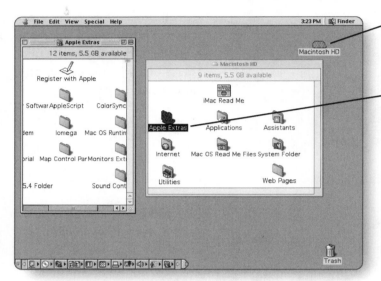

1. Double-click on the **hard disk icon**. The contents of the disk will appear in a window.

2. Double-click on the **Apple Extras folder** icon. The folder will expand into another window, displaying its contents.

NOTE

You can also open a document window by double-clicking on its icon on the Desktop. If the program for the document is not already running, double-clicking will automatically open the correct program. You will learn more about this process in Chapter 7, "Working with Application Software."

Making a Window Active

The Mac OS allows you to have many windows open at once. However, you can work with only one window at a time: the *active window*. All other open windows are *inactive*.

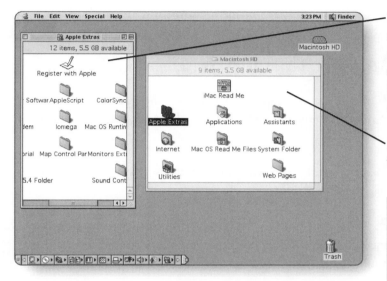

The active window always appears on top of all other open windows. An active window has horizontal lines in its title bar and its scroll bars are also filled in.

An inactive window has a gray title bar and empty scroll bars.

TIP

To make a window active, click anywhere inside the window.

Closing a Window

Although you can have many windows open at a time, your Desktop will become very cluttered if you don't close some windows when you finish with them.

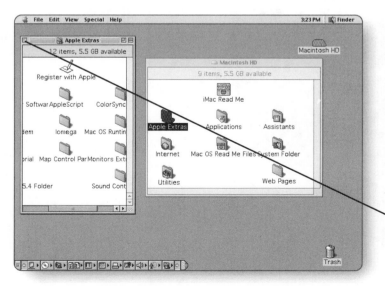

1. Click in the window's **Close box**. The window will close.

TIP

You can also close a window by pressing the key combination shortcut ⌘-W. See Chapter 4, "Using Menus," for more information on using Command-key combinations.

Moving a Window

Windows can overlap one another on the iMac screen. You may want to move a window to make its contents easier to see.

1. Click on the **window** you would like to move. The window will become active.

2. Press and hold the mouse button down on the **title bar** and drag the window to its new location. As you drag, an outline of the window will follow the mouse pointer.

3. Release the **mouse button.** The window will appear in its new location.

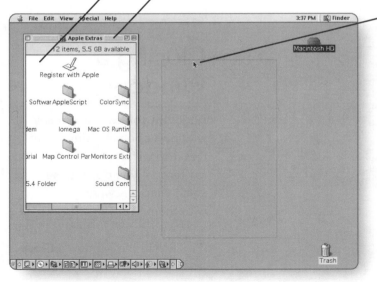

Resizing a Window

There are two ways to resize a window: one will give you complete control over the resulting size, whereas the other makes the window as big as possible.

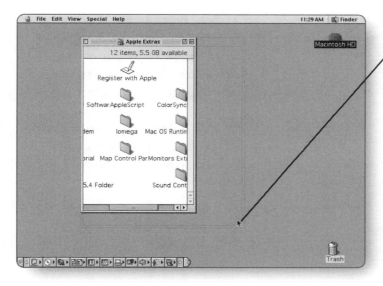

Using the Size Box

1. Press and hold down the mouse button to **drag** the **lower right corner** of the window in any direction. An outline of the window will become larger or smaller as you drag.

2. Release the **mouse button.** The window will be resized.

Zooming a Window

Clicking on the Zoom box at the far right of a window's title bar resizes the window to fill the entire screen or makes it large enough so that you can see the window's entire contents without scrolling. Clicking on it a second time returns the window to its original size.

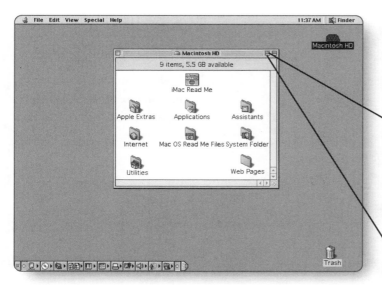

1. Click on the **Zoom box**. The window will be resized either to show all its contents without scrolling or, if the entire contents won't fit on the screen, to fill the entire screen.

2. Click on the **Zoom box** again. The window will return to its original size.

Turning a Window into a Tab

If you want a Finder window out of the way but easily accessible, you can turn it into a tab at the bottom of the screen. You can also expand the window back to its original size.

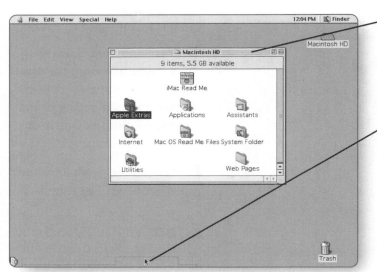

1. Press and hold down the mouse button to **drag** the window's **title bar** to the bottom of the Desktop screen. You will see an outline of a tab.

2. Release the **mouse button**. The tab will appear at the bottom of the screen.

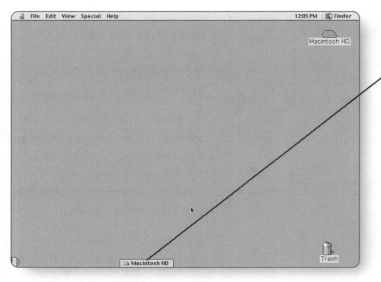

Expanding a Tabbed Window

1. Click on the **tab**. The window will expand, showing its title as a tab above the title bar.

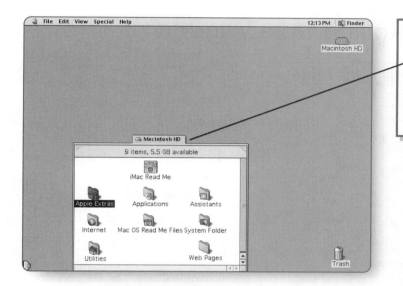

Changing a Tabbed Window into a Regular Window

When you are through working with a window as a tab, you can change it back to a regular window.

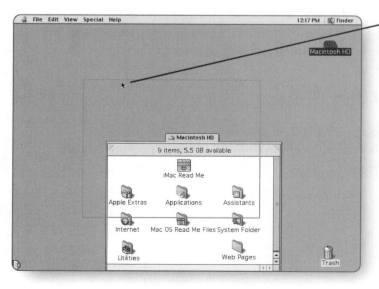

1. Press and hold down the mouse button and **drag** the window's **title bar** until an outline of the window shows up on the screen.

2. Release the **mouse button**. The window will appear as a regular window.

Rolling Up a Window

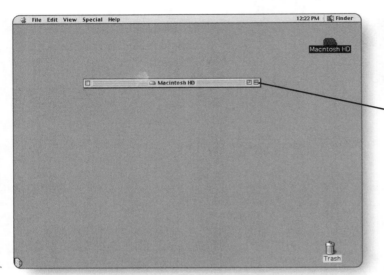

Another way to get a window out of the way without closing it is to roll it up into a *window shade*.

1. Click on the **Rollup box**. The window will roll up, leaving only its title bar visible.

> **TIP**
>
> To return a window to its original size, just click on the Rollup box again.

Special Types of Windows

The windows that you have seen so far have all been either standard *Finder windows* or *document windows*. However, the iMac has two additional types of windows that you will encounter frequently: dialog boxes and alerts.

Dialog Boxes

A *dialog box* is a window used to gather information necessary to perform a specific task. Dialog boxes have buttons that let you choose the final action to be taken.

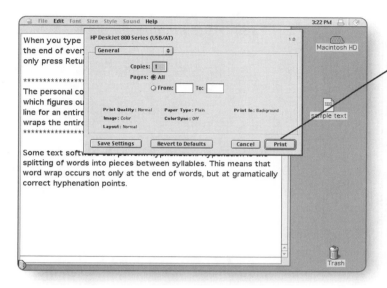

NOTE

In most cases, there will be a button with a heavy outline. This is the *default* button.

A default button is typically the most common action taken, such as clicking on OK. You can select the default button by clicking on it with the mouse pointer or pressing either the Return or Enter keys. There will usually be a Cancel button that allows you to cancel the current operation.

Alerts

An *alert* is a window, similar to a dialog box, which displays a warning or notifies you that an event has occurred. The display of an alert is usually accompanied by a sound from the computer's speaker (the *system beep*).

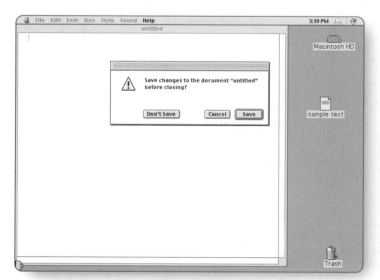

You must remove an alert from the screen before you can perform another action on your iMac.

NOTE

If you leave an alert on your iMac screen without closing it for a short period of time, the iMac will read the contents of the alert aloud.

4

Using Menus

A *menu* is a list of options from which you can choose. Menu options can be commands that you want the computer to perform or settings you choose. In this chapter, you'll learn how to:

- Make menu choices
- Use Command-key combinations for menu options
- Use the items in the Apple menu
- Work with pop-up menus
- Work with contextual menus

The Menu Bar

Nearly all iMac programs have a single menu bar across the top of the screen. (The exception is some games, which hide the menu bar until you press some specific key combination.) The leftmost three menus are identical in almost all programs. Any remaining menus are specific to whichever program you are working with at any given time.

Standard iMac Menus

From the left, the three standard iMac menus are as follows:

- **Apple menu**. The Apple menu is always at the far-left edge of the menu bar. The options in the Apple menu are the same regardless of the program with which you are working. You will read more about this menu later in this chapter.

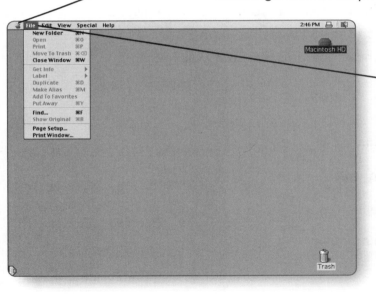

- **File menu**. The File menu contains options dealing with files, such as creating new documents, opening document files, or printing documents. Although the specific contents of the menu change from one program to another, the File menu is always just to the right of the Apple menu.

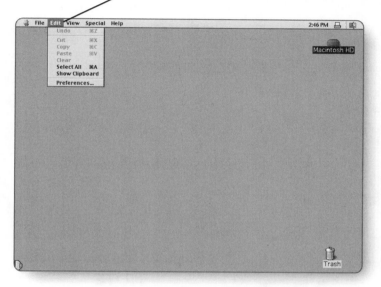

● **Edit menu**. The Edit menu contains options that allow you to edit parts of a document. The first two sections of the menu are the same in most programs (Undo, Cut, Copy, Paste, and Clear). You will learn to use these options throughout this book.

NOTE

If you look at the File and Edit menus, you will notice that some of the options are followed by ellipses (...). This indicates that choosing that menu option displays a dialog box.

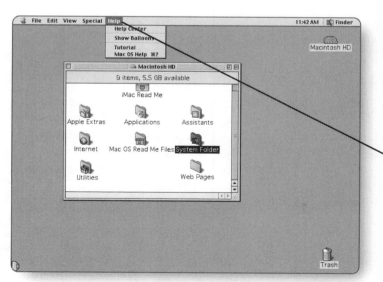

Making Menu Choices

The most common way to choose an option from a menu is to use the mouse.

1. Click on a **menu name** in the menu bar. The menu options will appear.

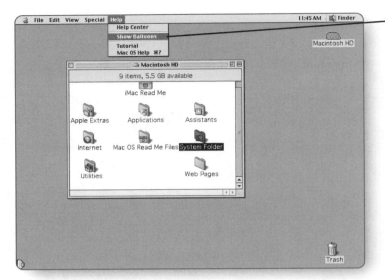

2. Move the **mouse pointer** and **click** on the **option** you want. The option will be highlighted and the action will be performed.

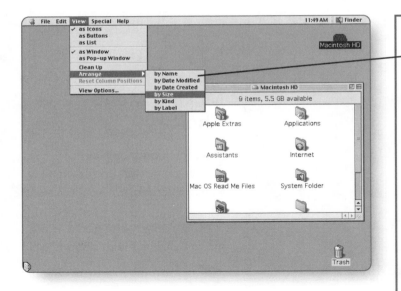

NOTE

Some menus have too many options to place them in a single list. Therefore, related menu options can be grouped together under a single heading and then displayed as a *submenu*. Menu options that have submenus associated with them have a right-pointing arrow at the right edge of the submenu.

Using Command-Key Combinations

As you become familiar with many of the actions you take with your iMac, you might find that choosing menu options with the mouse takes too long. A *Command-key combination* allows you to press a key or combination of keys to make a quick menu selection. You may remember from Chapter 1, "Anatomy of an iMac," that there are four modifier keys on the iMac keyboard. One or more of these keys can be combined with any of the other keys on the keyboard to produce a useful shortcut.

- The Command ⌘ key
- The Option ⌥ key
- The Control ⌃ key
- The Shift ⇧ key

You can find out what key combinations are available by looking at the menus. The key combinations are visible at the right edge of each. For example, if you look at the File menu, you will see that some options have the Command key symbol ⌘ followed by a letter.

TIP

To make a menu selection using a Command-key combination, press and hold the modifier key or keys needed and then press the letter, number, symbol, or function key associated with the modifier key or keys. Some key combinations are consistent for all Macintosh programs. For example, ⌘-Q always quits the program in which you are currently working.

Using the Apple Menu

The Apple menu lists programs and documents that you may need to access regardless of the application in which you are working. In this section, you will read about some of those programs and their uses.

Apple System Profiler

The Apple System Profiler contains useful information about your iMac such as the model name and number, version number of your system software, amount of memory, and the processor speed. You may be asked for this kind of technical information if you ever need to call in for Apple's technical support.

1. Move your **mouse pointer** over the **Apple icon** on the menu bar. The Apple menu will appear.

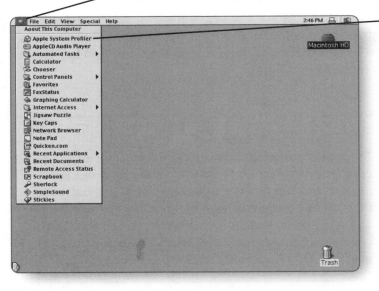

2. Choose the **Apple System Profiler** from the Apple menu.

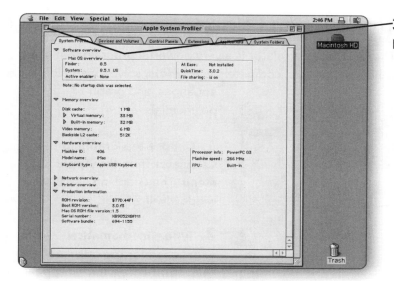

3. Click on the **Close box**. The Profiler window will close.

Calculators

The Mac OS is accompanied by two calculators—one that is easy to use but limited in function and another that is extremely powerful but rather complex.

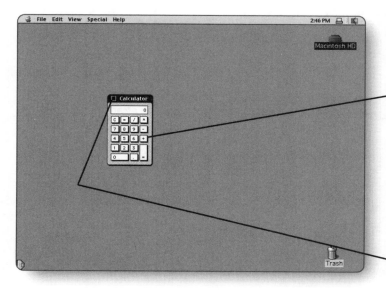

1. Choose Calculator from the Apple menu. The Calculator will appear.

2. Click on the **calculator buttons** with the mouse pointer. The results of your calculations will appear at the top of the Calculator window. You can use the numeric key pad on the right side of your keyboard for mouse-free calculation.

3. Click on the **Close box**. The calculator will close.

The Graphing Calculator

The Graphing Calculator is a very powerful program that can handle exponents, compute square roots, solve algebraic equations, and graph polynomials.

1. **Choose** the **Graphing Calculator** from the **Apple menu**. The Graphing Calculator window will appear.

2. **Type** a **mathematical expression** for the calculator to evaluate. The results will appear as you type.

3. **Choose Quit** from the File menu. The Graphing Calculator will close.

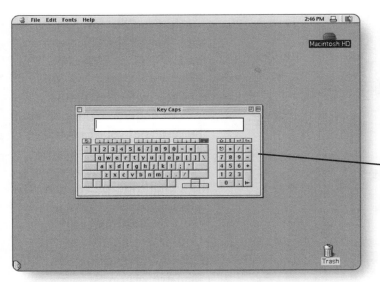

Keycaps

Using the Key Caps program, you can view the keys on your keyboard that represent other symbols, for example, Greek letters or small images.

1. **Choose Key Caps** from the **Apple menu**. The Key Caps window will appear.

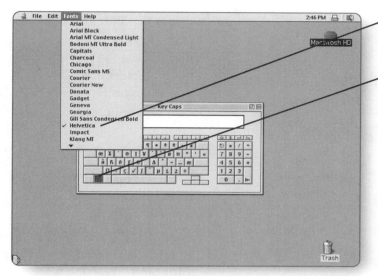

2. Choose a **font** that you would like to use.

3. Press the **Option key**. The display will change to show you the characters that will appear when the Option key is pressed.

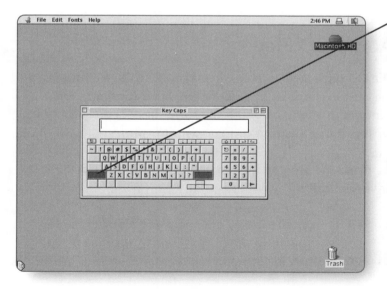

4. Press the **Shift key**. The display will change to show you the characters that will appear when the Shift key is pressed.

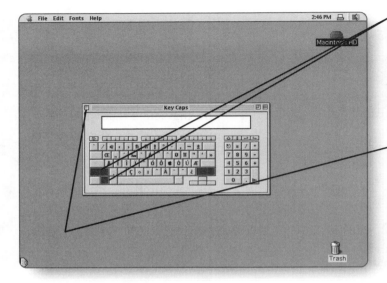

5. **Press** the **Shift and Option keys** at the same time. The display will change to show you to the characters that will appear when both the Shift and Option keys are pressed.

6. **Click** on the **Close box.** The window will close.

> ### NOTE
>
> Changing the appearance of text is discussed in Chapter 8, "Working with Text."

Audio CD Player

The CD drive in your iMac can play audio CDs, either using the built-in speakers or external amplified speakers. You control the operation of the CD player using a program that looks just like the front of a standard CD player.

1. **Press** the **colored button** on the front of the CD-ROM drive. The drive tray will open.

2. **Pull** the **tray** all the way out and **place** a **disc** in the tray.

3. **Push** the **tray** in gently.

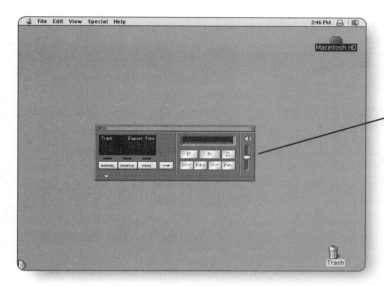

4. Choose Apple Audio CD Player from the Apple menu. The CD Player window will appear.

5. Click on the **buttons** on the CD Player window to control the playback of the audio CD, just as you would press buttons on the front of a regular CD player.

6. Press ⌘**-Q.** The program will close.

Stickies

Stickies are the electronic version of a Post-It note. You can place them all over your Desktop and have them pop up automatically whenever you start your iMac.

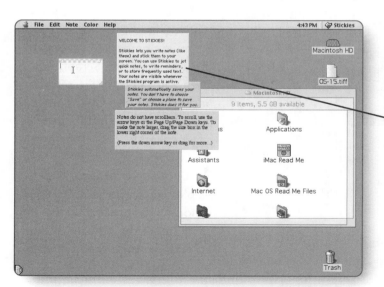

1. Choose Stickies from the Apple menu. Any Stickies that you have previously created will appear on the Desktop.

2. Create or **modify Stickies** as necessary. Stickies are really small text documents. You will learn to use them in Chapter 8, "Working with Text."

Removing Stickies

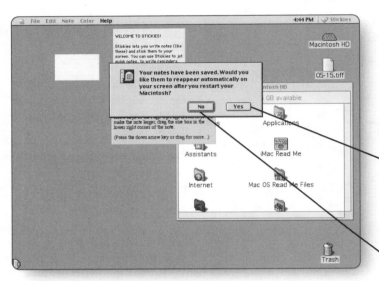

1. Press ⌘-Q. If you started Stickies by making a choice from the Apple menu, the iMac displays an alert asking if you would like Stickies to be started automatically each time you start your computer.

2a. Click on **Yes** to automatically start Stickies every time you start your computer.

OR

2b. Click on **No** to continue to use the menu selection to start Stickies.

Scrapbook

The Scrapbook provides storage for items that you need to access frequently. For example, if you have a return address that you use at the top of every letter you type, you can place the address in the Scrapbook. Then you can copy the return address from the Scrapbook and place it into your letters as often as you need.

1. Choose Scrapbook from the Apple menu. The Scrapbook window will appear. Use the scroll bar at the bottom of the Scrapbook window to view the built-in images.

Notepad

The Notepad is a simple way to keep notes on the desktop. It provides an eight-page blank message pad that keeps its contents even when the computer is turned off.

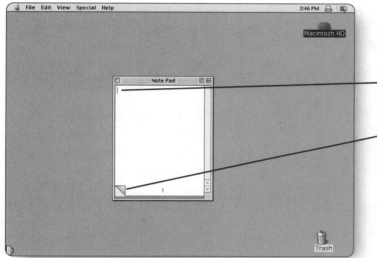

1. Choose Notepad from the Apple menu. The Notepad window will appear.

2. Type the **message** you want on the notepad.

3a. Click on the **turned up page corner.** You will move to the next page.

OR

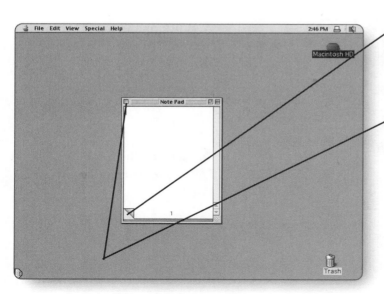

3b. Click on the **corner of the page** underneath the top page. You will move to the previous page.

4. Click on the **Close box.** The window will close and its contents will be saved.

Puzzle

When you are ready to take a break from more serious work, you can solve the jigsaw puzzle that is on your iMac. The picture is a map of the world.

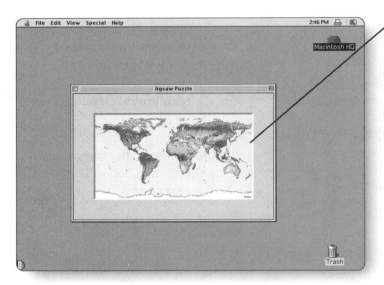

1. Choose Jigsaw Puzzle from the Apple menu. The puzzle window will appear either scrambled or in whatever condition you previously left it.

2. Press ⌘**-N** to create a new puzzle. A dialog box will appear asking you to select the size of the pieces.

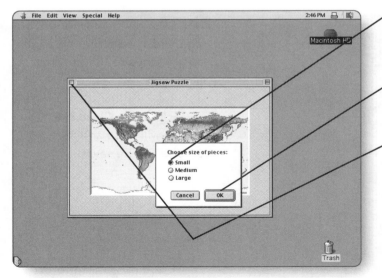

3. Click on the **Small radio button**. The option will be selected.

4. Click on **OK**. A new puzzle will appear.

5. Click on the **close box** when finished to exit the Jigsaw Puzzle.

Recently Used Items

The Apple menu includes two submenus, Recent Applications and Recent Documents, that provide quick access to items that you've used recently.

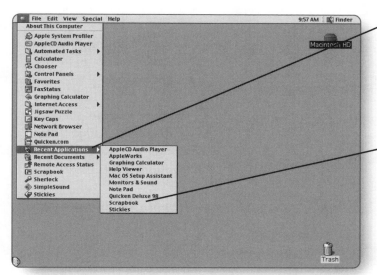

1. **Drag** the **mouse pointer** down the Apple menu until it reaches either the Recent Documents or Recent Applications menu item. The submenu will appear.

2. **Drag** the **mouse pointer** over the submenu until you come to the item you want. It will be highlighted.

3. **Release** the **mouse button**. The item you have chosen will open.

NOTE

You can modify the number of items that appear in the submenus or even the appearance of submenus in the Apple menu. You will read about configuring the contents of the Apple menu in Chapter 6, "Customizing Your iMac."

Pop-up Menus

A *pop-up menu* provides another way to select a single option from a list. Double arrows at the right edge of a visible menu option indicate that a pop-up menu is available.

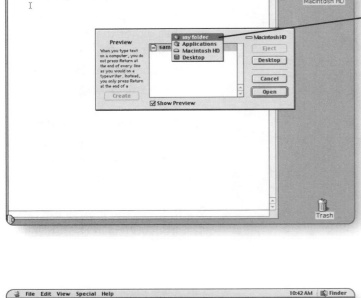

1. Click and hold the **mouse pointer** over a pop-up menu. The menu options will appear.

2. Drag the **mouse pointer** down the menu until you reach the option you want. The option will be highlighted.

3. Release the **mouse button**. Only the option you selected will appear.

Contextual Menus

A *contextual menu* is a pop-up menu that can appear for most items on the Desktop. The major benefit of such a menu is that it isn't necessary to move the mouse pointer to the menu bar to gain access to commands.

1. Move the **mouse pointer** to the item for which you want to display a contextual menu.

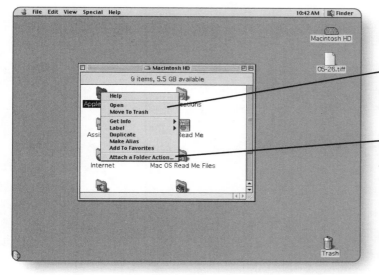

2. **Press and hold** the **Control key**.

3. **Press and hold** the **mouse button**. The contextual menu will appear.

4. **Drag** the **mouse pointer** down the menu until you reach the option you want. The option will be selected.

5. **Release** the **mouse button and the Control key**. The contextual menu will disappear and the option you want will appear.

5

Manipulating Folders and Files

The permanent storage found on disks is organized into folders and files so that you can work with the many items you'll accumulate over time. In this chapter, you'll learn how to:

- Understand how folders and files organize disk storage
- Create, open, and put items into folders
- Copy, move, and rename a file
- Delete files and folders
- Find items using Sherlock
- Work with aliases

It is not unusual for there to be more than 10,000 files stored on your iMac hard disk. If all those files were placed together in a single container, you would find it extremely time consuming to locate the one file that you want. The iMac has a way of organizing disk storage that can help get around that problem. You begin by looking at the storage organization and then manipulate the folders and files.

Understanding Disk Organization

The iMac refers to each disk that it can access as a *volume*, which can represent an entire disk or part of a larger disk. When a volume appears on the Desktop, it is *mounted*.

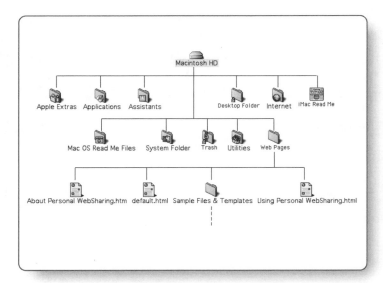

Each volume has its own organization for its contents, represented by a hierarchy of folders and files. As you can see in the illustration, the iMac's hard disk is at the top of the hierarchy. It is the top-level container. Each level in the hierarchy can contain folders or files. A folder is a container for still more folders and files. You can therefore use folders to create a hierarchical organization of the contents of any volume.

NOTE

The Desktop is actually a folder. When you look at the iMac's screen, though, you see just the opposite: The hard disk is on the Desktop. Internally, however, the iMac thinks of the Desktop as a folder on the hard disk.

NOTE

CD-ROMs have a folder and file hierarchy to organize their contents, just like hard disks. However, because a CD-ROM is a read-only disc, you can open its folders, but you cannot permanently make any modifications to them.

Working with Folders

Folders are the containers that you use to store other folders and files on a disk. They are most commonly used with the Finder. The instructions in this section apply only to the Finder. You rarely see a program that uses folders to organize groups of documents.

Opening Folder Windows

You open folders on all types of disks (for example, hard disks and CD-ROMs) the same way.

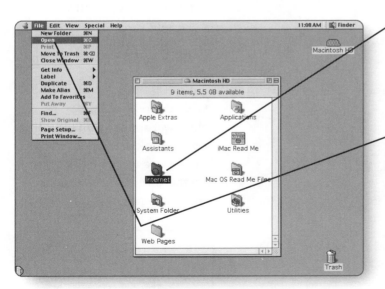

1a. **Double click** on the **folder icon**. The folder window will open.

OR

1b. **Click** on the **folder icon** to select it and then choose Open from the File menu. The folder window will open.

TIP

Instead of choosing Open, you can press ⌘-O.

TIP

To open more than one folder at once, click on the first folder to select it. Then hold down the Shift key and click on the next folder (a *Shift-click*). Keep Shift-clicking until all folders you want to open are selected. Then issue the Open command by either making the menu choice or pressing ⌘-O.

Creating and Naming a New Folder

You can create folders at any time on the hard disk to help you organize your files. It is usually most helpful to give folders names that are suggestive of their contents to make it easier to remember what you have done and where you have stored things.

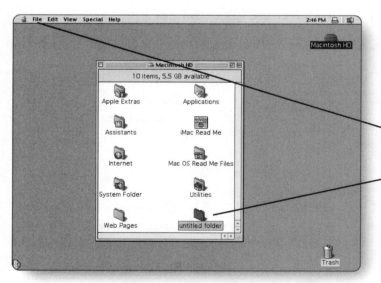

1. Open the **folder** or disk in which you want the new folder to be stored. Make sure that the folder you just opened is the active window.

2. Click on **File**. The File menu will open.

3. Click on **New Folder**. A folder will appear with the name "untitled folder." The characters in the name will be highlighted and there will be a rectangle around the name.

TIP

You can also create a new folder by pressing ⌘-N.

4. Type a **name** for the folder. Your typing will replace the highlighted text.

5. Press Enter. The new name will appear.

NOTE

File and folder names can contain any characters except a colon (:) and can be up to 32 characters long. Names must also be unique within a folder. This means that you can have more than one file or folder with the same name as long as they are in different containers in the disk storage hierarchy.

TIP

If you want to rename a folder or file, just click on its name, wait a few seconds for a rectangle to appear around the name, then type the new name in the box.

Placing Items in a Folder

The organization of a hard disk is not fixed. You can move items into and out of folders as needed.

Dragging

The easiest way to put a file or folder inside another folder is to drag it there.

1. Open folders until the icon of the folder into which you want to place something is visible.

2. Press and hold the mouse button to **drag** the **item** onto the folder's icon. The folder's icon will be highlighted. The item being moved will still appear in its original location and a gray version of the file or folder will appear over the destination folder.

3. Release the **mouse button**. The file or folder will appear in its new location.

To be totally accurate, the Mac OS *moves* a dragged file or folder when the destination is on the same volume as the file or folder's original location. On the other hand, if the original location is a different volume, the iMac *copies* the item being moved, leaving the item unchanged in its original location. To copy an item within the same disk hierarchy as opposed to moving it, hold down the Option key when you drag the item to its new location. There is no way to perform a move rather than a copy when going from one volume to another.

Spring-Loaded Folders

If you need to store something many layers down in a folder hierarchy, it can be awkward having to open up all the containing folders to reach the one you want. The Mac OS therefore provides *spring-loaded folders*, which open automatically as you drag.

1. Drag the **folder** or file you want to move onto the top folder in the destination hierarchy.

2. Hold the **folder** or file in place for a couple seconds until the folder underneath it automatically opens.

3. Drag the **folder** or file being moved on top of the next folder in the hierarchy in which you want to place it.

4. Repeat steps 2 and **3** until the item being moved is over the folder that is its final destination.

5. Release the **mouse button**. All the folders that have sprung open while you are dragging will close.

> **NOTE**
> Using the spring-loaded folder feature can take a bit of practice. If it doesn't work for you, don't worry. Come back and try it again when you have spent more time with your iMac. If you accidentally open a folder you did not mean to, simply drag it outside that folder's window, and it will disappear.

Changing the Way You See the Contents of a Folder

Up until this point, all the Finder windows you have seen have shown you large icons for the items within a folder. However, big icons, as attractive as they can be, aren't a very efficient use of window space. The iMac therefore lets you change the way in which you view folder contents.

To see the items in a folder in a *button format*, follow these steps:

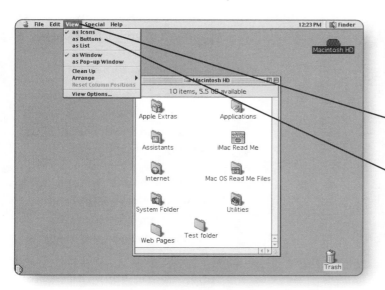

1. Open the **folder** for which you want to change the viewing method and make sure that it is the active folder.

2. Click on **View**. The View menu will appear.

3. Click on **as Buttons**. The display will change to buttons and, a ✔ will appear by the as Buttons option in the View menu.

To see the items in a folder in a *list format*, follow these steps:

1. Open the **folder** for which you want to change the viewing method, and make sure that it is the active folder.

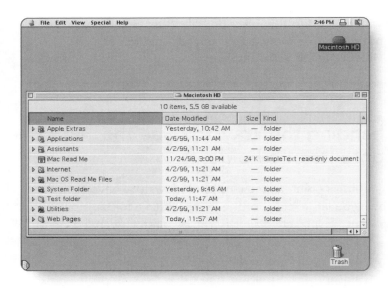

2. Choose as List from the **View menu**. The display will change to a list and, a ✔ will appear by the as List option in the View menu.

A List view provides much more information about the contents of a folder. By default, you see the date the item was last modified, the size of a file, and the type of an item.

> **NOTE**
>
> You can also have the iMac display the size of a folder. However, doing so significantly slows down the speed of your iMac. Therefore, it is better to leave that option turned off.

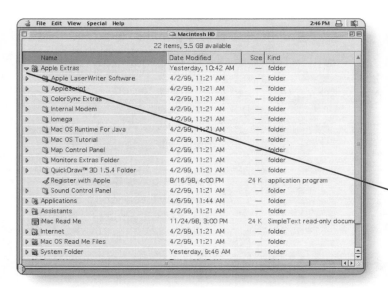

To expand a folder shown in List view, follow these steps:

1a. Click on the **right-pointing arrow** just to the left of the folder's name. The List view will expand to include the contents of the folder.

OR

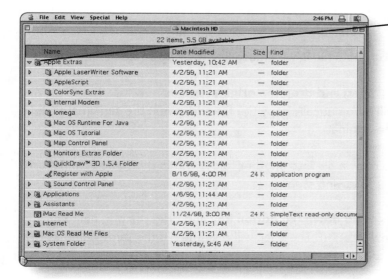

1b. Double-click on the **small folder icon**. The folder's window will open.

TIP

To collapse an expanded List view of a folder's contents, click on the down-pointing arrow to the left of the folder's name.

NOTE

You can change the way you view the contents of CD-ROM windows, but the change is temporary. The next time you use the disc, you will notice that the folders were returned to their original view.

Working with Files

A file provides a named storage location that may contain a document (for example, a letter, a graphics image, or a database containing related data) or a program (instructions that the computer can follow). The iMac distinguishes between these two types of files by calling them *documents* and *applications* (or *programs*). A document is a file that you create while you are working in a program.

Copying a File

Copying a file is very much like copying a folder.

1. Drag and drop the **original** into its new location. The iMac will automatically copy the file and give it the same name as the original.

To copy a file into another folder within the *same volume*, use the following steps:

1. Hold down the **option key** and drag the original to its new location. The iMac will give the file the same name as the original.

To make a copy of a file within the *same folder*, follow these steps:

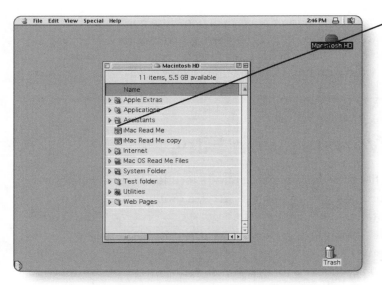

1. Click on the **file** that you want to copy. The file will be highlighted.

2a. Choose Duplicate from the **File menu**. The iMac will make a copy of the file and name it "*original name* copy."

TIP

You can also make a copy by pressing ⌘-D.

Moving a File

To move a file to a new location within the same volume, follow these steps:

1. Open windows until you see the folder into which the moved file will be placed. You do not need to open the destination folder.

2. Click on the **file**. The file will be highlighted.

3. Drag the **file** over the folder into which you want to place it. The destination folder will be highlighted.

4. Release the **mouse button**. The file will appear in its new location.

TIP

Remember that as far as the iMac is concerned, the Desktop is a folder. You can therefore move or copy any file or folder to the Desktop.

Deleting Files and Folders

When you no longer need a file or folder, you can delete it from a disk. There are several important things to consider before you delete a file or folder:

- Once an item has been deleted, you can't undelete it without special software. Such software is only somewhat successful, and if you have modified anything on the disk after performing the delete, recovery of a deleted file is nearly impossible.

- Deletion does not actually erase a file. The iMac merely marks the space occupied by the deleted file as available for reuse.

- When you delete a folder, you also delete its contents, including the contents of any nested folders. This is known as a *cascading delete*.

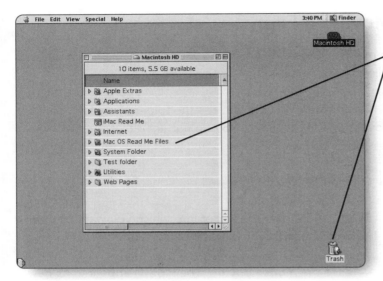

Deleting an Item

1. Drag the **item** that you want to delete into the Trash folder icon on the Desktop. If the trash folder was previously empty, the icon will change to show that there is something in the Trash folder.

TIP

You can also move an item to the Trash by clicking on the item and then pressing ⌘-Delete.

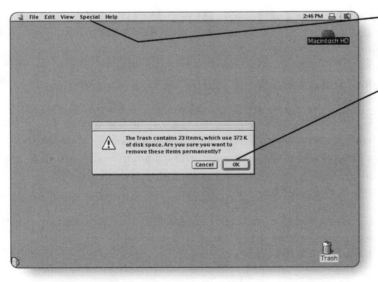

2. Click on **Empty Trash** from the **Special menu**. An alert will appear asking you to confirm the deletion.

3. Click on **OK**. The iMac will complete the deletion, and the Trash icon will return to its empty state.

NOTE

If you drag a CD-ROM icon to the Trash, the iMac will remove the icon from the Desktop and eject the disc. If you drag a hard disk icon to the Trash, the iMac will *unmount* the disk, making it inaccessible. There will be no damage to the hard disk, but with its icon gone from the Desktop, you will need to reboot the iMac to gain access to the hard disk again.

Removing Items from the Trash

You can return whatever is in the Trash can to its original location before performing step 3 to empty the trash.

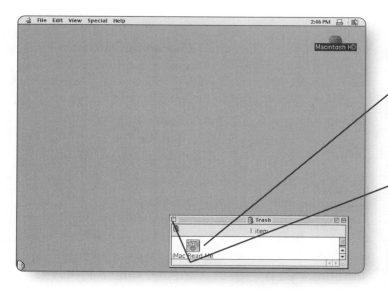

1. Double-click on the **Trash icon**. The Trash window will open.

2. Drag the **item** out of the Trash folder and onto the Desktop. The item will appear in its new location.

3. Click on the **Close box.** The Trash folder will close.

TIP

You can place an item back in its original location by clicking on it to select it and then choosing Put Away from the File menu or pressing ⌘-Y.

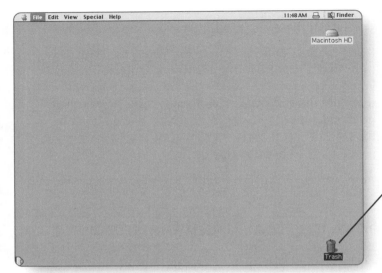

Getting Rid of the Empty Trash Warning

If you find the alert that appears when you empty the trash annoying, you can prevent the iMac from displaying it.

1. Click once on the **Trash icon.** It will be highlighted.

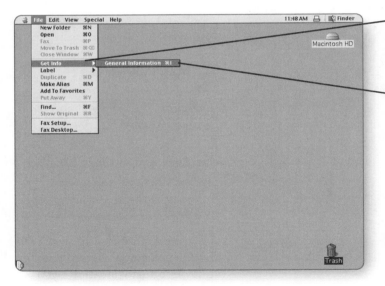

2. Choose Get Info from the **File menu.** A submenu will appear.

3. Choose General Information. The Trash Info window will appear.

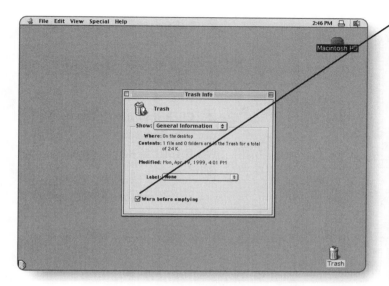

4. Click in the **check box** next to Warn before emptying. The ✔ in the box will disappear.

NOTE

The *check box* is used in dialog boxes to indicate whether an option should be turned on or off. If the box has a ✔ or an X in it, the option is chosen, or active. If the box is empty, the option is not chosen, or inactive.

Finding Files and Folders Using Sherlock

Despite giving files and folders meaningful names, the iMac has a program called Sherlock that can search all mounted volumes to look for files and folders.

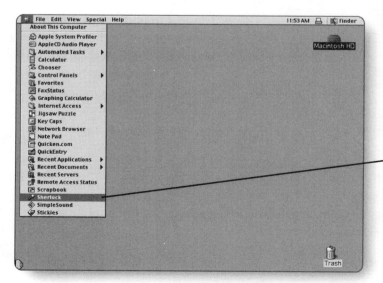

Performing a Search

To search for a file or folder by name, use the following steps:

1. Choose Sherlock from the **Apple menu**. The Sherlock window will appear.

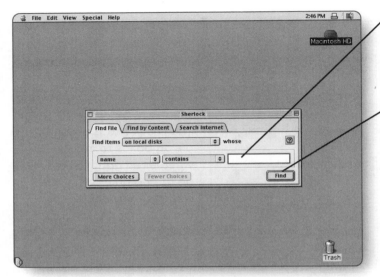

2. Type some or all the **name** of the file or folder you want to find in the text box. The text will appear in the box.

3. Click on **Find**. Sherlock will perform the search and display the results in a separate window.

Using the Results of a Search

Once Sherlock has found files and folders with names containing the text you entered, you can do several things.

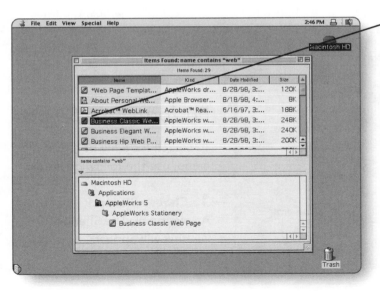

1. Click on the **item** in the list at the top of the search result window to find out where an item is located in the disk folder hierarchy. Sherlock displays the nested folders in the bottom of the window.

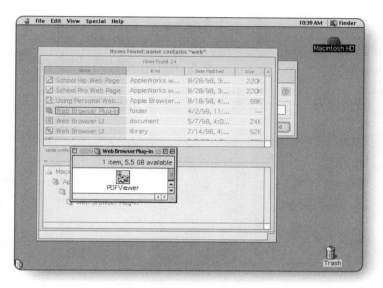

2. Double-click on the **item** to open a file or folder. If the item is a folder, the iMac will open the folder's window on the Desktop. If the item is a document, the iMac will open the document using the program that created it.

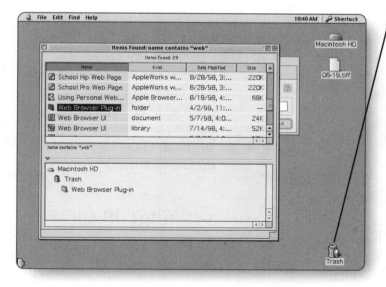

3. Drag the **item** from the list to the **Trash** to delete a file or folder. The item will be placed in the trash, and the display at the bottom of the search window will change to show the item's new location.

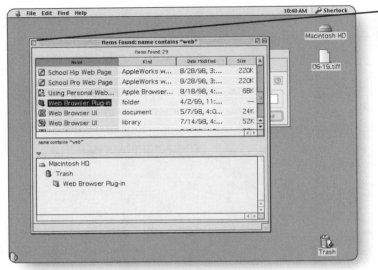

4. Click on the **Close box** when you are finished with your search. Sherlock will close.

Using Aliases

An *alias* is a placeholder that points to the actual location of a file or folder. Once you create an alias, you can leave the original in its current location and place the alias somewhere that is more convenient to access. For example, you might place an alias of a frequently-used file or folder on the Desktop. To use an alias, simply double-click on it.

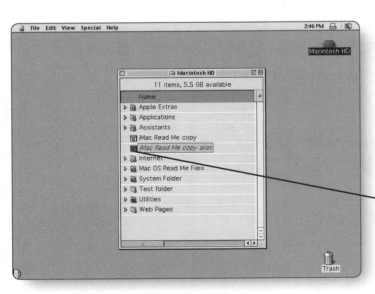

Creating an Alias

1. Find the **item** to which the alias will refer.

2. Click on the **item**. The item will be highlighted.

3. Choose Make Alias from the **File menu**. The iMac will create an alias file and name it "*original name* alias." The alias file's name will be highlighted so you can easily rename the alias.

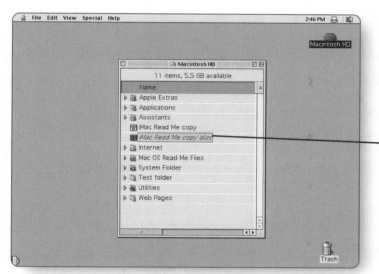

TIP

You can also make an alias by selecting the item and pressing ⌘-M.

4a. Type a new **name** for the alias. The new name will replace the text.

OR

4b. Press Enter to accept the name that appears.

TIP

You can move the alias to any convenient location, such as the Desktop. You can rename or move the alias at any time without affecting the original.

NOTE

If you move or rename the original to which an alias points, the iMac will no longer be able to find the original. Therefore, when you change an item that has an alias pointing to it, you must delete the old alias and create a new one.

Part I Review Questions

1. What are modifier keys and how do they help you? *See "Keyboard" in Chapter 1*

2. Name four iMac devices that use a USB port to connect to your computer? *See "Ports" in Chapter 1*

3. What is the difference between application software and system software? *See "Types of Software" in Chapter 1*

4. How do you turn on your iMac? *See "Turning on Your iMac" in Chapter 2*

5. How do you turn off your iMac? *See "Turning Your iMac Off" in Chapter 2*

6. How do you open a Finder window? *See "Opening a Finder Window" in Chapter 3*

7. What options are found in the Apple menu? *See "Using the Apple Menu" in Chapter 4*

8. How do you create a new folder? *See "Creating and Naming a New Folder" in Chapter 5*

9. How do you use Sherlock? *See "Finding Files and Folders Using Sherlock" in Chapter 5*

10. What is an alias? For what is it used? *See "Using Aliases" in Chapter 5*

PART II

iMac Essentials

6

Customizing Your iMac

The iMac is designed to let you customize your working environment. For example, you can change the color of the Desktop, the volume of the speakers, and the ways in which your software behaves. In this chapter, you'll learn how to:

- Understand the role of control panels
- Use common system configuration control panels
- Customize the contents of the Apple menu
- Enable and disable extension items with the Extensions Manager

Introducing Control Panels

Control panels are small programs that typically allow you to configure software. Most of the time, the customized settings are stored in a Preferences file, which can be found in the Preferences folder inside the System folder.

Control panels load into the main memory when the computer boots up and appear as icons. The control panel programs can be found in the Control Panels folder in the System folder, but there is a much easier way to access them.

1. **Choose Control Panels** from the **Apple menu**. The Control Panels submenu will appear.

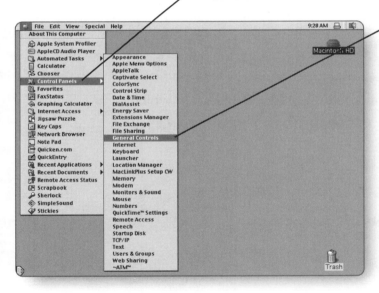

2. **Choose General Controls** from the submenu as an example of a control panel. The control panel's window will appear on the Desktop.

TIP

To close a control panel, simply click on its Close box.

Exactly what appears in the Control Panels submenu depends on the contents of the Control Panels folder. Many software installers add programs to this folder. For example, when you install Adobe PageMill, the installer also installs ATM (Adobe Type Manager).

> **NOTE**
>
> Notice how the ATM control panel name begins with a ~ so that it will appear alphabetically last on the Control Panels submenu and therefore the last control panel loaded when you boot. The ATM control panel turns the ATM program on and off. When ATM is on, it smoothes the appearance of large-sized PostScript screen fonts on the screen.

Using Basic Control Panels

In this section, you'll be introduced to the control panels that configure the look and feel of your iMac.

Adjusting Your Mouse Settings

If using your mouse seems difficult at first, you can modify the dragging speed and clicking tempo by accessing the Mouse control panel.

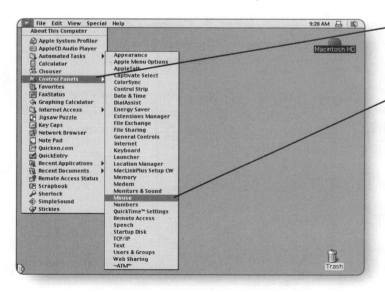

1. **Choose Control Panels** from the **Apple menu**. The Control Panels submenu will appear.

2. **Choose Mouse** from the submenu. The Mouse control panel will appear.

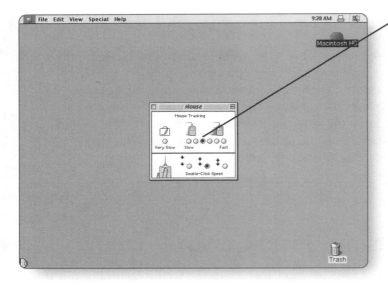

3. Customize the **mouse** settings to your liking. You can preview and test your preferences within the window.

4. Click on the **Close box**. The Mouse control panel will close.

Changing the Desktop Appearance

You can have a great deal of fun with Appearance, the control panel that lets you change the appearance of the Desktop. You can change Desktop patterns and colors, add or remove sound, choose system fonts, and so on.

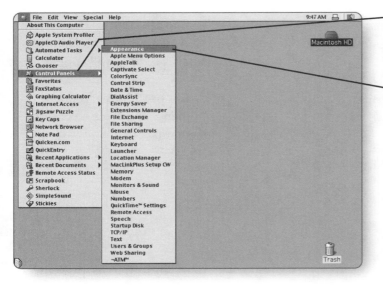

1. Choose Control Panels from the **Apple menu**. The Control Panels submenu will appear.

2. Choose Appearance from the submenu. The Appearance control panel will appear.

The Appearance control panel organizes groups of Desktop settings into *themes*. You can either use one of the themes provided by the iMac or create your own custom theme. The tabs at the top of the control panel provide access to all the elements that make up a theme. When you are through with your settings, you can give your custom theme a name so that you can access all the settings as a unit.

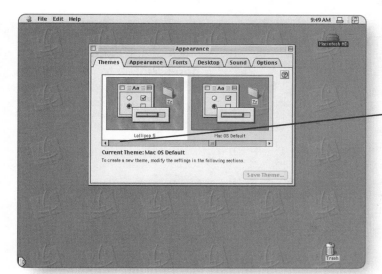

Choosing an Existing Theme

1. Scroll through the **themes** to select one. A sample of the theme will appear.

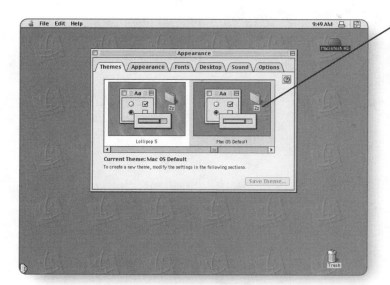

2. Click on the **sample** of the theme you want to use. The theme will appear on your Desktop.

Creating a Custom Theme

To create a custom theme, you can make changes using the remaining tabs of the Appearance control panel.

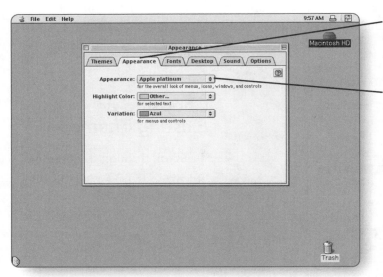

1. Click on the **Appearance tab**. The tab will move to the front.

- **Click** on the **Appearance pop-up menu** to control the overall look of scroll bars and close boxes.

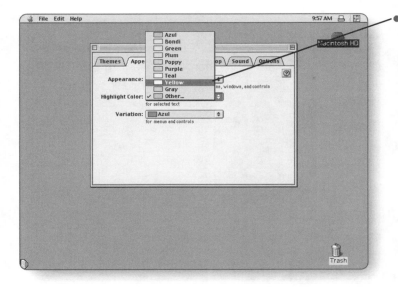

- **Click** on the **Highlight Color pop-up menu** to set the background color for selected text.

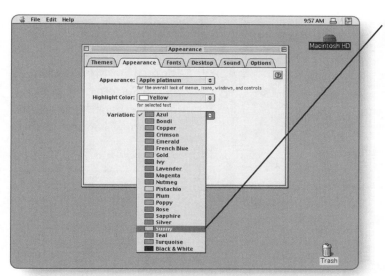

- **Click** on the **Variation pop-up menu** to set the color for menu and control highlighting.

2. Click on the **Fonts tab**. The tab will move to the front.

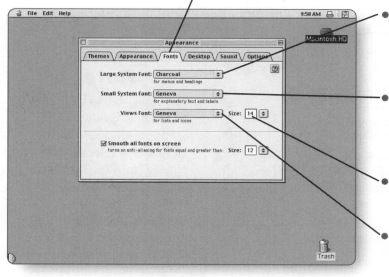

- **Click** on the **Large System Font pop-up menu** to select the font used for windows and menus.

- **Click** on the **Small System Font pop-up menu** to select the font used for text and labels.

- **Type** the **size** of the Views font if necessary.

- **Click** on the **Views Font pop-up menu** to select the font used in List views and for icon names in Icon views.

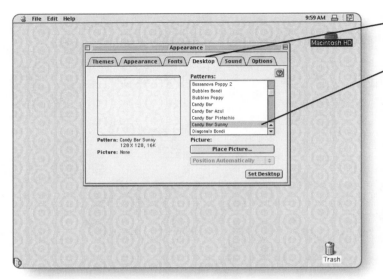

3. Click on the **Desktop tab**. The tab will move to the front.

- **Click** on a **Desktop Pattern** from the Patterns: list at the right of the panel. A sample of the pattern will appear at the left.

NOTE

If a desktop picture is active, you must click on Remove Picture before you can see the patterns or to place a new picture.

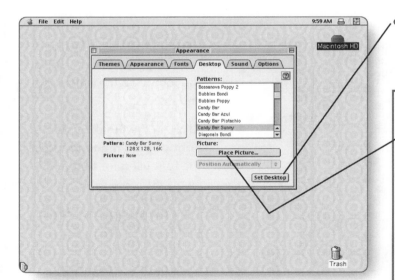

- **Click** on the **Set Desktop.** The pattern will be applied to the Desktop.

NOTE

You can also use a picture as the background of the Desktop. Click on Place Picture and select a picture from the list that appears from the Desktop Pictures folder. Click on Choose to return to the Desktop tab, then choose Set Desktop.

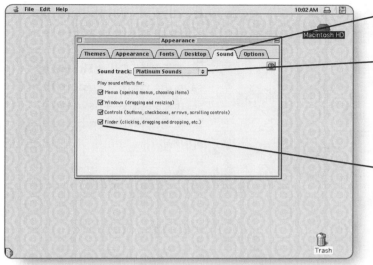

4. Click on the **Sound tab**. The tab will move to the front.

- **Click** on the **Sound track pop-up menu** to hear sounds when you work with the Finder.

TIP

You can place a ✔ in the boxes to hear different sounds while you use your iMac.

NOTE

You can choose None from the Sound track: pop-up menu to keep the sounds turned off.

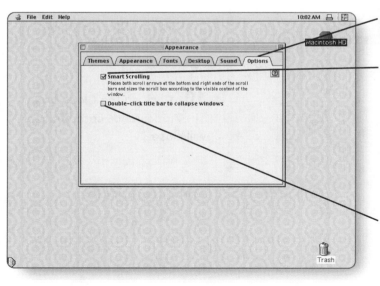

5. Click on the **Options tab**. The tab will move to the front.

- **Click** on the **Smart Scrolling check box** to remove the ✔ and turn off smart scrolling if you want. With smart scrolling off, the up arrow is at the top of a vertical scroll bar and the scroll box is a small, fixed size.

- **Place** a ✔ in the Double-click title bar to collapse windows check box if you want to be able to roll up a window by double-clicking on its title bar.

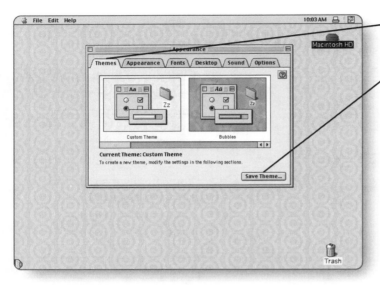

6. Click on the **Themes tab.** The tab will move to the front.

7. Click on **Save Theme** to save the current custom theme settings under a new name. The Save Theme dialog box will appear.

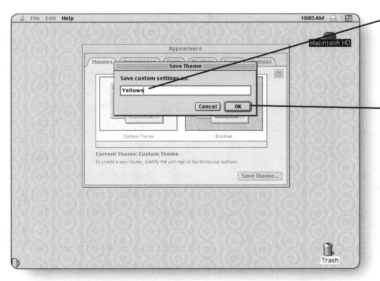

8. Type a **name** for the theme in the Save custom settings as: text box. The name will appear in the text box.

9. Click on **OK**. The theme will be saved using the name you selected.

10. Click on the **Close box.** The Appearance control panel will close.

Configuring Your Monitor and Adjusting Sounds

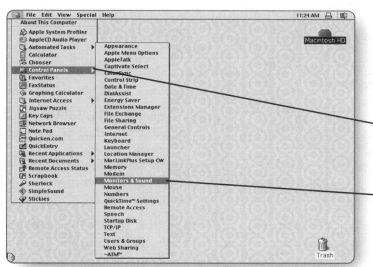

The Monitors & Sound control panel lets you change how your screen looks and the different sounds you hear as you use your iMac.

1. Choose Control Panels from the **Apple menu**. The Control Panels submenu will appear.

2. Choose Monitors & Sound from the Control Panels submenu. The Monitors & Sound control panel will appear.

Adjusting Basic Monitor Settings

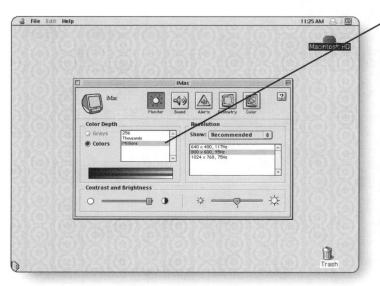

1. Click on the **Color Depth list** to choose the maximum number of colors you want your monitor to be able to display. Your choice will be highlighted.

NOTE

For most uses, you can leave the setting at millions of colors. However, you may run across some software—in particular, some games—that will only run if the color depth is set to 256 colors.

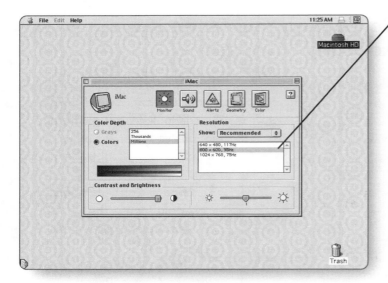

2. Click on a **screen resolution** from the list of resolutions located to the right of the window. The iMac will immediately reset the screen resolution.

NOTE

Resolution refers to the detail of an image on the screen. In general, a higher resolution means a larger Desktop area and smaller images.

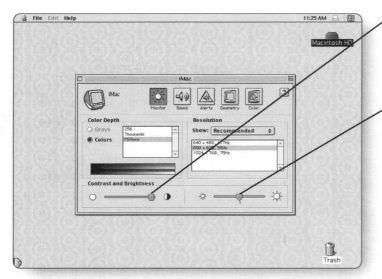

3. Drag the **Contrast slider** at the bottom-left of the window. The screen contrast will change as you drag the slider.

4. Drag the **Brightness slider** at the bottom-right of the window. The screen brightness will change as you drag the slider.

Adjusting Sound

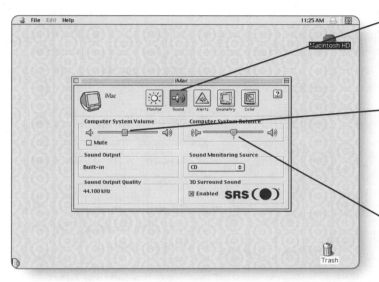

1. **Click** on the **Sound button** at the top of the Monitors & Sound control panel. The Sound panel will appear.

2. **Drag** the **Computer System Volume slider** to adjust the speaker volume. The iMac will play a sample sound when you release the mouse button.

3. **Drag** the **Computer System Balance slider** to adjust the balance of the speakers. The iMac will play a sample sound when you release the mouse button.

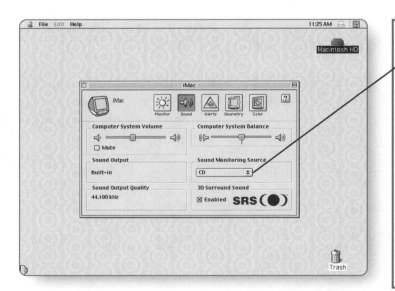

NOTE

You can use the Sound Monitoring Source pop-up menu to change the source of the iMac's sounds. Ordinarily, the iMac monitors the CD-ROM drive for sound. However, if you are recording sounds or if you have added voice recognition software to your iMac, the iMac will need to monitor the microphone port for sound.

Choosing an Alert Sound

The Alert panel of the Monitors & Sound control panel lets you choose your iMac's *beep sound*. Sounds play whenever the iMac needs to get your attention, for example, when an alert appears on the screen. You can also set the volume of the sounds from this control panel.

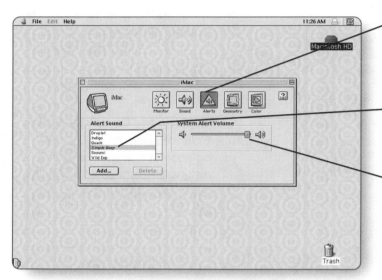

1. Click on the **Alerts button** at the top of the Monitors & Sound control panel. The Alert panel will appear.

2. Click on a **sound** in the Alert Sound list to select it. The iMac will play the sound.

3. Drag the **System Alert Volume slider** to adjust the volume of the beep sound. The iMac will play a sample sound when you release the mouse button.

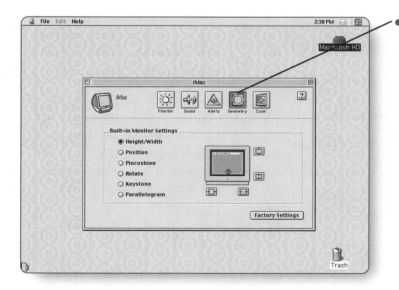

● Use the Geometry panel if you see problems with the image on your screen or it becomes distorted.

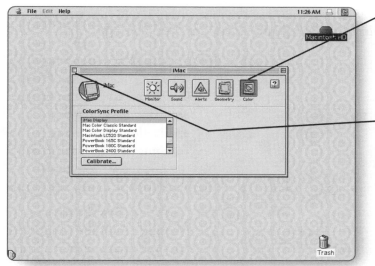

● Use the Color panel if you want to adjust the colors on the screen to closely match the colors that are printed by a color printer.

4. Close the **Display window** to exit the Monitors & Sound control panel.

Setting General Controls

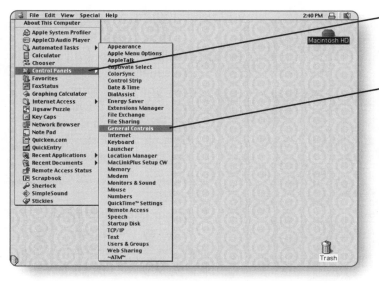

1. Choose Control Panels from the **Apple menu**. The Control Panels submenu will appear.

2. Choose General Controls from the Control Panels submenu. The General Controls control panel will appear.

Among the aspects of the iMac environment that you can affect from this control panel are the following:

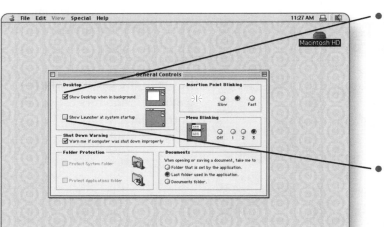

- This check box determines whether the contents of the Desktop are visible when you are working with another application. To hide the contents of the Desktop, remove the ✔ from the check box.

- This check box determines whether or not the Launcher appears when you start your iMac. You must place a ✔ in this check box for the Launcher to load automatically.

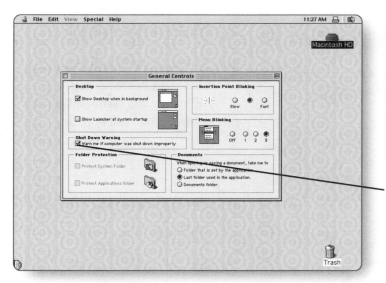

NOTE

The Launcher helps you personalize your iMac to give you quick access to items you use frequently. It is discussed in depth in Chapter 7, "Working with Application Software."

- If your iMac shuts down abruptly, without the benefit of the Shut Down command, the iMac will display an alert the next time you start your iMac warning you that an improper shut down occurred. You can disable that warning by removing the ✔ from the "Warn me if computer was shut down improperly" check box.

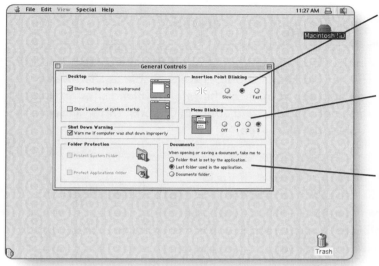

• The Insertion Point Blinking radio buttons control the flashing rate of the insertion point.

• The Menu Blinking radio buttons control the frequency at which menu options blink when you select them.

• The three Documents radio buttons control the default folder that a program uses each time it displays an Open File or Save File dialog box every time you run the program. The top radio button in the set uses the default folder set by the application itself. The middle radio button overrides that setting and uses the last folder you used the last time you opened or saved a file. The bottom radio button assumes that you have a folder named Documents on your hard disk and that you want to put all documents in that folder.

Using the Control Strip

The control strip appears across the bottom of the iMac's screen. Each small panel (control strip module) in the control strip is a pop-up menu. When you click on the icon, the menu appears with options that are ordinarily accessible through control panels.

> **NOTE**
>
> The modules that appear in the control strip are stored in the Control Strip Modules folder in the System Folder. Additional modules are available as shareware on AOL and at many of the safe download sites on the Internet that you read about in Chapter 15, "Wandering the World Wide Web."

The iMac rarely forces you to accept a particular type of configuration—including whether or not the control strip is present on the screen. If you consider it a hindrance, you can get rid of it or set up a key sequence to make it disappear and reappear.

1. Choose Control Strip from the Control Panels submenu of the Apple menu. The Control Strip control panel will appear.

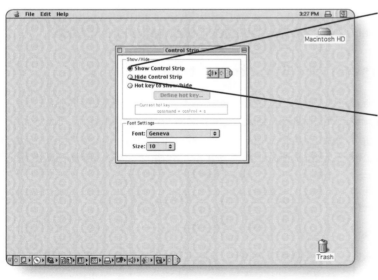

● **Click** on the **Show Control Strip radio button** to place the control strip on the screen. The control strip will appear.

● **Click** on the **Hide Control Strip radio button** to remove the control strip from the screen. The control strip will disappear.

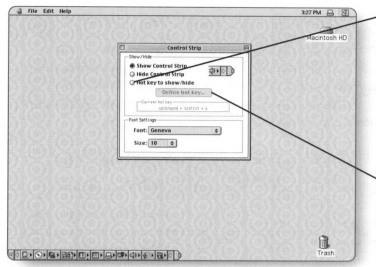

2. Click on the **Hot key to show/hide radio button** to define a *hot key* (a key combination that performs a specific action) to toggle the appearance of the control strip on the screen. The Define Hot Key button will become active.

3. Click on **Define Hot Key** if you are going to be using a hot key. An untitled dialog box for defining the hot key will appear.

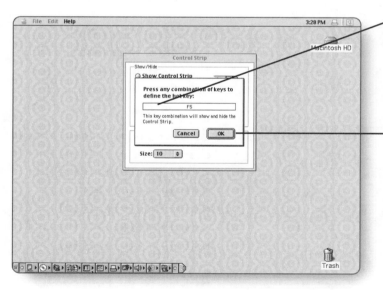

4. Press the **key or key combination** that will define the hot key. The name of the key or keys will appear in the middle of the dialog box.

5. Click on **OK**. The dialog box will close and you will return to the Control Strip control panel.

6. Click on the **close box** to close the Control Strip window.

Configuring the Date and Time

When you initially configured your iMac, you set the date and time. You will probably never need to change them unless you move to another time zone. However, the Date & Time control panel does give you some control over the format of date and time displays.

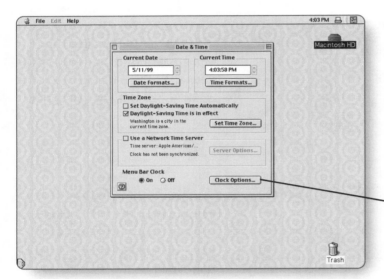

Configuring the Menu Bar Clock

To configure the digital clock that appears in the menu bar, follow these steps:

1. Choose Date & Time from the Control Panels submenu.

2. Click on **Clock Options** in the Date & Time control panel. The Clock Options dialog box will appear.

3. Click on one or more of the **check boxes** in the Menu Bar Display Format area to add or remove elements from the display. Your changes will appear in the Sample area at the bottom of the dialog box.

4. Click on the **Font pop-up menu** to choose a font for the menu bar clock. Your changes will appear in the Sample area at the bottom of the dialog box.

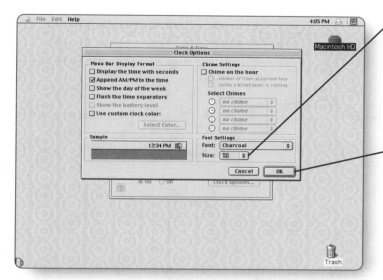

5. **Click** on the **Size pop-up menu** to choose a type size for the menu bar clock. Your changes will appear in the Sample area at the bottom of the dialog box.

6. **Click** on **OK**. You will return to the Date & Time control panel.

Setting Speech Characteristics

The Speech control panel handles settings for talking alerts and other applications that speak. You can change the speaking voice and configure how talking alerts will work.

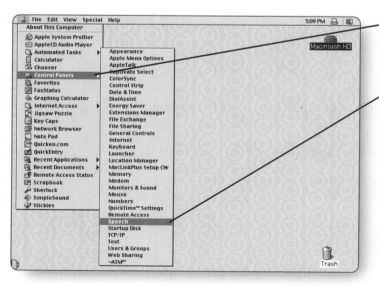

1. **Choose Control Panels** from the **Apple menu**. The Control Panels submenu will appear.

2. **Choose Speech** from the Control Panels submenu. The Speech control panel will appear.

The Speech control panel has two options. The Voice panel sets the speaking voice and rate of speech. The Talking Alerts panel configures what is spoken when an alert appears.

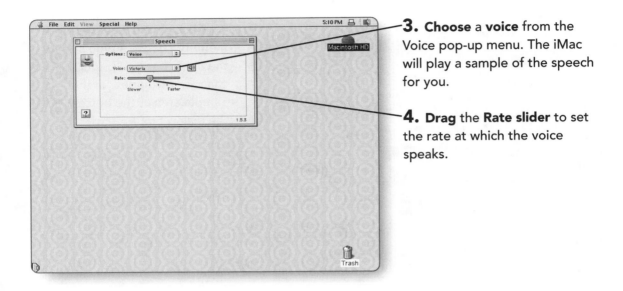

3. Choose a **voice** from the Voice pop-up menu. The iMac will play a sample of the speech for you.

4. Drag the **Rate slider** to set the rate at which the voice speaks.

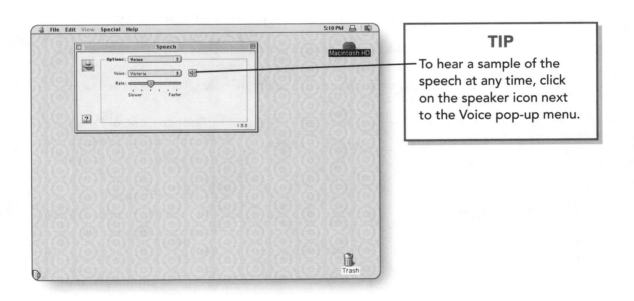

TIP

To hear a sample of the speech at any time, click on the speaker icon next to the Voice pop-up menu.

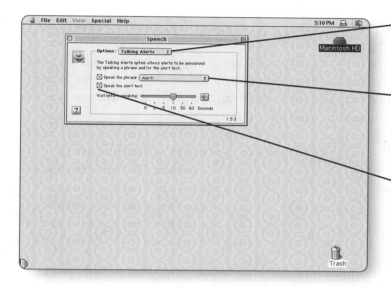

5. Choose Talking Alerts from the Options pop-up menu. The Talking Alerts panel will appear.

6. Choose the **phrase** to be spoken when an alert appears from Speak the phrase: pop-up menu.

7a. Click in the **Speak the alert text box** to remove the X and prevent the content of the alert from being read.

OR

7b. Leave the **X** in the box to hear the content of an alert.

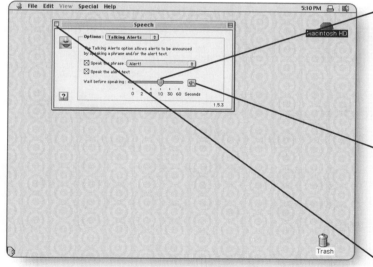

8. Drag the **Wait before speaking: slider** to set the length of time an alert must be on the screen before it is read aloud.

TIP

To hear a sample of your talking alert settings, click on the microphone icon to the right of the delay slider.

9. Close the **Speech window** by clicking the close box.

TIP

You can disable talking alerts by removing the checks from both check boxes in the Talking Alerts panel.

Modifying Apple Menu Items

Usually the options that appear in the Apple menu are determined by the contents of the Apple Menu Items folder, which can be found inside the System Folder. Options can be programs, documents, aliases, or folders.

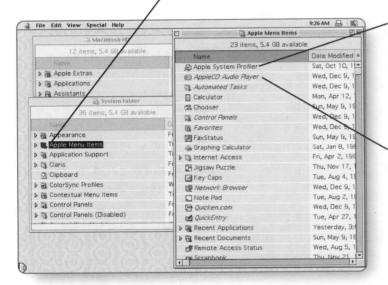

Small programs that are accessible only from the Apple menu—such as the Chooser, Key Caps, or the Graphing Calculator—are placed directly in the Apple Menu Items folder.

Other programs, such as the AppleCD Audio Player, are referenced by aliases. The names of aliases appear in italics inside the folder, but not in italics when listed in the Apple menu.

Adding and Removing Items from the Apple Menu

To add an item to the Apple menu, use the following steps:

1. Create an **alias** for the item (see Chapter 5, "Using Aliases").

2. Drag the **alias** into the Apple Menu Items folder inside the System folder.

3. Click on the **Close box** of the Apple Menu Items folder. The iMac will add the new item as an option in the Apple menu.

To remove an item from the Apple menu, follow these steps:

1. Open the **Apple Menu Items folder** in the System Folder.

2. Drag the **item** you want to remove onto the Desktop, into another folder, or even into the trash.

3. Click on the **Close box** of the Apple Menu Items folder. The iMac will remove the item from the list of Apple menu options.

Configuring the Apple Menu

Some of the configuration of the Apple menu is handled by a control panel. To set the Apple menu options, follow these steps:

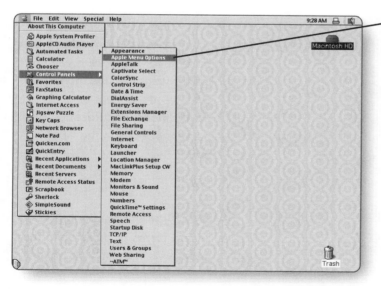

1. Choose Control Panels from the **Apple menu**. The Control Panels submenu will appear.

2. Choose Apple Menu Options from the Control Panels submenu. The Apple Menu Options control panel will appear.

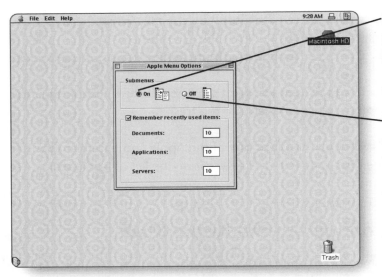

3a. **Select** the **On radio button** if you want folders to act as submenus.

OR

3b. **Click** on the **Off radio button** if you don't want folders to act as submenus. In that case, when you choose the name of a folder from the Apple menu, the iMac will open the folder's window.

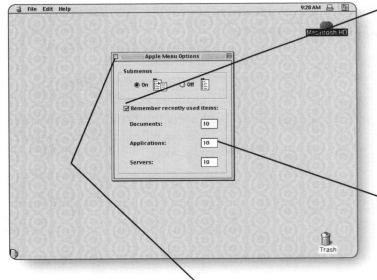

4a. **Click** on the **Remember recently used items: check box** to remove the check if you no longer want to have the Recent Documents, Recent Applications, and Recent Servers options in the Apple menu.

OR

4b. **Type** the **number of recent items** to be listed in the submenus in these text boxes.

5. **Click** on the **Close box** to close the control panel window. The iMac will apply any changes you made to the Apple menu.

Using the Extensions Manager

The Extensions Manager helps you manage all the add-on programs that are automatically loaded into the main memory when you boot your iMac.

Occasionally extensions may not be able to coexist with one another in main memory (called an *extension conflict*). Typical symptoms of an extension conflict include unexpected program crashes or your computer suddenly freezes while attempting to load extensions.

One of the main purposes of the Extensions Manager is to help you identify extension conflicts. By turning them off one-by-one you'll be able to identify which extension is causing the problem.

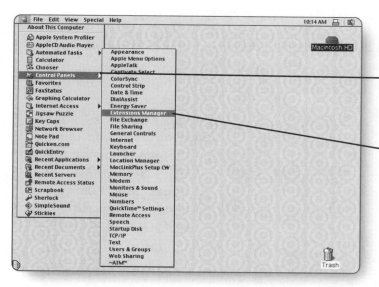

To access the Extensions Manager, follow these steps:

1. Choose Control Panels from the **Apple menu**. The Control Panels submenu will appear.

2. Choose Extensions Manager from the Control Panels submenu. The Extensions Manager window will appear.

NOTE

Use caution when working with the Extensions Manager. It is an advanced feature of the system software.

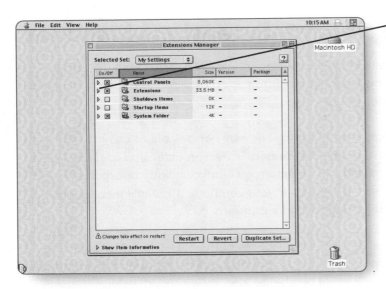

3. Click on the **right-facing triangle** next to a folder of items. The folder will expand so you can see its contents. Folders with enabled contents (those that contain items that are being loaded at system startup) will have an X in the check box to the left of the folder icon.

Disabling and Enabling Items

To disable an item to prevent it from being loaded at system startup, use the following steps:

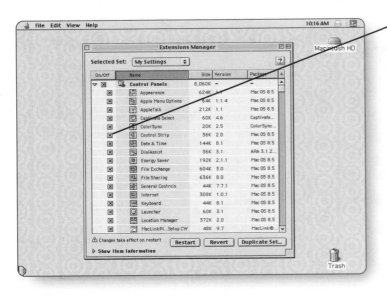

1. Click on the **X** to the left of an item. The iMac will disable the item, preventing it from being loaded into main memory.

2. Repeat Step 1 until you have finished disabling all the items that you don't want to load.

3. Click on the **Close box.** The Extensions Manager window will close.

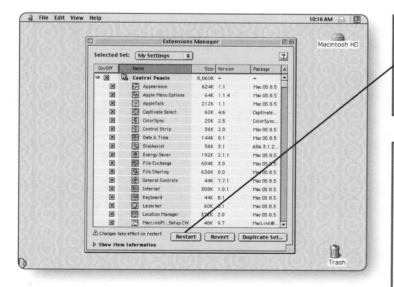

TIP

Be sure to restart your iMac so that your changes will take effect.

TIP

One quick way to check for an extension conflict is to boot without extensions. To do so, hold down the Shift key while restarting the iMac. You can release the Shift key as soon as you see Extensions Disabled appear underneath the Mac OS logo.

7

Working with Application Software

When you are not interacting with the Finder to manage disk storage, you will usually be working with a program. The iMac is famous for the consistency of basic program operations. In particular, the way in which you interact with documents to create, open, close, save, and print them is generally the same from one program to another. In this chapter, you'll learn how to:

- Start a program
- Work with documents
- Exit a program
- Handle multiple programs running at the same time
- Use the Launcher

Starting a Program

Starting a program is also known as *running* or *launching* it. Depending on the program and the way you have it configured, launching a program may open a new, blank document for you, open the document you last used, or open no document at all.

For the examples in this chapter and in Chapter 8, you can use a program called SimpleText, a text editor that is supplied with the iMac.

NOTE

Although your iMac comes preloaded with many programs, others have not been installed and are supplied on CD-ROMs. You will therefore need to install them before you can use them. Instructions for installing software can be found in Appendix D, "Adding Software."

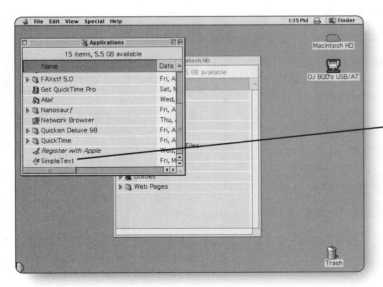

To launch a program, follow these steps:

1. Find the **application** in the disk hierarchy.

2. Double-click on the **application icon**. The program will open. Depending upon the program, a new untitled document will open.

TIP

You can also launch an application by clicking on its icon to highlight it and then either choosing Open from the File menu or pressing ⌘-O.

Handling Documents

The work that you create on your iMac will be saved in documents. Once you have saved the contents of a document, you can close it and later return to that document, open it with the application you used to create it, and continue working with it again.

Creating a New Document

A new document provides you with a blank surface on which you can type, draw, compute, and so on. The process for creating a new document is the same for most Macintosh programs.

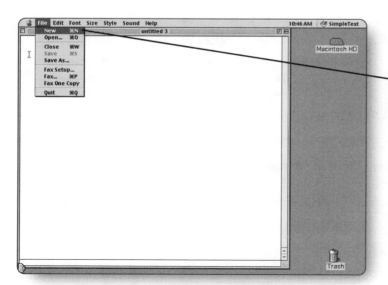

1. Launch the **program** you want to use.

2. Choose New from the **File menu**. The program will create the new document and name it "untitled."

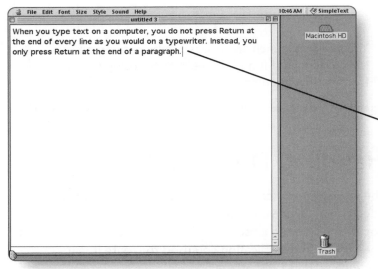

If you happen to have more than one new document that has not been given a name, "untitled" will be followed by a sequence number, as in "untitled 3."

3. Type some **text**. What you type will appear to the left of the insertion point. Entering text is discussed in more detail in Chapter 8, "Working with Text."

Saving a Document

A document with which you are working is kept in main memory. Unless you save it permanently on a disk, any changes you have made to the document since it was last saved will be lost when you exit the program.

NOTE

The wise computer user adheres to the SOS directive: "Save Often, Silly." How often? Somewhere between every 5–15 minutes, depending on how critical the document.

The way in which you save a document depends on whether you want to save it using the same name, replace the existing version of a document, or save a copy using another name.

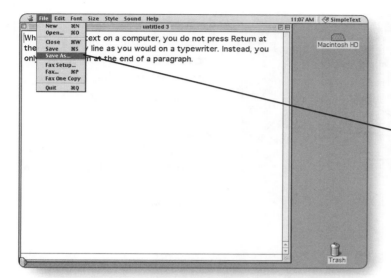

Save As

To save a document for the first time, you use the Save As menu option.

1. Choose Save As from the **File menu**. The Save As dialog box will appear.

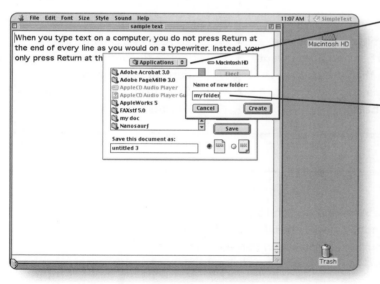

2a. Locate the **folder** where you want to save the document.

OR

2b. Click on new to create a new folder. **Type** a **folder name** in the text box, then **click** on **Create**.

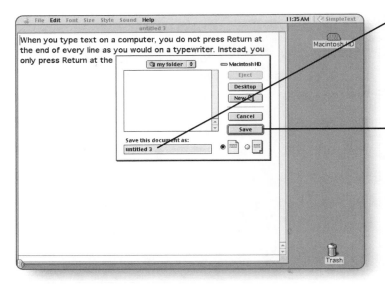

3. Type a **name** for the document in the Save this document as: text box at the bottom of the dialog box. The text will appear in the box.

4. Click on **Save**. If no file exists with the same name in the current folder, the iMac will save the file and close the dialog box, returning you to your document.

NOTE

If the current folder contains a file with the same name, the iMac displays an alert asking if you want to replace the existing file with the new one or abort the save. To abort saving a copy of a document, click on the Cancel button.

TIP

To resave a previously saved document under its current name, choose Save from the File menu or press ⌘-S.

NOTE

Use the Save As menu option to save a copy of a document under a new name. Choose Save As from the File menu, type a new name in the Save this document as: text box, then click on the Save button.

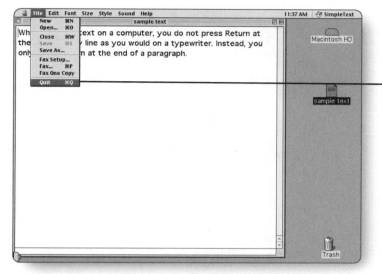

Quitting a Program

1. **Choose Quit** from the **File menu**. The application will close.

TIP

You can also quit an application by pressing ⌘-Q.

Saving a Document When You Quit

If you have any documents that have been modified since you last saved them, most programs will give you a chance to save those changes before you exit the program and lose the work:

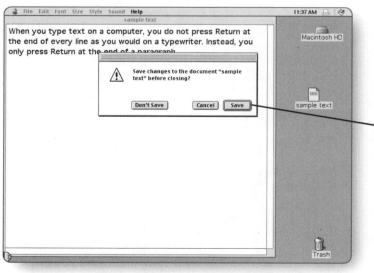

1. **Click** on **Quit** from the **File menu**. The program will display an alert warning you of unsaved changes and asking you what action you would like to take.

2a. **Click** on **Save** to save the document. If the document has not yet been named, the Save File dialog box will open.

OR

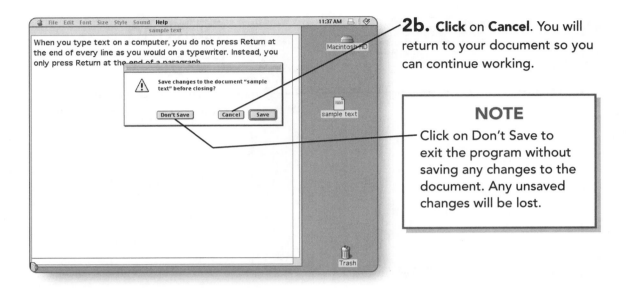

2b. **Click** on **Cancel**. You will return to your document so you can continue working.

NOTE

Click on Don't Save to exit the program without saving any changes to the document. Any unsaved changes will be lost.

Opening Existing Documents

You open a document stored on a disk so you can view, edit, or print the contents.

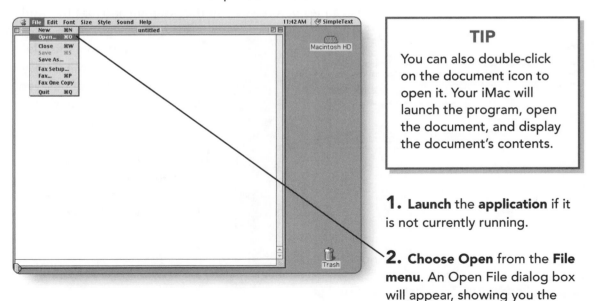

TIP

You can also double-click on the document icon to open it. Your iMac will launch the program, open the document, and display the document's contents.

1. **Launch** the **application** if it is not currently running.

2. **Choose Open** from the **File menu**. An Open File dialog box will appear, showing you the contents of the current folder.

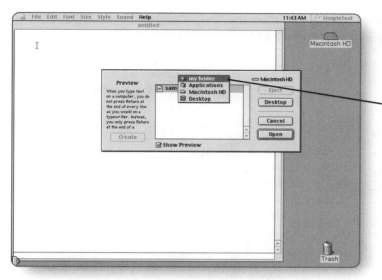

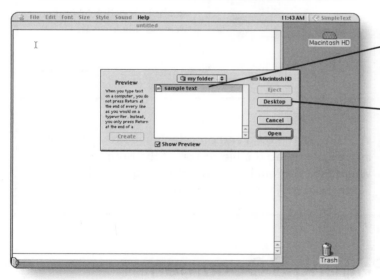

There are several techniques you can use to navigate through the folder and file hierarchy on the disk to find the correct folder:

- Use the pop-up menu at the top of the dialog box to move to a folder directly above the current folder in the disk folder hierarchy. The top level in this hierarchy is the Desktop even though it is on the bottom of the list. The selected folder will become the current folder and its contents will be displayed in the list in the dialog box.

- Double-click on a folder in the list of items to display its contents.

- Click on the Desktop button to go directly to the Desktop. The Desktop folder will become the current folder, showing you all items on the Desktop, providing access to all mounted disk volumes.

Once you have located the file you want to open, you can proceed to open the file.

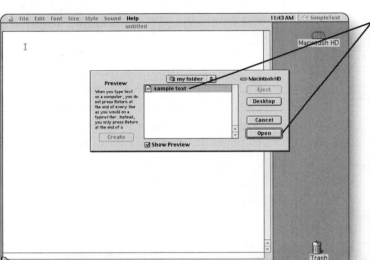

1a. **Click** on the **file** to highlight it and **click** on **Open**. The iMac will open the file and display its contents.

OR

1b. **Double-click** on the **file name**. The iMac will open the file and display its contents.

> ### TIP
> To abort the file opening process, click on the Cancel button.

> ### TIP
> You can use the drag and drop technique to open a file as well. Just drag the file on top of the program icon. When the program icon appears highlighted, drop the file by releasing the mouse button.

Printing a Document

A paper copy of a document is known as a *hard copy*. Assuming that you have a printer attached to your iMac, you can print the contents of any document you create, documents that you access via the Internet, and in some cases, documents created by programs. Consult the instructions that came with your specific printer to find out how to attach it to your iMac.

Choosing a Printer

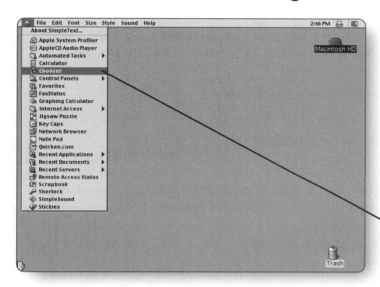

Your iMac can print to more than one type of output device. For example, when you send a fax, you print to a special type of file that can be sent as a fax. The iMac can also be connected to more than one printer; therefore, before you begin printing, you must choose which printer you want to use.

1. Select Chooser from the **Apple menu**. The iMac Chooser window will appear.

On the left side of the window you will see one icon for several types of printers possibly available on your iMac.

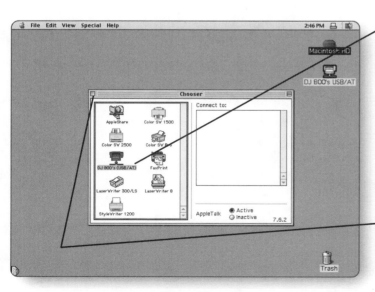

2. Click on the **printer icon** for the type of printer you have. If your printer is turned on, its name will appear highlighted in the list at the right of the window. (The instructions that came with your printer should tell you what type you have. See your printer manual for the proper set up of your printer.)

3. Click on the **Close box** to close the Chooser window. If this is the first time you have chosen this printer, the iMac will place a Printer icon on the Desktop. You will use this special file to help you manage printing activities.

NOTE

Once you have chosen a printer, you don't need to choose it again unless you want to change the printer. The setting is retained by the iMac even when power is turned off.

Using Page Setup

You use Page Setup to choose print settings such as the size of the paper and the orientation of the page. Once these settings are in place, you do not need to change them unless you switch paper sizes, change document orientation, or choose a different printer.

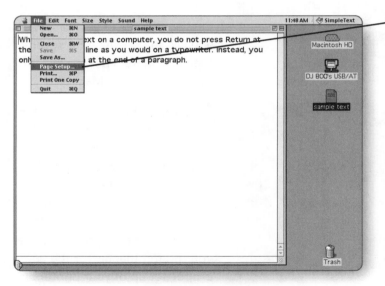

1. Choose Page Setup from the **File menu**. The Page Setup dialog box will appear.

2. Click on the **landscape button** if you want to change the page orientation from *portrait* (taller than it is wide) to *landscape* (wider than it is tall).

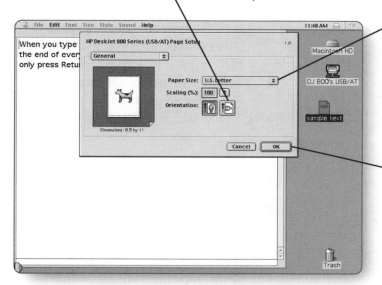

3. Click on a **paper size** from the Paper Size: pop-up menu. A list of paper sizes will appear. The exact sizes you see in the menu will depend on the printer that has been selected in the Chooser.

4. Click on **OK**. You will return to the program you were using before the dialog box appeared.

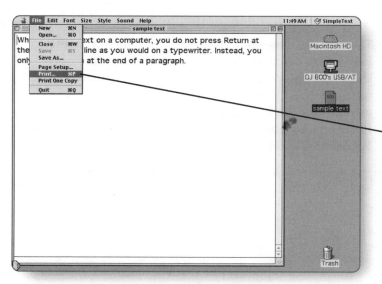

Printing a Document

1. Open a **document** to be printed.

2. Choose Print from the **File menu**. The Printer Dialog box will appear.

3. Type the **number of copies** to be printed in the Copies: text box if you want more than one copy of the document. The number will appear in the text box.

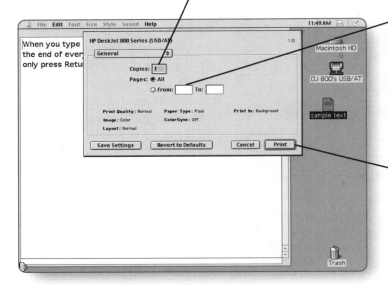

4. Type the **page range** to be printed in the From: and To: text boxes if your document has several pages and you don't want to print the entire document. The page numbers will appear in the text boxes.

5. Click on **Print**. Your document will be printed.

TIP

There are also two ways to print a document from the Finder. You can drag the document on top of the Desktop Printer icon. Or, you can click on the document to select it and then choose Print from the Finder's File menu. The iMac will launch the program, display the Printer dialog box, create the print file, quit the application, and return you to the Finder.

Running More than One Application at a Time

The iMac can have more than one program open at the same time. This is known as *multitasking*, and means the programs that are in main memory take turns using the CPU. Although only one program can actually run at any given instant, the sharing of the CPU and switching from one program to another occurs so fast that it appears to you as if multiple programs are actually running simultaneously.

The application with which you are working is known as the *foreground application*. All other open programs are called *background applications*. You decide which application is the foreground application.

- Click on any visible window for the program you want to use. The iMac will make the program the foreground application and will place its windows on top of all other windows on the screen.

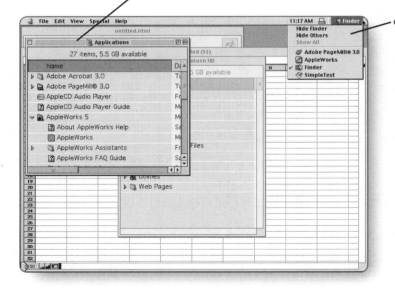

- Use the Application menu, which is located at the far right of the menu bar. It lists all programs currently running.

Using the Launcher

One of the handiest features of the iMac is the Launcher, a program that can help you organize aliases of document files, folders, and programs you access frequently. The Launcher turns each alias into a button that you can click on or drag and drop to.

1. **Choose Control Panels** from the **Apple menu**. The Control Panels submenu will appear.

2. **Choose Launcher** from the Control Panels submenu. The Launcher window will appear on the Desktop.

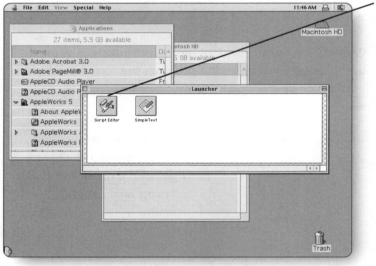

- **Click** on a **button** to open a document file, folder, or program.

  OR

- **Drag** a **document file** onto a program button to open the file. If the program is not running, the iMac will launch it for you.

Adding Aliases to the Launcher

Until you add your own items to the Launcher, it contains only two aliases. The Launcher is most useful when you add aliases to it representing items that you need to access quickly.

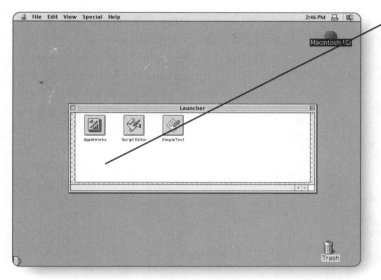

1. **Drag** a **document file, folder, or program icon** to the Launcher window. The iMac will create an alias and store it in the Launcher Items folder inside the System Folder. The new button will appear in the Launcher window.

Creating Launcher Sections

Although the Launcher automatically alphabetizes the aliases you add to it, as the number of buttons increases, it becomes increasingly hard to find what you need quickly. You may therefore want to create categories into which you place aliases. When you have finished, the Launcher will have one button for each category of aliases.

1. **Double-click** on the **Launcher Items folder** in the System Folder. The Launcher Items folder will appear.

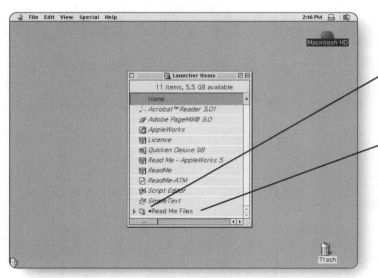

2. **Create** a **new folder**. The new folder will appear.

3. **Type Option–8** to insert a bullet (•) as the first character of the folder name.

4. **Type** in a **name** for the section right after the bullet. The new name will appear next to the bullet.

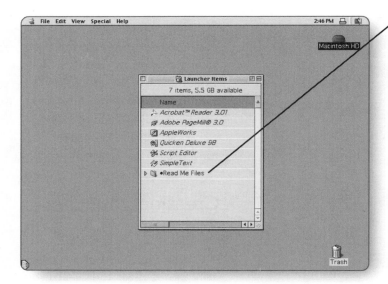

5. **Drag** any **aliases** that should be part of the new section into the folder. Any aliases that are not placed in a folder whose name begins with a ● will become part of the Applications section.

6. **Repeat steps 2** through **5** for all sections you would like to create.

TIP

Although there is no limit to the number of sections you can have in the Launcher, if you have more than three, the buttons at the top of the window showing the section names become too small to display much text. You will find the Launcher most effective if you restrict the number of categories to no more than three (in addition to the Applications section, which you can't delete).

8

Working with Text

The ability to manipulate and format text has been part of the Macintosh since 1984. Text appears just about everywhere: on the Desktop, in documents, and in dialog boxes. Fortunately, the way in which you enter and modify text is remarkably consistent, regardless of where that text happens to be used. In this chapter, you'll learn how to:

- Enter, select, and modify text
- Copy and paste text
- Work with fonts and styles
- Find and replace text

Typing, Selecting, and Modifying Text

The most basic operations that you perform with text are typing, selecting, and modifying the text.

Entering Text

When you first approach an empty area for entering text—regardless of whether the area is a document or a text box within a dialog box—you will see a *flashing insertion point* at the far left. This straight line indicates where the typed text will appear. As you type, the insertion point will move to the right. You will also notice that the mouse pointer changes to an I-beam whenever it is over an area in which text can be typed.

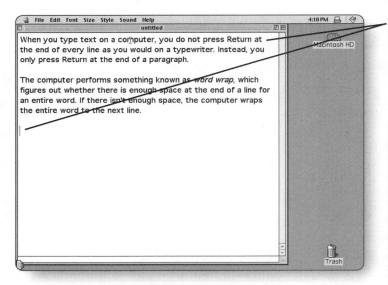

1. Type some **text**, pressing the Return key only at the end of a paragraph. The insertion point will move to the right as you type.

NOTE

There's no need to press Return at the end of a line. Most programs use *word wrapping:* if a word is too long to fit completely on a line, the program "wraps" the entire word, moving it down to the beginning of the next line.

Moving the Insertion Point

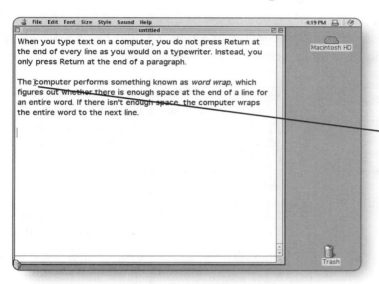

If you need to modify text or insert some text in the middle of a document, you must place the insertion point somewhere else in the document.

1. Move the **I-beam** to the location where you would like to insert text.

2. Click the **mouse button**. The insertion point will appear in its new location.

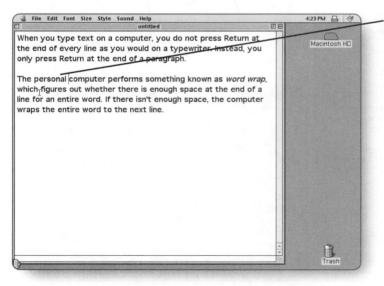

3. Type some **text**. The new text will appear at the new location, and the program will adjust word wrap to accommodate the new text.

Selecting Text

Most of the editing you do will be on a block of text. When a block of text is highlighted, it is referred to as being *selected*. There are three techniques for selecting text:

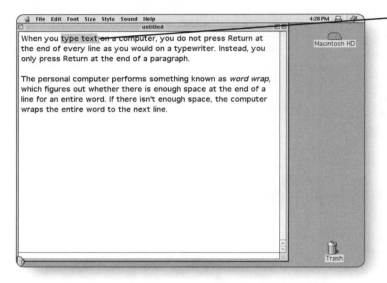

- If the amount of text you need to select is relatively small, click and drag the I-beam over the text you want to select.

- Double-click on a single word to select it.

- To select a large block of text, place the insertion point at the beginning of the text you want to select, then scroll to the end of the text block. Shift+click (hold down the Shift key while clicking the mouse button) at the end of the text you want to select. The text between the insertion point and the Shift+click location will be highlighted.

Modifying Text

The simplest way to change existing text while you are typing is to use the Delete key, which deletes one character at a time to the left of the insertion point.

1. Place the **insertion point** to the right of the first character to be deleted. The insertion point will appear in its new location.

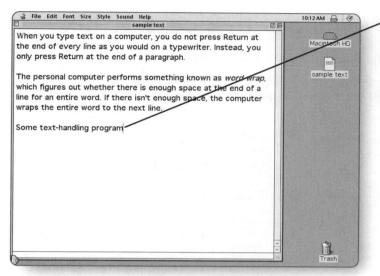

2. Press the **Delete key** once for each character to be deleted. The character to the left of the insertion point will disappear each time you press Delete.

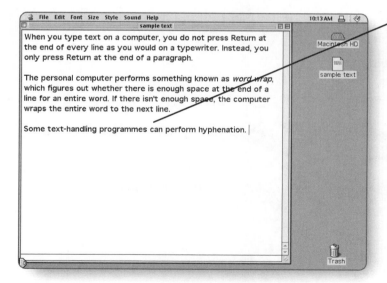

3. Type some **text**. The new text will appear to the left of the insertion point.

Working with Blocks of Text

The most powerful text-editing techniques available are those that work with blocks of selected text. You can replace, delete, move, and duplicate selected text.

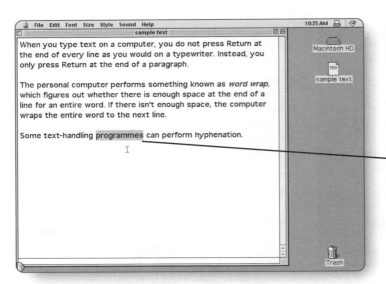

Replacing Selected Text

Replacing selected text lets you easily delete a block of text and then replace it with new typing.

1. Select the **text** you want to replace. The text will be highlighted.

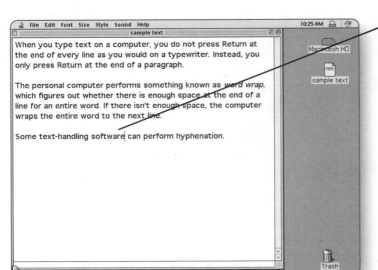

2. Type the **replacement text**. The selected text will be deleted, and the new typing will appear in its place.

Deleting Selected Text

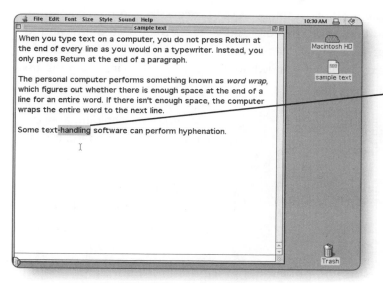

To simply delete a block of text without entering replacement text, do the following:

1. Select the **text** you want to delete. The text will be highlighted.

2a. Press the **Delete key**. The selected text will be deleted.

OR

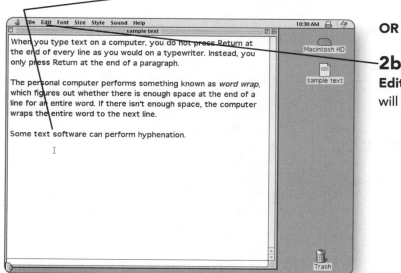

2b. Choose Clear from the **Edit menu**. The selected text will be deleted.

Moving Selected Text

One of the best things about processing text on a computer is that you can move blocks of text around without having to retype anything. Moving text involves deleting the block of text, storing it somewhere temporarily, then inserting the text at a new location.

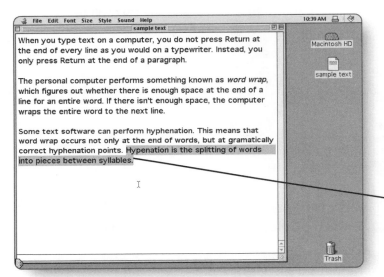

The temporary holding area is known as the *Clipboard*. It can hold just about any type of data, text, or graphic. However, it can only hold one item at a time (one image or one block of text). When you place something on the Clipboard, it replaces whatever was there previously.

1. Select the **text** you want to move. The text will be highlighted.

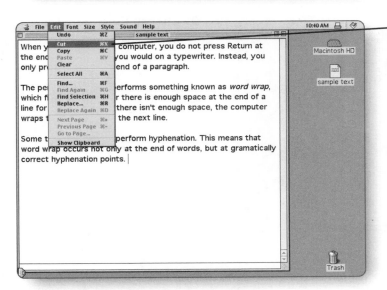

2a. Choose Cut from the **Edit menu.** The text will be deleted from the document and placed on the Clipboard.

OR

2b. Press ⌘-X. The text will be deleted from the document and placed on the Clipboard.

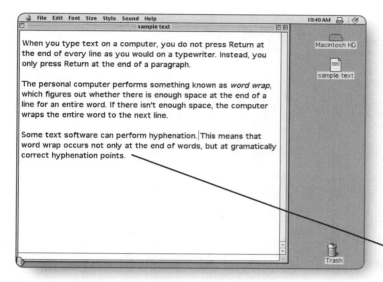

TIP

You can cut (or copy) text from one document and paste it into another. If you want to paste text into a different document, you must make the new document's window the active window before pasting the text.

3. **Place** the **insertion point** where you want the text from the Clipboard to be inserted.

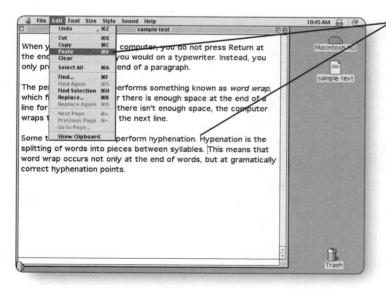

4a. **Choose Paste** from the **Edit menu**. The text on the Clipboard will be inserted to the left of the insertion point.

OR

4b. **Press** ⌘-**V**. The text on the Clipboard will be inserted to the left of the insertion point.

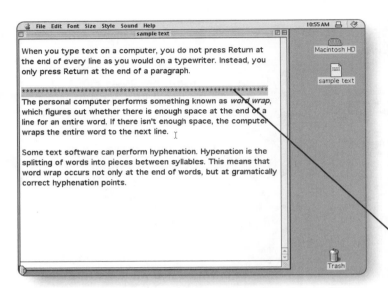

Duplicating Selected Text

If you want to copy a block of text, and place the copy somewhere else, you can use a variation of the cut-and-paste technique in the previous section that leaves the original document unchanged.

1. Select the **text** to be copied. The text will be highlighted.

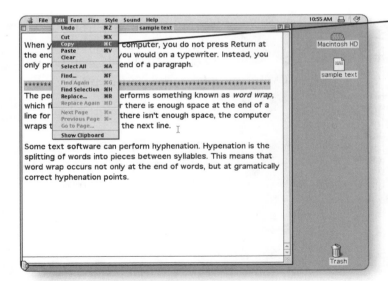

2a. Choose Copy from the **Edit menu**. The selected text will be copied to the Clipboard without changing the original document.

OR

2b. Press ⌘-C. The selected text will be copied to the Clipboard without changing the original document.

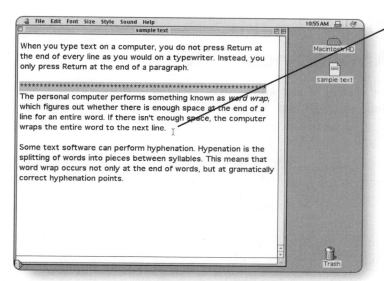

3. Place the **insertion point** where you want to insert the text. The insertion point will appear in its new location.

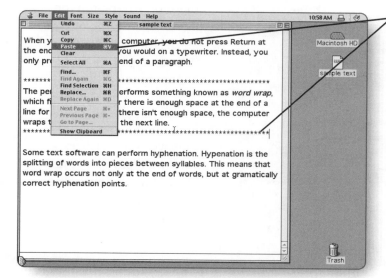

4a. Choose Paste from the **Edit menu**. The text will be copied from the Clipboard and inserted into the document.

OR

4b. Press ⌘-V. The text will be copied from the Clipboard and inserted into the document.

NOTE

The contents of the Clipboard remain unchanged until you copy another item into it.

Changing the Appearance of Text

The Macintosh has always been capable of working with many kinds of styled text. You can take advantage of the iMac's capabilities to use a variety of text styles.

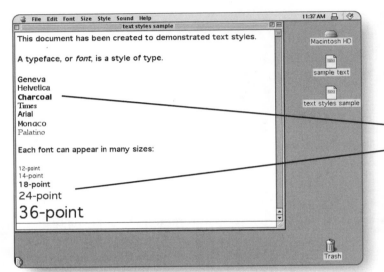

Understanding Text Characteristics

There are three aspects of text over which you have control:

- **Font**. The style of type.

- **Size**. The height of type is measured in *points*. Therefore, 12-point type is shorter than 14-point type, which is still smaller than 18-point type.

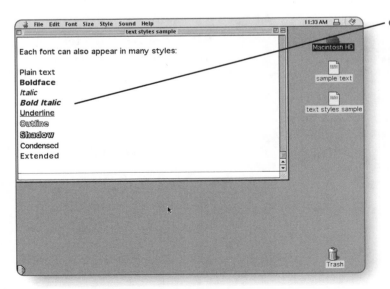

- **Style**. Text styles include enhancements such as boldface (heavy text), italic (slanted text), bold italic (slanted heavy text), and underline.

Changing the Font

Although your iMac comes with a set of standard Macintosh fonts, many programs install additional fonts.

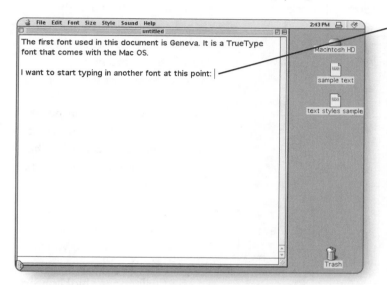

1a. **Place** the **insertion point** at the location in the document where you want to use a new font. The insertion point will appear in its new location.

OR

1b. **Select** the **text** for which the font is to be changed. The text will appear highlighted.

2. **Click** on the **Font menu.** The Font menu will appear.

3. **Click** on the name of the **font.** If text has been selected, the program will change the font of the selected text. If no text is selected, the new text you type will appear in the chosen font.

Changing Font Size

When you are typing a letter, you usually type everything in a single font size. However, if you are typing a report that has hierarchical section headings, you may want to make the outer headings larger than the headings nested within them. You will therefore need to change the size of the font.

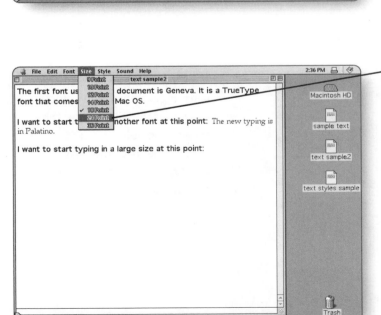

1a. Place the **insertion point** at the location where you want the new font size to begin. The insertion point will appear in its new location.

OR

1b. Select the **text** to which the new size is to be applied. The text will appear highlighted.

2. Choose a **font size** from the Size menu. If text has been selected, the program will change the size of the selected text. If no text is selected, the new text you type will appear in the chosen size.

NOTE

You will notice that some or all of the sizes in the Size menu appear in outlined type. These are the sizes that will give you the best appearance for the current font. However, you can select any size, regardless of whether it is outlined.

TIP

The easiest to read and most commonly used font size is 12-point.

Modifying Style

Styles are different from other text characteristics in that they are *additive*. Therefore, when you choose a new style, it is in addition to any other styles currently in effect. This means that you can use more than one style at a time. Bold italic, for example, is a combination of boldface and italic.

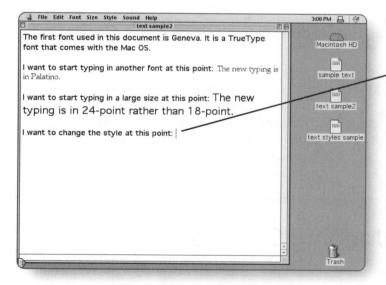

To change the style of text, follow these steps:

1a. Place the **insertion point** at the location in the document where you want the new style will begin. The insertion point will appear in its new location.

OR

1b. Select the **text** to which you want to apply the new style. The text will appear highlighted.

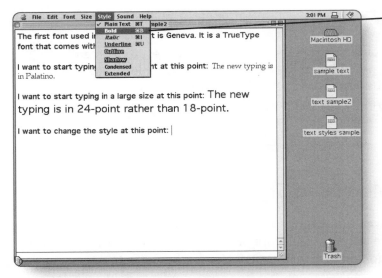

2. Choose a **style** from the **Style menu**. If text has been selected, the application will change the style of the selected text. If no text is selected, new typing will appear in the chosen style.

> **TIP**
> The key combinations for the basic styles are as follows:
>
> Plain Text = ⌘-T
> Boldface = ⌘-B
> Italic = ⌘-I
> Underline = ⌘-U

> **NOTE**
> Underlining was used on a typewriter in place of italics, which was only available with typeset materials. Therefore, most things that you might be in the habit of underlining, such as the title of a book in a bibliography, should use the italics style rather than the underline style.

Undoing Changes

Imagine that you have accidentally deleted some text or that you don't like the style you just applied. Do you have to retype the deleted text or set the text style back to plain text? Not if you catch the error immediately after doing it! You can undo your most recent action.

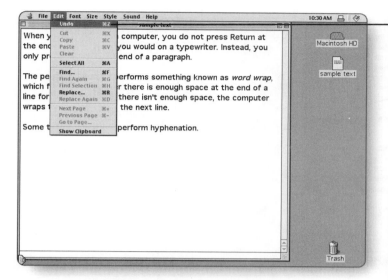

1a. **Choose Undo** from the **Edit menu**. The program will undo your most recent action.

OR

1b. **Press ⌘-Z**. The program will undo your most recent action.

TIP

Some programs maintain a history of the actions you take. You can therefore undo more than once. Each undo takes you back one action.

Finding and Replacing

The longer a document becomes, the more difficult it may be to find a specific part of the document that you want to edit. To make that easier, many programs provide a way to search for specified characters and, if desired, replace them with other characters. This is often called *Find and Replace*.

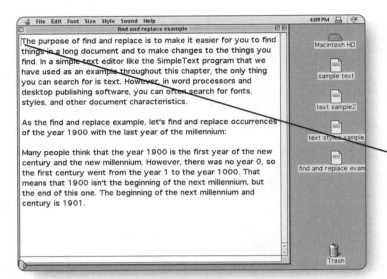

Finding Text in a Document

If you just want to find text in a document without changing it, use the following steps:

1. Place the **insertion point** at the location in the document where you want the search to begin.

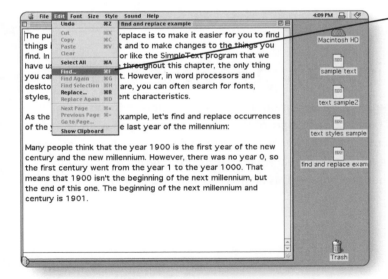

2. Choose Find from the **Edit menu**. The Find dialog box will appear.

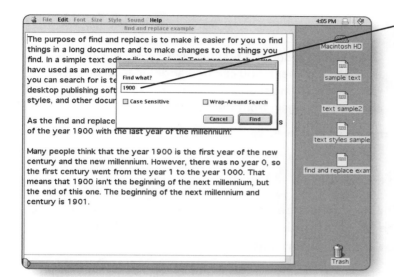

3. Type the **text** you want to find in the Find what? text box.

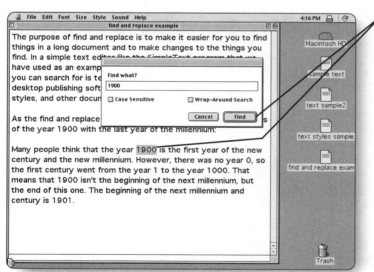

4. Click on **Find**. The program will locate the first occurrence of the text and highlight that text.

NOTE

The most common key combination for the Find command is ⌘-F. Occasionally, however, you may find that a different key has been used.

TIP

Once you've found the first occurrence of your search text in a document, you can find additional occurrences without displaying the Find dialog box again. Just choose Find Again from the Edit menu.

Replacing

The Replace feature lets you both search for text and replace the found text with new text automatically. To find and replace text, follow these steps:

1. **Place** the **insertion point** at the location in the document where you want to find and replace text.

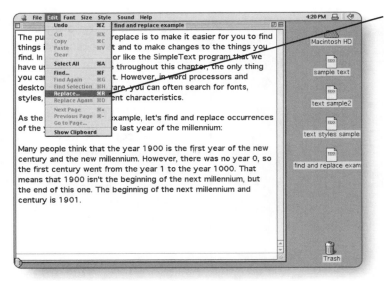

2. **Choose Replace** from the **Edit menu**. The Replace dialog box will appear.

3. Type the **text** that you want to find in the Find what? text box.

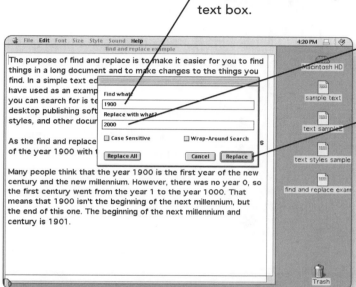

4. Type the **replacement text** in the Replace with what? text box.

5. Click on **Replace**. The program will find the first occurrence of the text and replace it with the replacement text.

TIP

If you want to replace the next occurrence of the same search text with the same replacement text, use the Replace Again option from the Edit menu.

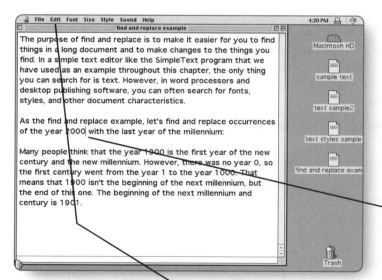

Replacing All

It is also possible to replace all occurrences at once of a block of text with the same replacement text. This is known as *Replace All*.

1. Place the **insertion point** at the location in the document where you want the search to begin.

2. Choose Replace from the **Edit menu**. The Replace dialog box will appear.

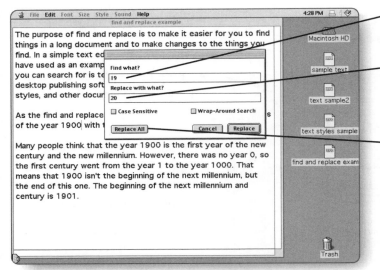

3. **Type** the **search text** in the Find what? text box.

4. **Type** the **replacement text** in the Replace with what? text box.

5. **Click** on **Replace All**. The program will find all occurrences of the search text and replace them with the replacement text.

NOTE

Although it is a powerful tool, Replace All can also be dangerous because it can have unintended effects. For example, if you want to change Mary Smith's last name to Jones, you set up the Replace dialog box to find Smith and replace it with Jones. Unfortunately, if there was also a person named Smithson, when you replace all, you not only end up with Mary Jones, but also with Jonesson.

---

6. When finished with Simple Text, **click** on the **close box** and return to the iMac desktop.

9

Getting Help

Because the iMac is designed for computer users of all levels, it offers a great deal of help as you work. The Help menu provides various types of Help. Like the Apple menu, it is available with all programs. However, the Help menu's options change considerably depending on the program with which you are working. In this chapter, you'll learn how to:

- Use the basic tutorials
- Turn on Balloon help
- Discover the Help Center
- Get help with the Apple Guide

Viewing the Tutorials

Apple has included two interactive multimedia presentations with your iMac that will reinforce the basics you learned in the previous chapters. The first deals with using the mouse; the second focuses on the Desktop. You can view these tutorials at any time, although it's a good idea to go through them before you start working intensively with application software.

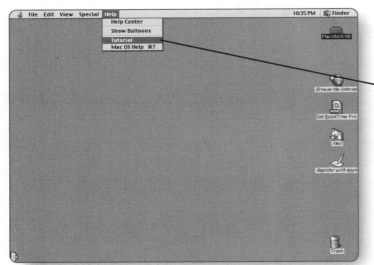

1. **Choose Tutorial** from the **Help menu**. The screen will go black as the iMac launches the tutorial. An introductory screen will appear.

2. **Click** on **Mouse Skills**. The tutorial will lead you through several exercises, eventually returning to the introductory screen.

3. **Click** on **Desktop Skills**. When finished, you'll return to the introductory screen.

4. **Click** on **Quit**. The tutorial will end, and you will return to the Finder.

Using Balloon Help

Balloon Help, which is available with many programs, provides cartoon-like balloons that appear when you move the mouse pointer over some element on the screen. A balloon contains information that identifies the element and provides you with information about how to use it. Balloons are most useful when you are just learning to use your iMac or a new program.

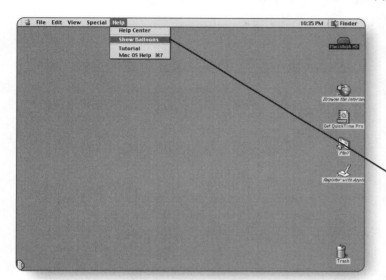

1. Choose Show Balloons from the **Help menu.**

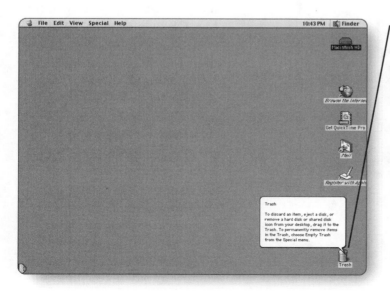

2. Move the **mouse pointer** over an item on the screen that you want to know more about. A balloon will pop up with information about the item.

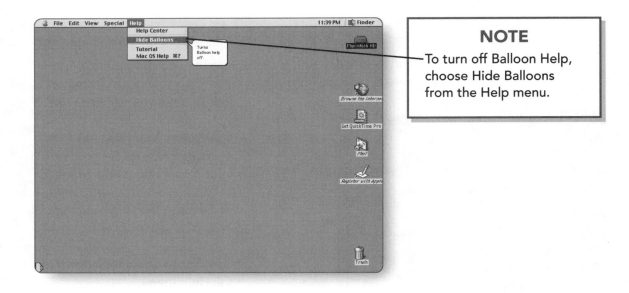

NOTE

To turn off Balloon Help, choose Hide Balloons from the Help menu.

Visiting the Help Center

The Help Center is a reference that helps you become more familiar with your iMac. It contains three documents: About Your iMac, AppleScript Help, and Mac OS Help. The iMac and Mac OS Help contain lots of valuable information for the new user. The Help Center can search through all its documents, or let you browse.

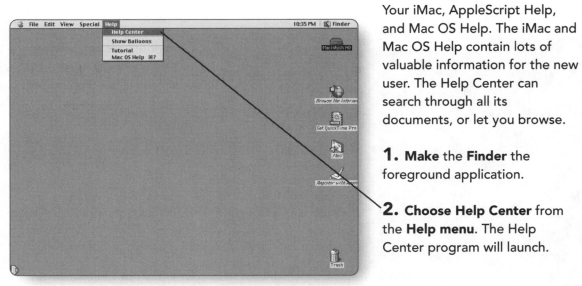

1. Make the **Finder** the foreground application.

2. Choose Help Center from the **Help menu**. The Help Center program will launch.

The initial Help Center screen has a table of contents that lists the three Help Center documents. When you look at the titles of those documents in color on your iMac screen, they will appear as blue underlined text. They are *hyperlinks*, text that, when clicked on, displays another part of the document.

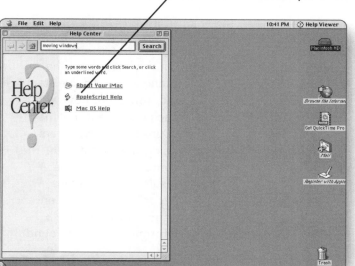

NOTE

Hyperlinks are used extensively throughout the World Wide Web. You will learn more about them in Chapter 15.

Searching in Help Center

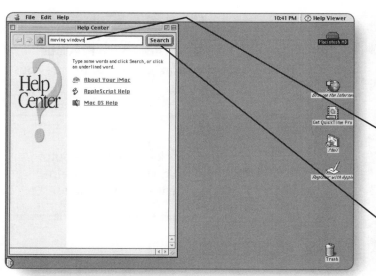

One way to find information in the Help Center is to ask the iMac to match search phrases that you type in. To search the Help Center, follow these steps:

1. Type a **word or phrase** describing a subject you want to learn more about. The text will appear in the text box.

2. Click on **Search**. The Help Center window changes to show you the results of the search.

3. Click on the **topic name** that best fits your search. The Help Viewer will take you to that page.

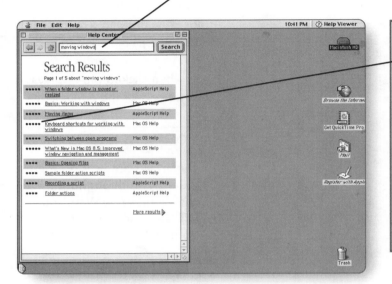

NOTE

On the left side of the listing are up to five stars that represent how well each document matches your search—five stars being the best match. The center column of the result listing contains hyperlinks to Help Center pages where more information can be found.

4a. Click on **Next** to move to the next page.

OR

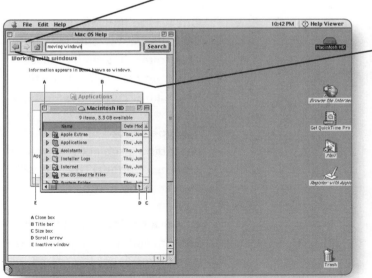

4b. Click on the **Previous button** to move to the previous page.

TIP

Click on the Home button to go back to the Help Center opening page.

Browsing the Help Center

You can browse through the Help Center rather than searching for information on a specific topic. This is a good strategy when you are interested in learning a wide variety of iMac techniques.

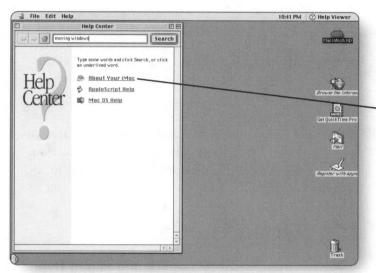

1. Open the **Help Center**. Make sure that you are looking at the Help Center's opening screen.

2. Click on a **Help Center section document name**. The opening page for that document will open. A list of topics will appear at the left side of the page. Each of these topics is a hyperlink that you can click on to display a list of subtopics.

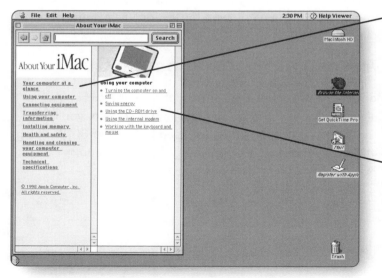

3. Click on a **topic** in the left pane. A list of subtopics will appear in the right pane. Each of the subtopics is a hyperlink that will take you to a page containing information about the subtopic.

4. Click on a **subtopic** to read the page. The subtopic page will appear.

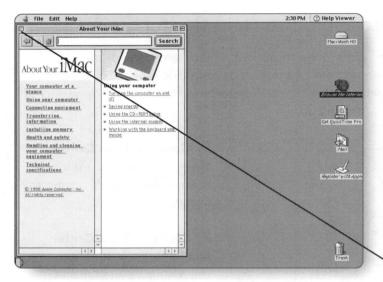

NOTE

The exact contents of a Help Center page vary depending on the topic. A Help Center page may also contain a link that will open a *Control Panel* (a small program such as the Launcher used for software configuration) or take you to an Apple Guide entry.

5. Click on the **Close box** when you are finished with the Help Center. The window will close.

NOTE

Apple Guides are also accessible through the Help Center, where documents refer to an Apple Guide section with links that look like blue diamonds.

Using Apple Guide

Apple Guide is a form of Help that takes you step by step through various programs. Program-specific Guides are accessible from the program's Help menu, usually with the name of the program followed by "Guide" as a menu option.

Opening a Program-Specific Guide

Many of the programs that came with your iMac have Apple Guides available. For the examples in this section, you'll be using SimpleText, the text editor used in Chapter 8, "Working with Text." Access a Guide by using the Help menu.

1. **Launch** the **SimpleText program** if it is not already running. The program will appear.

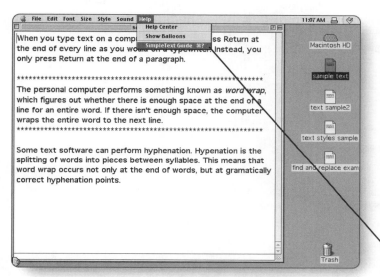

2. **Choose SimpleText Guide** from the **Help menu**. The SimpleText Guide opening page will appear.

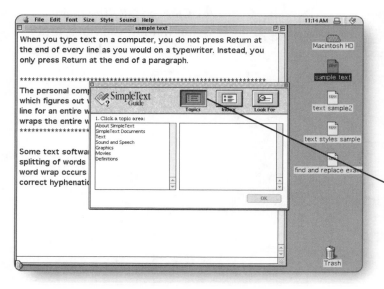

Selecting a Topic

The main Guide page allows you to look at the topics available using three different methods: by topic, index, or keyword search. To choose a topic, follow these steps:

1. **Click** on the **Topics button** in the SimpleText Guide opening page. A list of topic areas will appear on the left side of the page.

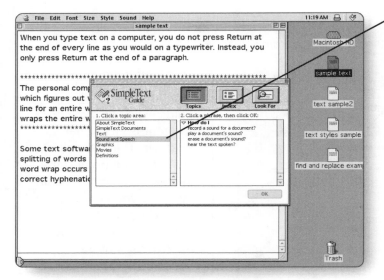

2. Click on a **topic**. it will appear highlighted, and a list of subtopics will appear on the right.

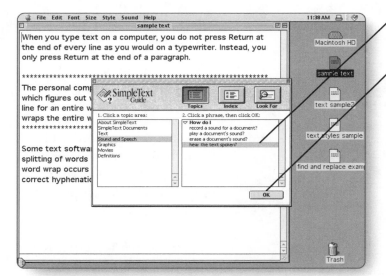

3. Click on a **subtopic**. It will be highlighted.

4. Click on **OK**. The main Guide window will close, and a window for the chosen topic will open.

Following a Topic's Steps

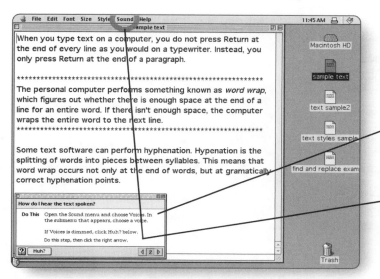

Guides lead you through a topic step by step, with lots of visual clues to help you along. Don't run ahead of the Guide; if you do, it will force you to back up.

1. **Read** the **descriptive information** on the first page of the topic window.

If the next step involves a menu to open, it will be circled in bright red.

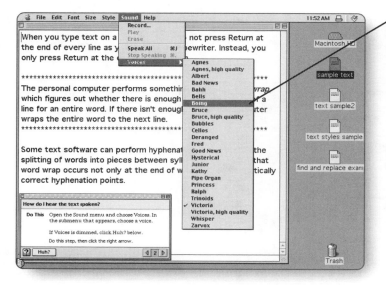

2. **Click** on the **menu** as directed. The menu will appear. The Guide will show you which option to choose by underlining the correct menu choice and displaying it in red.

What you will see at this point depends, of course, on the specific action requested by the menu option.

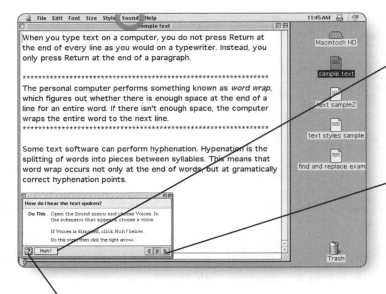

TIP

You can click on the Huh? button if you don't understand a step and want more information about it.

3. Click the **right arrow** to continue through each step of the Guide. As you would expect, exactly what you will see depends on the topic you have chosen.

TIP

Click on the question mark icon to return to the main Guide window.

NOTE

You can return to the previous step at any time by clicking the left arrow.

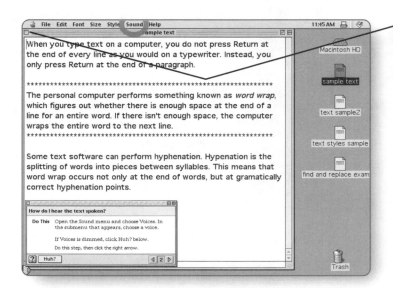

4. Click on the **Close box** to exit the Guide. The Guide window will close.

Searching for an Apple Guide in the Help Center

1. Open the **Help Center** if necessary. The Help Center will appear.

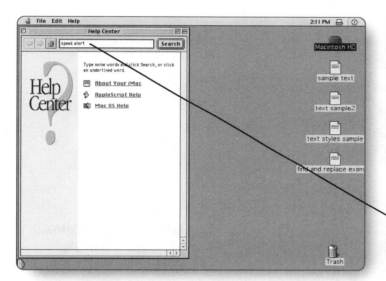

2. Type a **search word or phrase** in the Search box. The text will appear in the box.

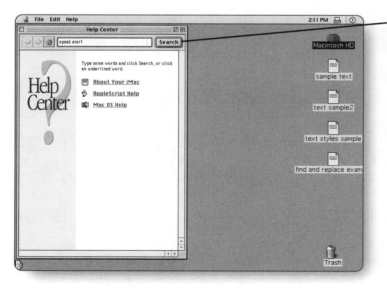

3. Click on **Search**. The results of your search will appear.

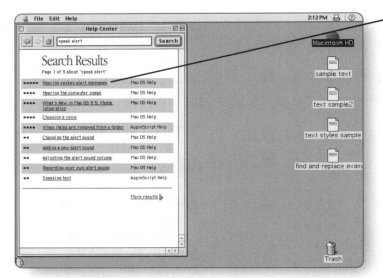

4. Click on the **hyperlink** in the list that best corresponds to the information you want. The Help Center page with the information you chose will appear.

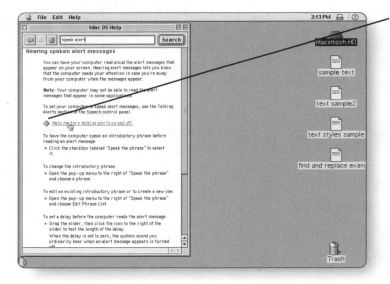

5. Click on the **hyperlink** with a diamond at the left. This represents a link that will open an Apple Guide. The Apple Guide window will appear.

6. Follow the **directions** presented by the Apple Guide.

Part II Review Questions

1. What is a Desktop theme? *See "Changing the Desktop Appearance" in Chapter 6*

2. How do you adjust the volume of the iMac's speakers? *See "Adjusting Sound" in Chapter 6*

3. What is the Control Strip and if desired, how do you remove it? *See "Using the Control Strip" in Chapter 6*

4. How do you use the Save and Save As options and when should you use them? *See "Saving a Document" in Chapter 7*

5. How do you print a document? *See "Printing a Document" in Chapter 7*

6. What is the Launcher and how do you use it? *See "Using the Launcher" in Chapter 7*

7. What does it mean for text to be selected? *See "Selecting Text" in Chapter 8*

8. What type characteristics can you change in an iMac document? *See "Changing the Appearance of Text" in Chapter 8*

9. How do you use Balloon Help? *See "Using Balloon Help" in Chapter 9*

10. How do you use an Apple Guide? *See "Using Apple Guide" in Chapter 9*

PART III

The iMac's Bundled Programs

10

Touring AppleWorks

AppleWorks is an *integrated package*, a piece of software that contains several different application programs that are tightly connected. Each of these programs, a *module*, is the equivalent of a stand-alone program that you might purchase separately. However, the tight coupling between the modules not only makes each of the modules easier to use, but also makes it easier for you to share data between them. AppleWorks can handle text, graphics, and numeric analysis with equal ease. In this chapter, you'll learn how to:

- Use the individual modules of Appleworks
- Use an AppleWorks Assistant to create a newsletter

NOTE

An in-depth exploration of AppleWorks is well beyond the scope of this book. To learn AppleWorks thoroughly, look for a book written specifically for AppleWorks or ClarisWorks 5. ClarisWorks 5 is the same program as AppleWorks; Apple renamed the software when it began shipping with the iMac.

Creating a Document with an Assistant

To use an assistant to create an AppleWorks document, you must first run the AppleWorks program. After that, you can select which assistant you want to use.

Starting AppleWorks

To launch AppleWorks, you must first find its icon on the hard disk.

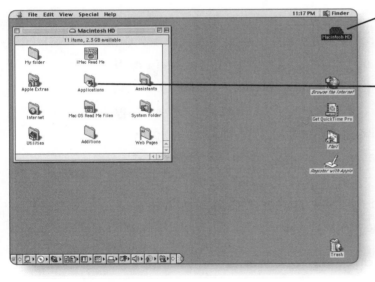

1. Double-click on the **iMac hard disk** icon. The hard disk window will appear.

2. Double-click on the **Applications folder**. It will open.

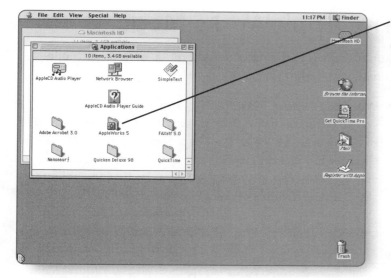

3. Double-click on the **AppleWorks 5 folder**. It will open.

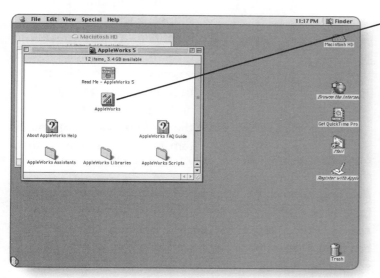

4. Double-click on the **AppleWorks icon.** The Mac OS will launch the program and display the New Document dialog box.

TIP

If you use AppleWorks frequently, you may want to place an alias for the application in the Launcher for easy access.

The AppleWorks Modules

AppleWorks is made up of several modules with each one serving a different function.

- **Word processing**. A *word processor* is designed to allow you to enter, edit, and format text. It has all the capabilities of a text editor, such as the SimpleText program you saw in Chapter 8, "Working with Text," but also includes more sophisticated formatting capabilities, such as the ability to set margins, number of columns, and so on. Word processors are the most widely used type of application software today.

- **Drawing**. A *drawing*, or *object graphics*, program lets you create images from shapes. Each shape retains its identity as a shape so you can move it, resize it, color it, and so on. Object graphics are used for creating technical and business images and therefore provide tools more familiar to the draftsman than to the painter.

- **Painting**. A *paint*, or *bit-mapped graphics*, program is used for artistic graphics and therefore provides tools that are similar to those artists use, such as brushes. Although you can draw shapes, once you have finished drawing something, it loses its individual identity and becomes part of the overall canvas, just as oil paint becomes a part of an entire painting once it is applied to a canvas.

- **Spreadsheet**. A *spreadsheet* is the electronic equivalent of an accountant's ledger sheet. You can use it for anything that requires computations of a table of numbers, such as analyzing household finances or planning the cost of a trip. Spreadsheet programs can also draw graphs from data stored on them.

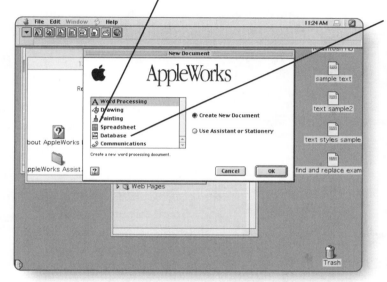

- **Data management**. *Data management* programs provide the ability to store, organize, and retrieve data. The AppleWorks data management module lets you design forms to use for data entry, forms for querying data, and forms for viewing data you have retrieved. You use this module when you have collections of data with the same structure, such as the data that go into an address book.

<table>
<tr><td>

NOTE

AppleWorks also has a Communications module. However, with the importance of the Internet, there is very little use for this module anymore and it will probably be removed from the package in the next release.

</td></tr>
</table>

Designing a Newsletter in AppleWorks

In the next section, you'll create a newsletter document that uses a wide range of the capabilities of AppleWorks.

One way to generate an AppleWorks document is to start from scratch and create a new word processing, spreadsheet, drawing, painting, or database document. Another way is to use an AppleWorks Assistant, a series of dialog boxes that let you enter information about what you want on the document. AppleWorks then formats the document for you from where you can go on to customize it. AppleWorks provides assistants for a number of common documents, such as business letters, calendars, and newsletters.

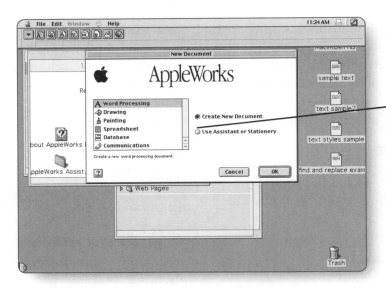

Starting the Newsletter Assistant

1. Click on the **Use Assistant or Stationery radio button**. The listing in the New Document dialog box will change to show you a list of all available Assistants.

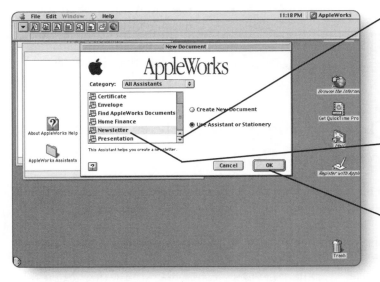

2. Scroll through the **list** of assistants from the New Document dialog box (make sure the Use Assistant or Stationery radio button has already been selected.)

3. Click on the **Newsletter** to select it. The name will be highlighted.

4. Click on **OK**. AppleWorks will run the Newsletter Assistant and display the assistant's first page.

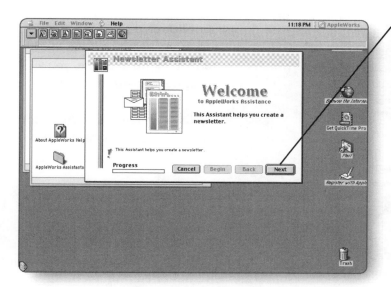

5. **Click** on **Next**. The Newsletter Assistant will continue to the next page beginning a series of questions that will help set up your document.

Choosing a Format

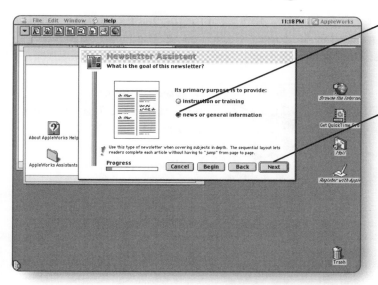

1. **Click** on the **radio button** which best describes the general purpose of the newsletter.

2. **Click** on **Next**. The Assistant will continue to the next page.

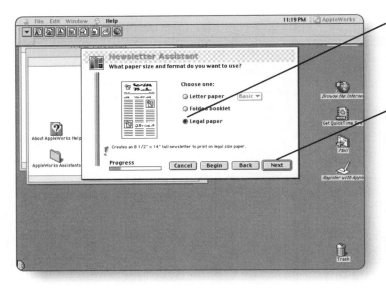

3. **Click** on a **radio button** to select the paper size and format. In this example, you'll be using legal-sized paper.

4. **Click** on **Next**. The Assistant will continue to the next page.

Adding Your Masthead Content

A masthead is a printer's term for the name of a publication, displayed at the top of the first page. The Newsletter Assistant makes it easy to create a title for your newsletter.

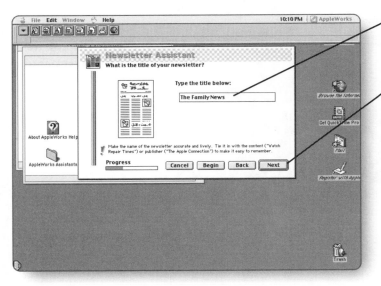

1. **Type** a **title** for your newsletter in the Type the title below: text box.

2. **Click** on **Next**. The Assistant will continue to the next page.

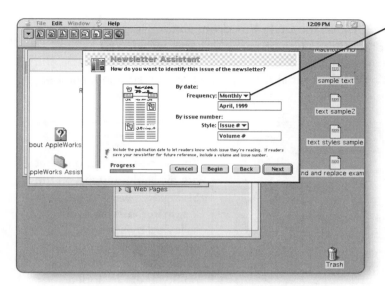

3. Click on the **Frequency box** down arrow. The options in the pop-up menu will appear.

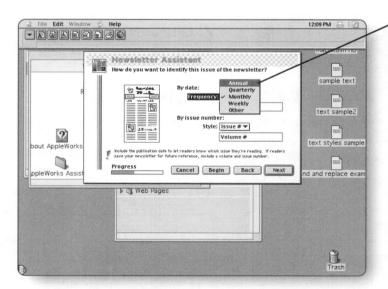

4. Click on **Annual** to select the frequency with which your newsletter will appear. For this exercise, you'll be creating a yearly newsletter.

TIP
You can edit the text in the Frequency: text box, if necessary.

5. Click on the **Style box** down arrow. The numbering options in the pop-up menu will appear.

6. Edit the **text** in the Style text box by adding a number after the # sign.

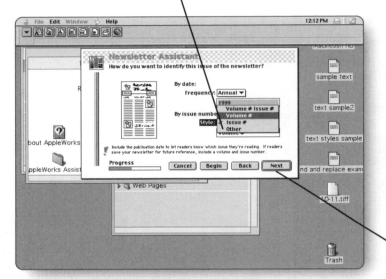

7. Click on **Next**. The Assistant will continue to the next page.

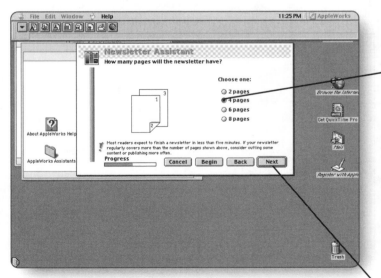

Making Other Formatting Choices

1. Click on the **radio button** to indicate the number of pages in the newsletter.

2. Click on **Next**. The Assistant will continue to the next page.

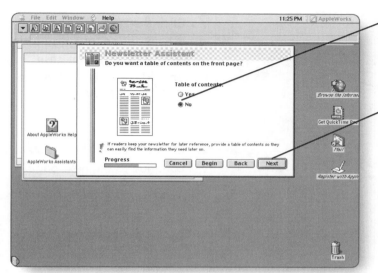

3. Click on the **radio button** to indicate whether or not you want a table of contents for the newsletter.

4. Click on **Next**. The Assistant will continue to the next page.

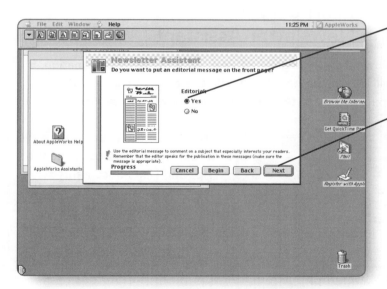

5. Click the **radio button** to indicate whether or not you want space set aside for an editorial message.

6. Click on **Next**. The Assistant will continue to the next page.

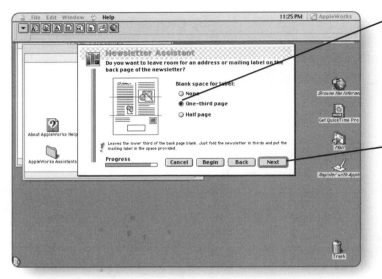

7. Click the **radio button** to choose an option for space for an address label. In this case, you should choose to leave one-third of a page for the mailing label.

8. Click on **Next**. The Assistant will continue to the next page.

Finishing Up with the Newsletter Assistant

Now that you've given the Assistant the basic information, it will lay out the newsletter. The basic layout will provide spaces to place text and graphics for customization.

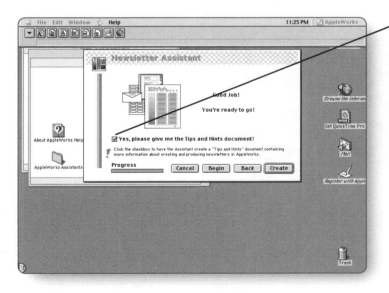

1. Click in the **check box** to the left of "Yes, please give me the Tips and Hints document" to remove the check mark. This will prevent the tips and hints document from opening on top of the newsletter layout.

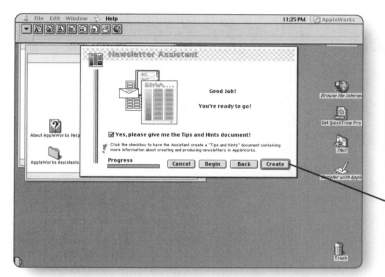

TIP

To read the tips and hints, leave the check in the check box. When you've finished reading the tips and hints, close that document.

2. Click on **Create**. AppleWorks will lay out the newsletter and display it in a new, untitled document.

Now you have the basic layout for the newsletter.

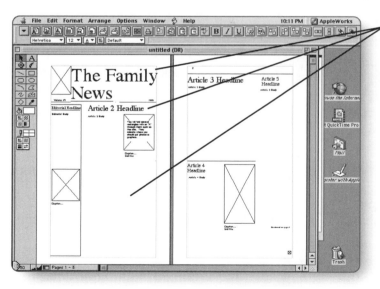

1. The title is in place, styles and sizes are chosen for headlines and article text, and areas have been set aside for the text.

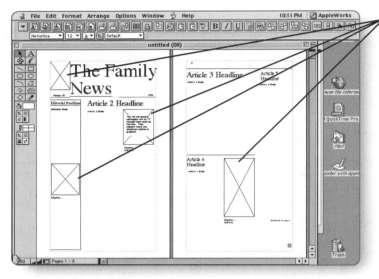

2. The boxes with Xs in them are placeholders for graphics. You can modify your layout or use the layout as shown and simply add the text and graphics.

Saving Your Newsletter

1. Choose Save As from the **File** menu. The Save As dialog box will appear.

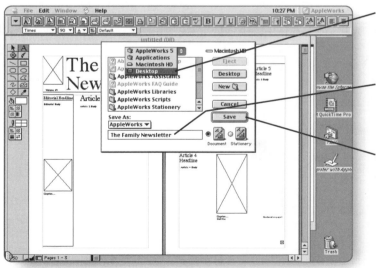

2. Click on the **folder** where you want to store the document. It will be highlighted.

3. Type a **Name** for the document in the Save As: text box.

4. Click on **Save**. AppleWorks will save the document for you.

Using the Zoom Function

When you are working on the layout of a document, you may want to make the document smaller so that more of it will fit on the screen, giving you an overview of the entire layout.

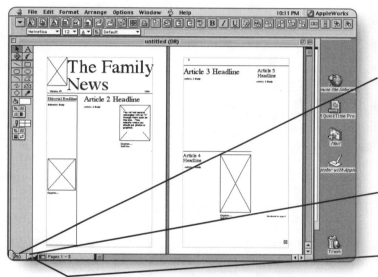

The zoom controls are found in the lower-left corner of every AppleWorks window.

- The leftmost bottom corner of the window contains a pop-up menu from which you can choose a zoom percentage. The percentage is based on the full size of the document.

- The second button zooms out, making the document smaller.

- The third button zooms in, making the document larger.

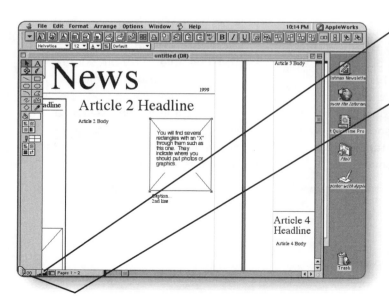

1. Click on the **zoom in control**. You'll see more detail but less area of the document.

2. Choose 50% from the **zoom pop-up menu**. The display will return to its original size.

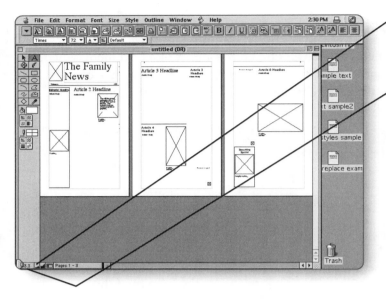

3. **Click** in the **zoom out control**. You'll see a larger area of the document but less detail.

4. **Choose 50%** from the **zoom pop-up menu**. The display will return to its original size.

Filling in Your Newsletter Text

The newsletter layout already contains places and styles set for the titles and bodies of newsletter articles. Now you'll replace the placeholder text with your own text. As you type, the text will flow to fill the text box.

TIP	TIP
For a printer-quality look, be sure to press Return at the end of a paragraph, rather than at the end of each line. Also try typing only one space between a period and the beginning of the next sentence which is another professional convention.	You'll be able to try out some new text selection techniques here: double-clicking text selects a word; triple-clicking selects a line; and quadruple-clicking anywhere in a paragraph selects the entire paragraph.

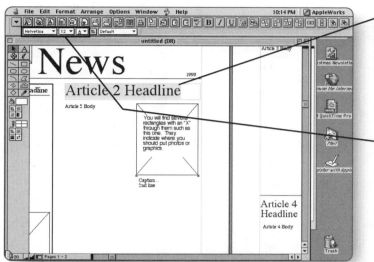

1. Triple-click on an **article headline placeholder**. The entire headline placeholder will be selected.

NOTE

All text can have the font, size, or style modified using the pop-up menus in the tool bar.

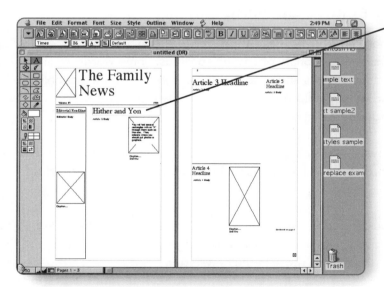

2. Type a new **headline**. The new headline will replace the selected placeholder.

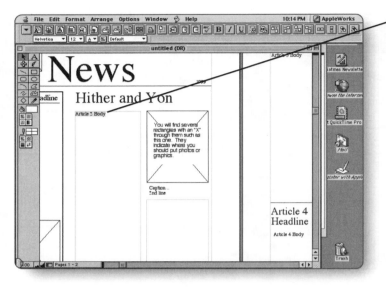

3. Triple-click on an **article body text placeholder**. The placeholder will be selected and an outline of the text block will appear. This outline shows where text will flow as you type.

4. Type the **text** of the article. The text will appear in the text block.

Checking Spelling

Spell-checkers typically match the words in a document against a dictionary of correct spellings. Some words, such as technical terms and proper names, won't be in the dictionary and will be indicated as incorrect. They can, however, be added to a dictionary of your own.

However, a spell-checker doesn't look at the context in which words are used, so you should always proofread for a perfect document.

You can use the spell-checker in AppleWorks anywhere text appears, either in a word processing document or in text blocks such as those in the newsletter.

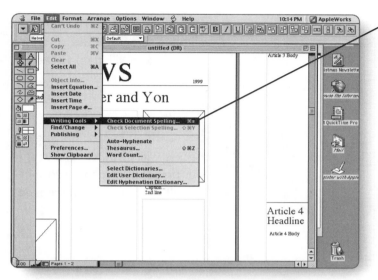

1. Choose Check Document Spelling from the Writing Tools submenu of the Edit menu. The Spelling dialog box will appear, displaying the first word that the spell checker can't find in its dictionary. The word will also be highlighted in the text. The spell checker will also present any recommended alternate spellings.

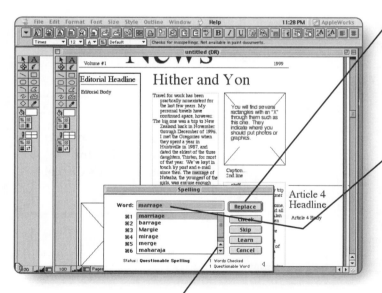

2a. Click on **Replace**. The misspelled word will be replaced by the highlighted suggestion. The spell-checker will jump to the next incorrect word.

OR

2b. Type a **word** in the Word: text box and **click** on **Replace**. The word you typed will replace the misspelled word and the spell-checker will jump to the next incorrect word.

OR

2c. Scroll through the **list** of suggested correct spellings, **click** on the **word** you want, and **click** on **Replace**. The word you chose will replace the misspelled word and the spell-checker will jump to the next incorrect word.

OR

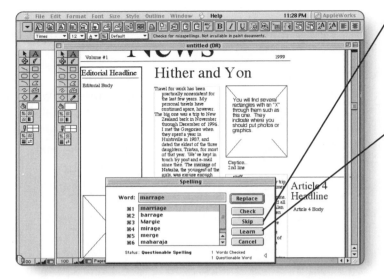

2d. Click on **Skip**. The word will be left uncorrected, and the spell checker will jump to the next incorrect word.

OR

2e. Click on **Learn**. The spell-checker will add the word to your personal dictionary so that it won't be caught as misspelled again.

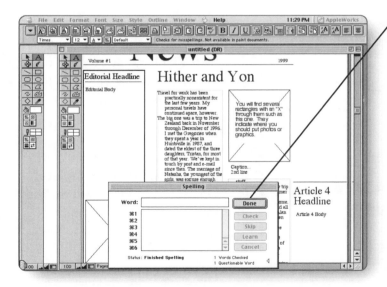

3. Click on **Done** when the spell-checker has reached the end of the text.

TIP

To stop checking spelling at any time, click the Spelling window's Cancel button.

Using AppleWorks Graphics

There are several ways to include graphics in an AppleWorks document:

- Create them with either the drawing or painting modules and then use copy and paste to place them in another document.

- Copy and paste graphics from one of AppleWorks's graphics libraries.

- Copy and paste graphics from another source into an AppleWorks document. In particular, you may decide to purchase some *clip art*, royalty-free images.

In this section, you'll be introduced to using the graphics libraries and creating your own art in a paint document.

Preparing to Add Graphics to the Newsletter

When AppleWorks created the newsletter document, it *locked* the graphics placeholders, making it impossible to modify them in any way. Locking elements in a document is a technique typically used to keep layout elements in place while you are working with other parts of the document. You need to unlock the placeholders if you want to change, delete, or replace a graphic with new images.

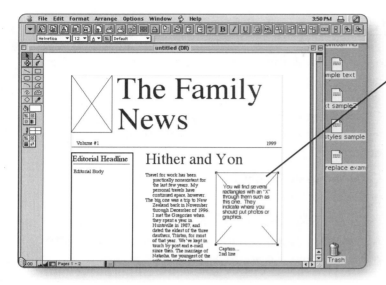

Unlocking Graphic Placeholders

1. **Click** on the **graphic placeholder** you want to replace. You'll see the outline of the placeholder. There will be a small square at each corner. These are the placeholder's *handles*, which you can drag to change the placeholder's size. Because the placeholder is locked, the handles will be gray.

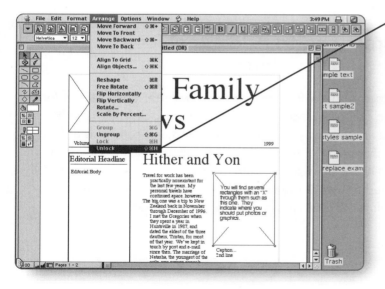

2. **Choose Unlock** from the **Arrange menu**. The placeholder's handles will turn black.

3. **Press** the **Delete key** on your keyboard. The placeholder will disappear.

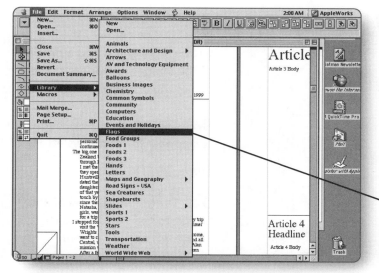

Choosing a Library Graphic

AppleWorks comes with a number of graphics libraries, each of which contains multiple images. You can copy an image from any library and place it in your document.

1. Choose a **graphic** from the Library submenu of the File menu. The library's window will open.

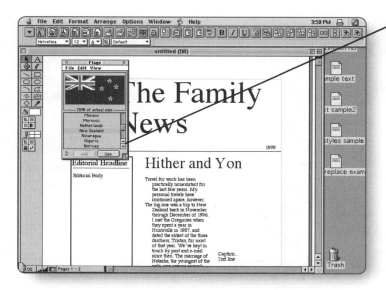

2. Scroll through the **library window** until you find the name of the image to place in the document.

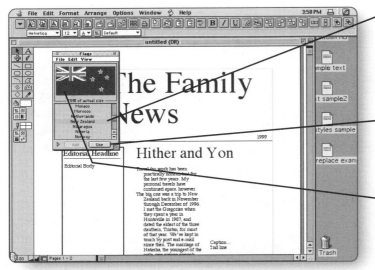

3. Click on the **image name** to select it. The name of the image will be highlighted and a preview of the image will appear at the top of the window.

4a. Click on **Use**. The image will appear in your newsletter.

OR

4b. Drag the **preview of the image** to the newsletter. The image will appear in your newsletter.

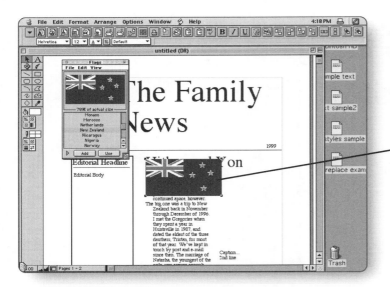

Adjusting Graphics

Once you have placed a graphic in your document, you can drag to position it and adjust the size of the image to fit.

1. Click on the **image** to select it. When selected, the image will have a handle at each corner.

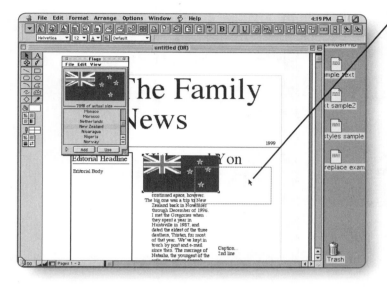

2. **Drag** the **image** to its new location in the document. An outline of the graphic will travel with the mouse pointer as you drag.

3. **Release** the **mouse button**. The image will appear in its new location.

To change the size of a graphic image:

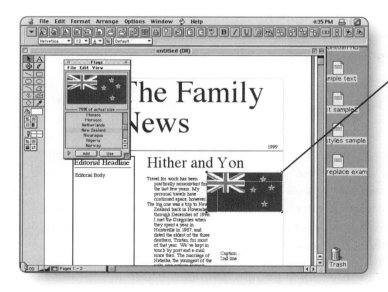

1. **Click** on the **image** to select it.

2. **Move** the **mouse pointer** over one of the image's handles.

3. **Drag** the **handle** to change the size of the image. An outline of the new size of the image will be visible as you drag.

TIP

If you want the image to retain its original proportions as you change its size, hold down the Shift key while you drag a handle.

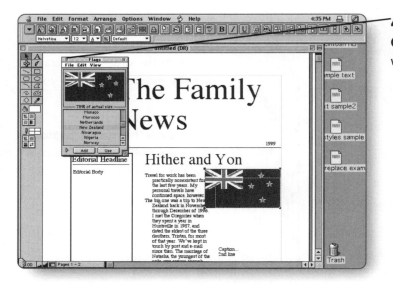

4. Click on the library window's **Close box** to remove the window from the screen.

Creating Art in a Draw Document

In this section, you'll be introduced to the draw module to create your own graphics. As an example, you'll create a flagpole for the flag that was inserted into the newsletter.

Creating a New Drawing Document

To begin the flagpole drawing project, you'll be opening a new drawing document. Although the newsletter has been created in a drawing document, using a second document to create the flagpole has two advantages: It will be less confusing because you won't have the newsletter elements intruding on your work and you'll get experience working with multiple documents.

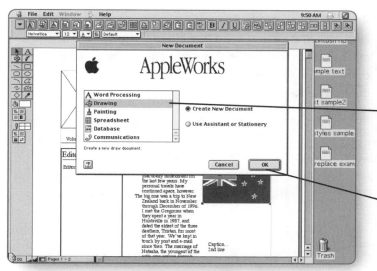

1. Click on **New** from the **File menu** or press ⌘-N. The New Document dialog box will appear.

2. Click on **Drawing** in the list of document types to select it. The type of document will be highlighted.

3. Click on **OK**. AppleWorks will create a new untitled drawing document, placing it on top of the newsletter document.

Creating and Editing Graphic Objects

The left side of the drawing window contains a palette of tools that you can use to create elements of the drawing.

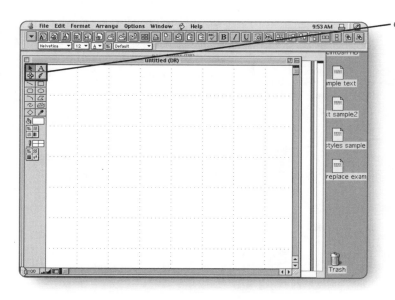

• **Mode buttons.** The Mode buttons determine the drawing mode. Select the arrow to work with any of the object graphics tools. Use the "A" tool to create a text block like those in the newsletter. The + button creates a spreadsheet block, and the brush button creates a painting block. When you are working with text, spreadsheet, or painting blocks within a draw document, all the functions of the other modules are available.

Regular shape tools. These tools draw graphic objects with well-known and predetermined shapes, such as lines, ovals and circles, rectangles and squares, and round-cornered rectangles. You'll be using two of these shapes to create the flagpole.

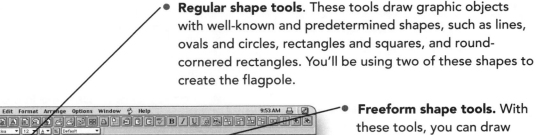

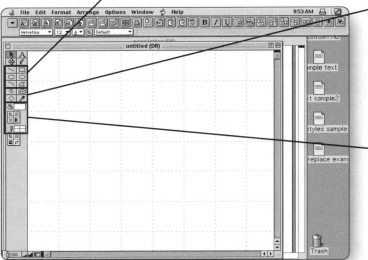

Freeform shape tools. With these tools, you can draw objects, including arc, polygons, and diamonds. There is also a freeform drawing tool that lets you draw any shape you need.

Color, fill, and line tools. These tools determine colors, fills, and line characteristics. You'll be using some line and fill colors to create the flagpole.

Most of the document is taken up by the drawing area, which is filled by a grid. You can use this grid to make it easier to position and size objects precisely.

Drawing a Flagpole

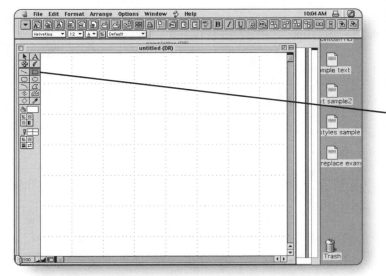

1. **Click** on the **rectangle tool**. The tool will be selected.

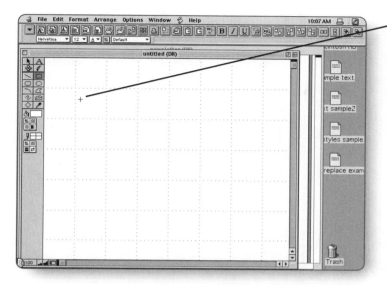

2. Move the **mouse pointer** into the drawing area. The mouse pointer will change to a cross hair. When you are drawing a regular shape, the cross hair anchors the top left corner of the shape.

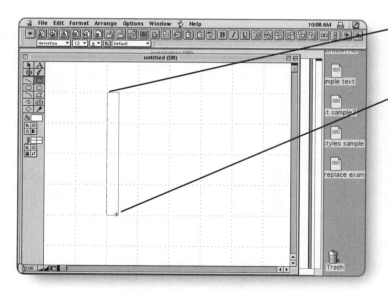

3. Move the **cross hair** to a corner made by the crossing of two grid lines.

4. Click and drag down and to the **right** from the cross hair's location. A rectangle shape will follow you as you drag.

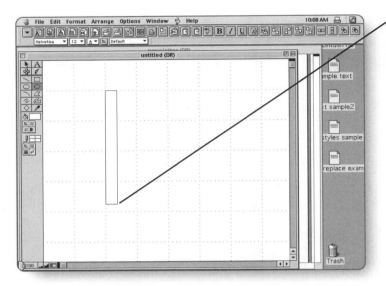

5. **Release** the **mouse button** when the rectangle is approximately ½-grid square wide and four-grid squares tall.

6. **Click** on the **oval tool**. The tool will be selected.

7. **Move** the **mouse pointer** into the drawing area. The mouse pointer will change to a cross-hair shape.

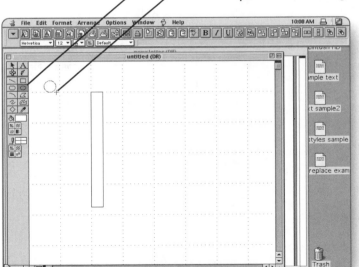

8. **Press and hold** the **Shift key**.

9. **Click and drag down** and to the **right**, keeping the Shift key pressed.

10. **Release** the **mouse button** and the **Shift key** when the circle fills approximately ¼ of a grid square.

TIP

Holding down the Shift key as you drag gives you a circle instead of an oval, a square instead of a rectangle, or a perfectly straight line.

11. Click on the **circle object** to select it, if necessary. Handles will appear at the corners. (In the case of a circle, the handles are at the four corners of an imaginary square that completely encloses the circle.)

12. Drag the **circle** until it is sitting on top of the rectangle. An outline of the circle will be visible as you drag.

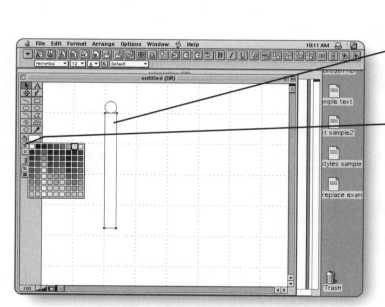

13. Click on the **rectangle** to select it. Handles will appear at each of the rectangle's corners.

14. Press and hold the **mouse button** down on the fill color icon. The fill color palette will appear.

15. Drag across the **top row** of the fill color palette.

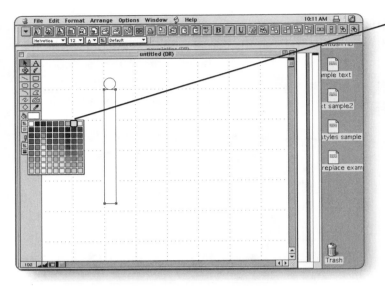

16. **Release** the **mouse button** when the second square from the right in the top row of the palette is surrounded by a black box. The square will be filled with the selected color.

17. **Repeat steps 13–16** for the circle.

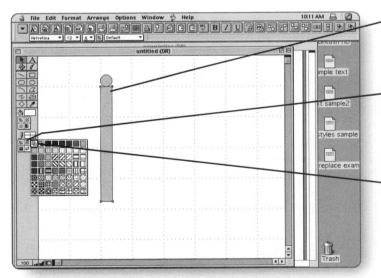

18. **Click** on the **rectangle** to select it. Handles will appear at each of the rectangle's corners.

19. **Press and hold** the **mouse button** down on the line pattern icon. The line pattern palette will appear.

20. **Drag** to the **top left square** of the palette and **release** the **mouse button**. The line around the rectangle will disappear.

21. **Repeat steps 15–20** for the circle.

Copying and Pasting Your Graphic

Now that the flagpole is complete, copy it onto the newsletter. The procedure for copying and pasting graphics is exactly the same as that for copying and pasting text.

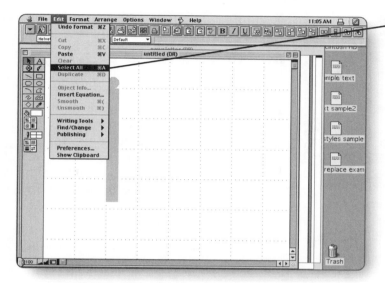

1a. Choose **Select All** from the **Edit menu**. Both objects will be selected and handles will appear at the corners of an imaginary rectangle surrounding the objects.

OR

1b. Click on **one object** to select it. **Shift and click** on the **second object** to add it to the selection. Both objects will be selected and handles will appear at the corners of an imaginary rectangle surrounding the objects.

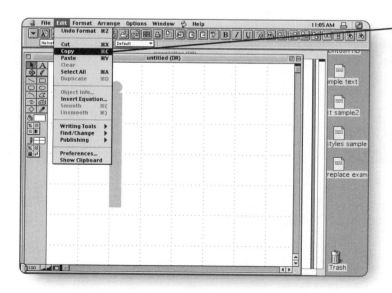

2. Choose **Copy** from the **Edit menu** or press ⌘-C. The objects will be copied to the Clipboard.

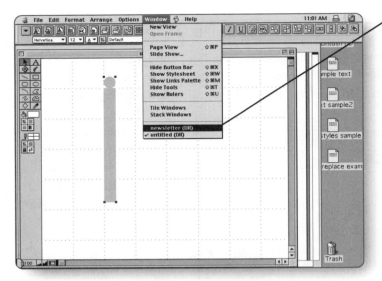

3. **Choose** the name of your **newsletter** from the **Window menu**. The newsletter window will become the front window, hiding the window that has the flagpole.

TIP

AppleWorks lists the names of all open AppleWorks windows at the bottom on the Window menu. This makes it easy to switch between documents, even if some documents are hidden by others on the screen.

4. **Choose Paste** from the **Edit menu** or press ⌘-V. The flagpole appears on top of the newsletter. Both objects are still selected.

Arranging Graphics in Your Newsletter

Pasting graphics into a new document places them in the middle of the document and on top of all other objects, which is usually not where you want them to be. You must therefore rearrange the objects.

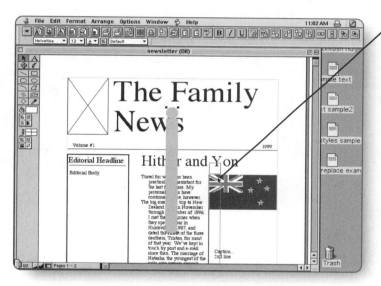

1. Move the **mouse pointer** anywhere on top of the selected objects and **drag** them so that the top-left corner of the rectangle is aligned with the top-left corner of the flag. An outline of the selected objects will follow the mouse pointer as you drag.

2. Release the **mouse button**. The flagpole will be resting on top on the flag.

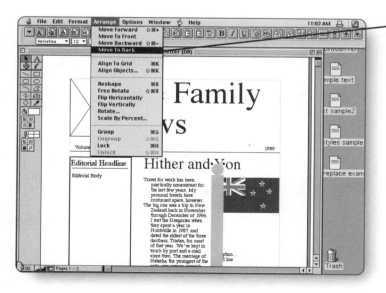

3. Choose Move to Back from the **Arrange menu**. The flagpole will be moved underneath all other objects on the newsletter.

4. Save the **document** if you plan to work on it more later.

TIP

Objects in a drawing document are layered on top of one another. Each new object that is added is placed on top of all others. You can change that layering by using the first four options of the Arrange menu.

11

Organizing Your Finances

Quicken is the most popular, personal, financial management program today. You can use it as a substitute for a paper check register. It can also balance your checkbook and help you maintain a budget. This chapter provides an overview of using Quicken to maintain a checking account. In this chapter, you'll learn how to:

- Set up a checking account
- Add charge accounts
- Enter transactions into your check register
- Reconcile your checking account

Getting Started with Quicken Deluxe

Quicken Deluxe, or just "Quicken," is an application program that you launch by double-clicking on its icon or by double-clicking on a document that the program created.

1. Install Quicken, if it is not already on your hard drive. Instructions for installing software can be found in Appendix D, "Adding Software." The remainder of this chapter assumes that the Quicken folder has been stored in the Applications folder, which is stored on your hard disk.

2. Open the **Quicken folder**.

3. Double-click on **Quicken Deluxe 98**. If this is the first time you have run Quicken, you'll see a dialog box asking you to personalize your copy of the program.

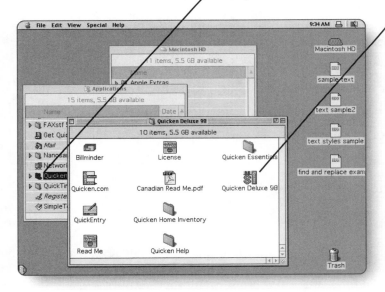

NOTE

After the initial setup process, you do not need to do it again. You can launch Quicken by double-clicking on the icon for the file in which your Quicken data are stored.

Setting Up Quicken

When you run Quicken for the first time, the program will take you through the process of identifying yourself, registering the software, and configuring a new file.

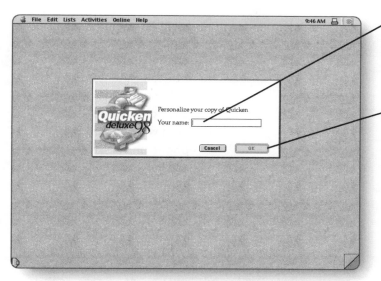

1. Type your **name** in the Your name: text box. The OK button the dialog box will become active.

2. Click on **OK**. A dialog box describing your registration options will appear.

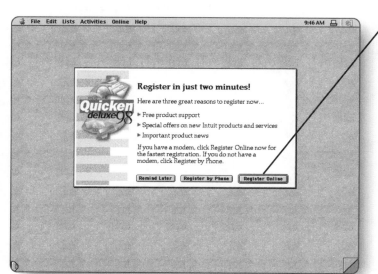

3. Click on **Register Online**. This assumes that your iMac is connected to a telephone line. The registration form will appear.

4. Type the **registration information**. Press the Tab key to move from one text entry box to the next or click in a text box with the mouse pointer to make it active. The Connect button will become active.

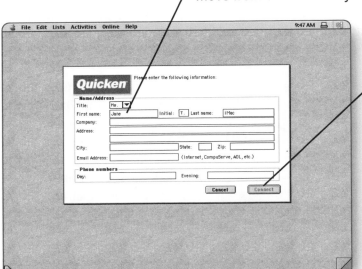

5. Click on **Connect**. Quicken will dial a toll-free telephone number, connect with the remote computer, and register the software. When the registration is complete, Quicken will hang up the telephone and display a dialog box asking you what you want to do next.

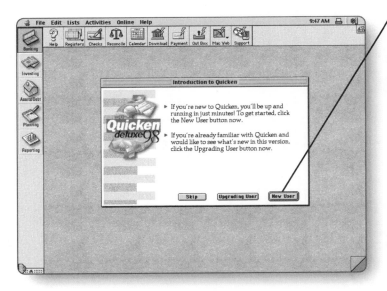

6. Click on **New User**. Quicken will display the first window of the Quicken Apple Guide (small message box in the bottom-left of the screen) for configuring the program.

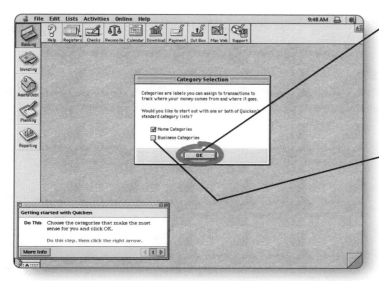

7a. **Click** on **OK** if the Quicken file will be used to manage your home finances. Quicken imports the home categories and gets ready to set up accounts.

OR

7b. **Click** on the **check box** next to Business Categories and **click** on **OK** if you are going to be using this Quicken file to manage business expenses. Quicken imports the business categories and gets ready to set up accounts for you.

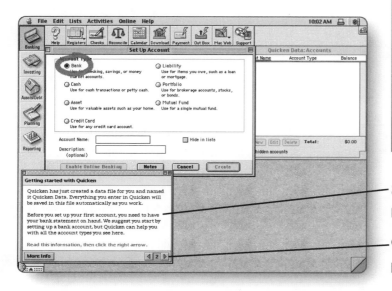

NOTE

The process for working with managing home finances is virtually identical to the one for working with business categories.

8. **Read** the **Apple Guide page**.

9. **Click on** the **right arrow** to proceed.

Creating Bank Accounts

The first task will be to set up your bank accounts. Before beginning this part of the setup, you should have the most recent statement for each account available as well as all the transactions (deposits and withdrawals) that have been made since that statement.

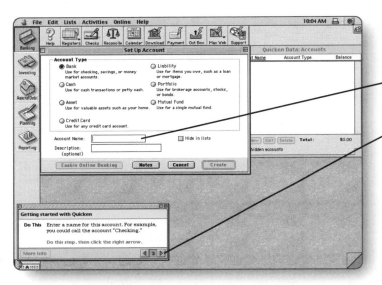

Configuring the Account

1. **Type** an **account name** in the Account Name: text box.

2. **Click** on the **right arrow** on the Apple Guide page. The Guide will move to the next page and show you where the next typing should appear.

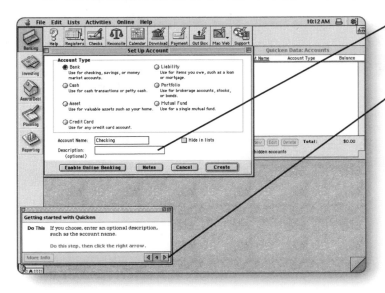

3. **Type** a **description** of the account in the Description: text box.

4. **Click** on the **right arrow** on the Apple Guide page. The Guide will move to the next page and the Create button will be active.

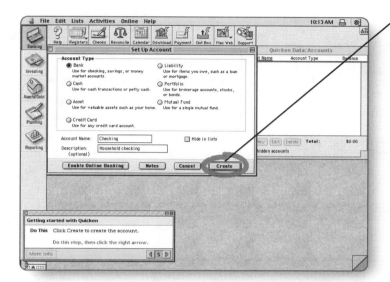

5. Click on **Create**. The Apple Guide will advance to the next page and Quicken will create an account register.

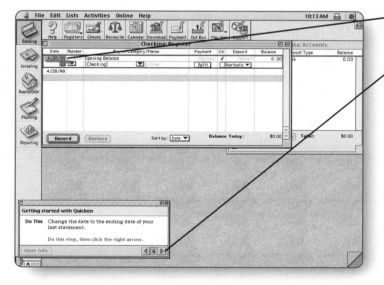

6. Type the **date** on which your last account statement was cut.

7. Click on the **right arrow** on the Apple Guide page. The Guide will move to the next page.

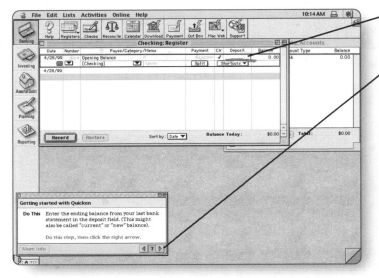

8. Type the **statement closing balance**.

9. Click on the **right arrow** on the Apple Guide page. The Guide will move to the next page.

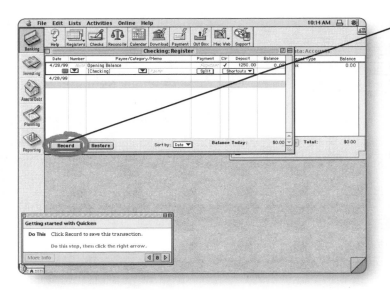

10. Click on **Record.** Quicken will store the data you have entered. The Guide will move to the next page.

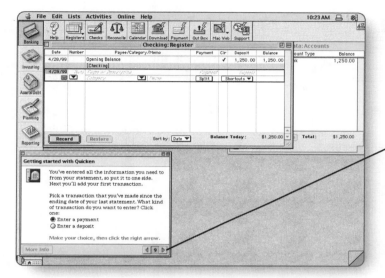

Entering the First Transaction

At this point, you are ready to enter the transactions made since the last statement was cut.

1a. Click on the **right arrow** of the Guide Window if you want to enter a payment. The Guide moves to the next page.

OR

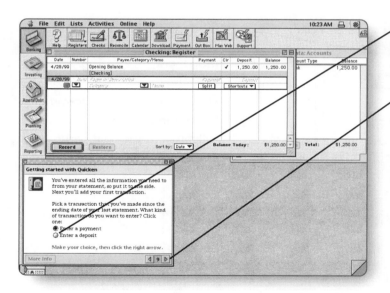

1b. Click on the **option button** next to Enter a deposit to enter a deposit

2. Click on the **right arrow** of the Guide Window. The Guide moves to the next page. For this example, you will enter a payment.

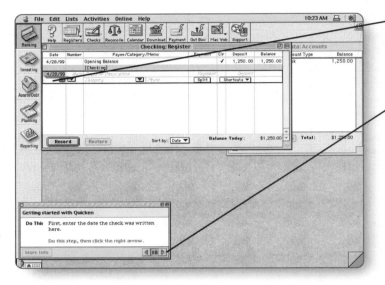

3. Type the **date of the transaction**. Your typing will replace the current date, which Quicken entered automatically.

4. Click on the **right arrow** of the Guide window. The Guide will move to the next page.

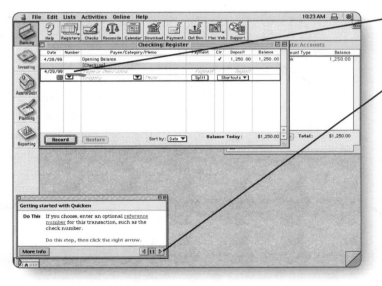

5. Type the **check number** if a check was used for this transaction.

6. Click on the **right arrow** of the Guide window. The Guide will move to the next page.

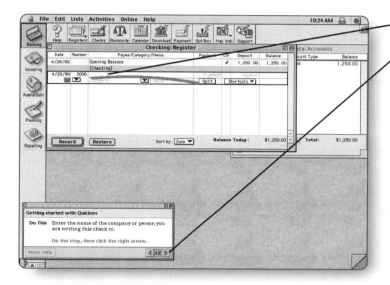

7. **Type** the **payee**.

8. **Click** on the **right arrow** of the Guide window. The Guide will move to the next page.

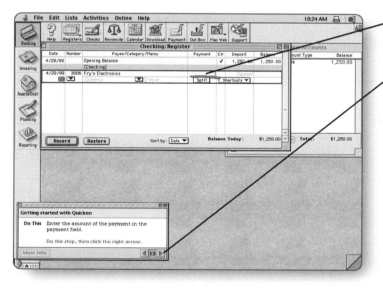

9. **Type** the **amount** of the check.

10. **Click** on the **right arrow** of the Guide window. The Guide will move to the next page.

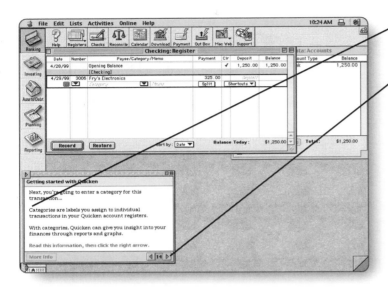

11. **Read** the **definition** of a category in the Guide page.

12. **Click** on the **right arrow** of the Guide window. The Guide will move to the next page.

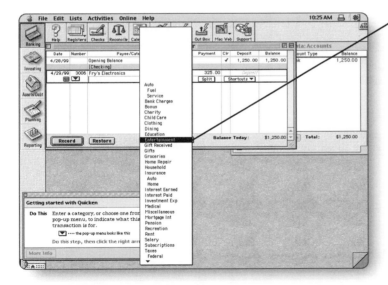

13. **Click** on a **category** from the category pop-up menu. It will be highlighted.

14. **Click** on the **right arrow** of the Guide window. The Guide will move to the next page.

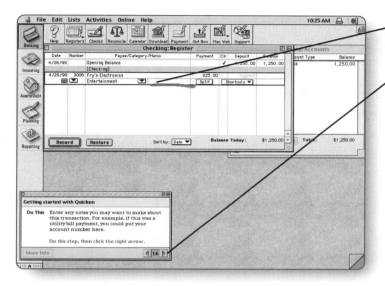

15. Enter any **notes** that you want about the check.

16. Click on the **right arrow** of the Guide window. The Guide will move to the next page.

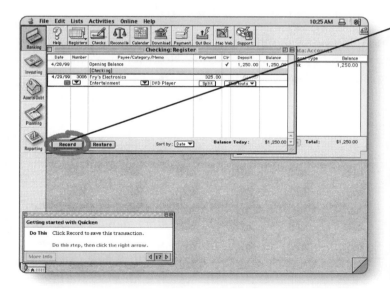

17. Click on **Record**. Quicken stores the transaction and creates a register entry below it for the next transaction.

TIP

Quicken is one of the few programs in which you do not need to use a Save command to save data to a disk file. Quicken automatically writes data to disk as you work.

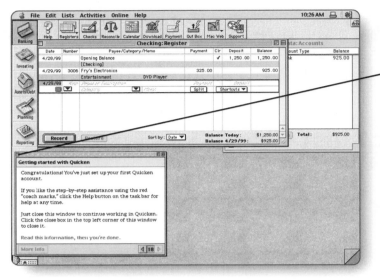

18. **Read** the **last page** of the Guide.

19. **Click** on the Guide window's **Close box** to remove the Guide from the screen. You will now be ready to create accounts and enter transactions as needed.

Creating Charge Accounts

The Apple Guide stepped you through creating a checking account and entering a transaction. However, that's as far as the Guide can take you. You'll therefore need to create additional accounts on your own; something you can do at any time.

To create a charge account:

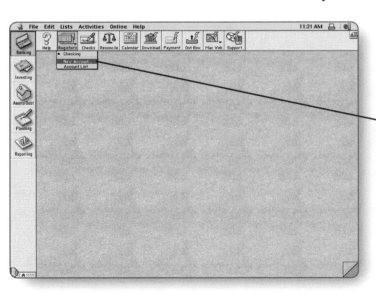

1. **Click** on **New Account** from the Registers menu. The Set Up Account dialog box will appear.

2. **Click** on an **option button** to choose the type of account you want to enter. The dialog box will change to present options appropriate to the type of account.

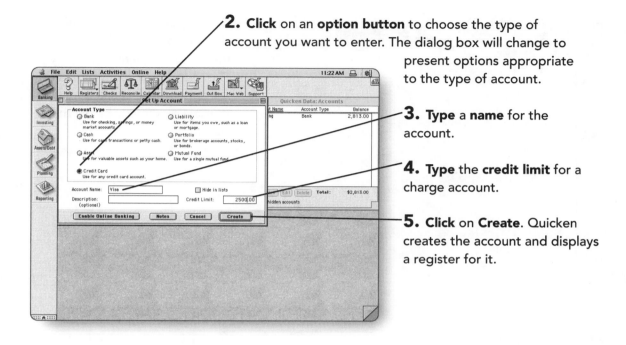

3. **Type** a **name** for the account.

4. **Type** the **credit limit** for a charge account.

5. **Click** on **Create**. Quicken creates the account and displays a register for it.

Entering Data in Your Register

Once your accounts are created, use Quicken like a paper register. Every time you write a check, use your ATM/debit card, make a deposit, or charge something on a credit card, you enter the transaction to a Quicken register.

Writing Checks

The process for recording a written check is similar to what you just completed when you went through the Apple Guide earlier in this chapter. For check writing you won't need to click through the Guide pages again, but you will need to know how to get a new line on the register to record a check transaction.

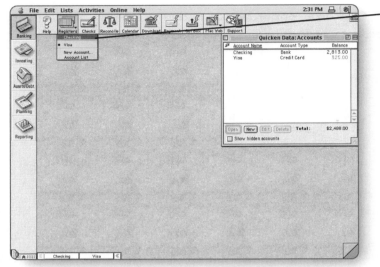

1. Choose the **name** of the checking account register from the Registers menu if necessary. The checking account register will appear with space for a new transaction directly below the last transaction.

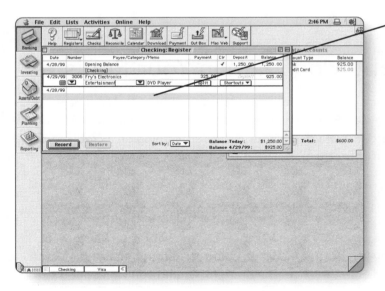

2. Click on the **space** for the new transaction to begin entering the check.

Making Deposits

Recording a deposit is very similar to writing a check. The major difference is that it doesn't have a check number.

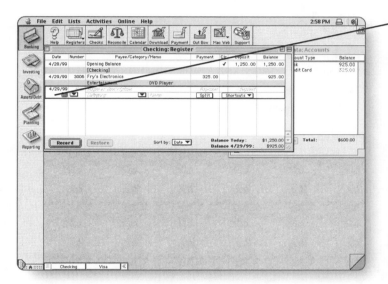

1. **Click** on the **date** if you want to change it. Quicken automatically fills in the current date.

2. **Modify** the **date**, if necessary.

TIP

You can increase and decrease the date by using the + and – keys respectively.

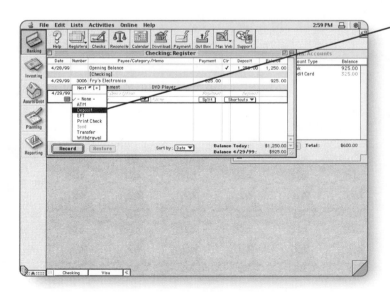

3. **Choose Deposit** from the pop-up menu in the Number column.

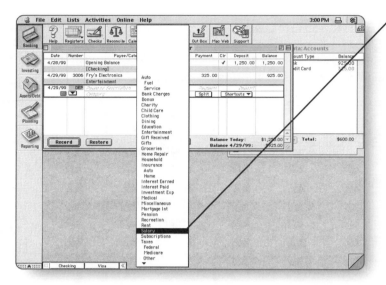

4. Click on the **source** of the deposit from the pop-up menu in the Payee/Category/Memo column.

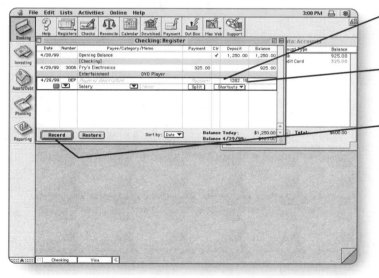

5. Click on the **Deposit column** to get an insertion point.

6. Type the **amount** of the deposit.

7. Click on **Record**. Quicken stores the deposit and creates space for the next transaction.

Recording Credit Card Charges

Credit card charges are recorded in the special credit card register. However, payments are posted in the checking account register. When you choose the credit card account as the source of the payment, the amount by which the account will be credited is automatically transferred to the credit card register.

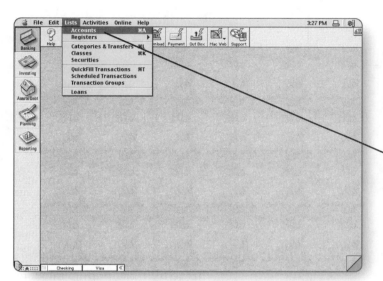

1. Choose Accounts from the **Lists menu**. The Quicken Data: Accounts window will appear.

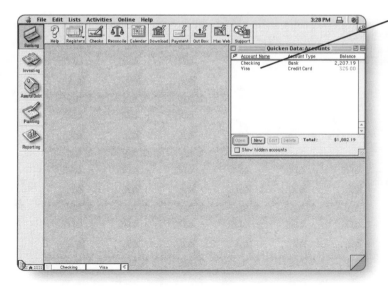

2. Double-click on the **credit card account**. The credit card register will open.

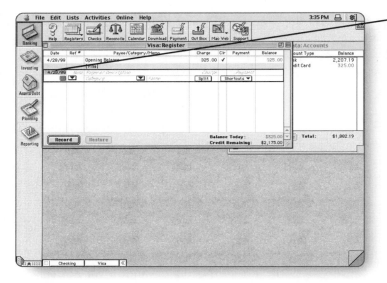

3. Click on the **date** to get an insertion point if you want to change the date.

4. Edit the **date** as needed.

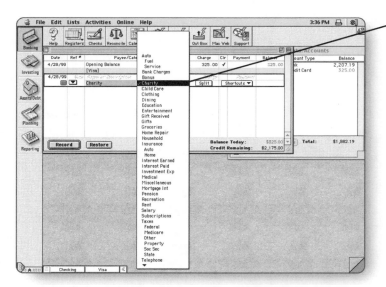

5. Click on a **category** for the charge from the pop-up menu in the Payee/Category/Memo column. It will be highlighted.

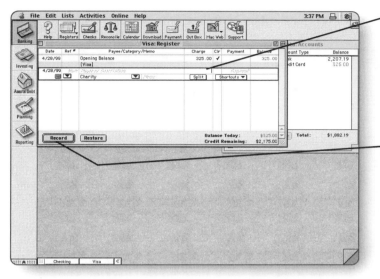

6. Click on the **Charge column.** An insertion point will appear in the column.

7. Type the **amount** of the charge.

8. Click on **Record**. Quicken will store the credit card charge and make space for the next transaction.

Reconciling Your Checking Account

Reconciling a checking account involves making the account agree with what the bank says. The process involves telling Quicken which transactions appear on the statement, what extra charges have been added (for example, service charges), and the balance on the statement.

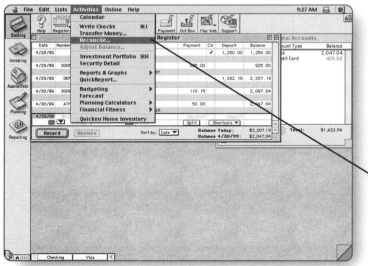

1. Double-click on **Checking** from the **Accounts menu**. The checking account register will open.

2. Choose Reconcile from the **Activities menu**. The Reconcile Startup dialog box will appear.

3. **Click** on the **Beginning Balance: text box**.

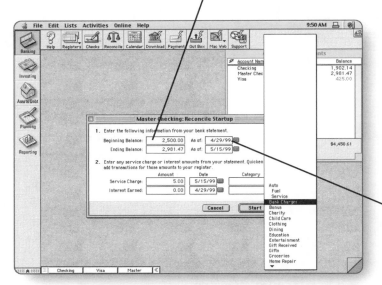

4. **Type** the **beginning balance** on the account statement if the value entered by Quicken is not correct.

5. **Press** the **Tab key**. The As of: text box next to the Beginning Balance: text box will be selected.

6. **Type** the **beginning date** of the statement if the date entered by Quicken is not correct.

7. **Press** the **Tab key**. The Ending Balance: text box will be selected.

8. **Type** the **ending balance** on the statement.

9. **Press** the **Tab key**. The As of: text box next to the Ending Balance: text box will be selected.

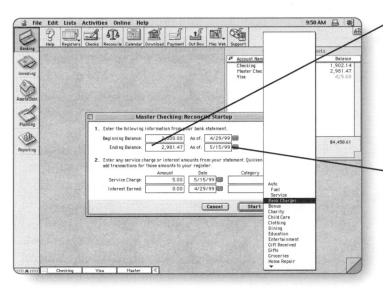

10. **Type** the **ending date** of the statement if the date entered by Quicken is not correct.

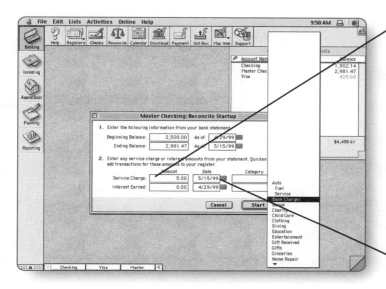

11. Click on the **Service Charge:** text box if the bank subtracted checking account fees from your account.

12. Type the **amount** of the service charge if necessary.

13. Press the **Tab key**. The Date: text box next to the Service Charge: text box will be selected.

14. Type the **date** the service charge was deducted from your account if necessary.

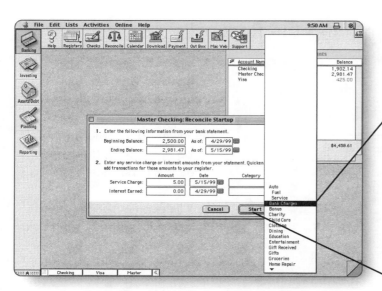

15. Press the **Tab key**. The Category: text box next to the Date: text box will be active and a pop-up menu will appear.

16. Choose a **category** for the service charge from the pop-up menu if necessary.

17. Repeat steps **10–15** if your checking account earned interest to record the interest earned.

18. Click on **Start** to begin the reconciliation of the account. The Reconcile dialog box will appear. Quicken also adds transactions for the service charge and interest earned to the check register if you entered amounts for them.

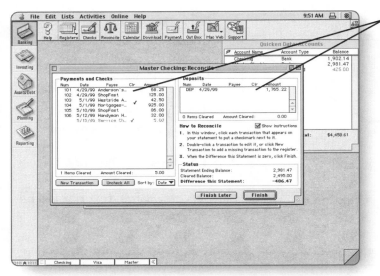

19. Click next to each **item** in the **Clr column** that has been cleared on the statement. Quicken will place a check mark next to the item and deduct its value from the total of outstanding items.

20. Repeat step 18 for all items on the statement.

Finishing the Reconcile

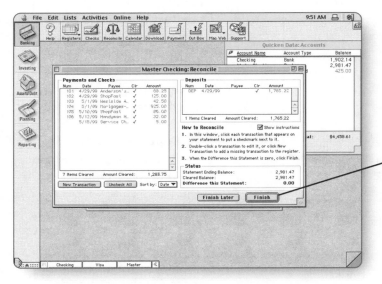

What you do at this point depends on whether your account is in balance. If the "Difference This Statement" in the lower-right corner of the dialog box is 0.00, then the account is in balance.

1. Click on **Finish**. The Reconcile Complete dialog box will appear.

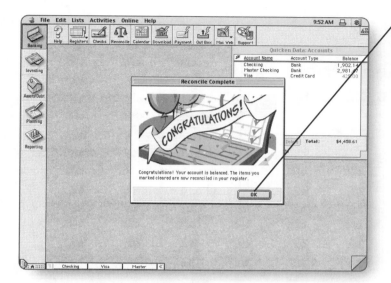

2. **Click** on **OK**. The Reconcile Complete dialog box will close and you will be able to continue with other tasks.

Adjusting Your Account Balance

If your account is not in balance, you can enter any missing transactions or modify existing transactions to correct errors. If you absolutely can't find the error, you can ask Quicken to adjust the account balance to match the statement.

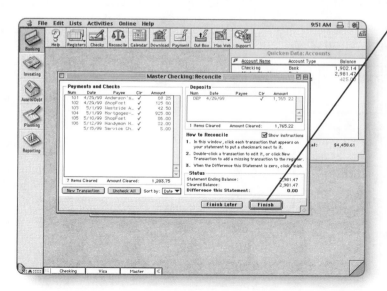

1. **Click** on **Finish**. Quicken will display a dialog box explaining that the account is not in balance.

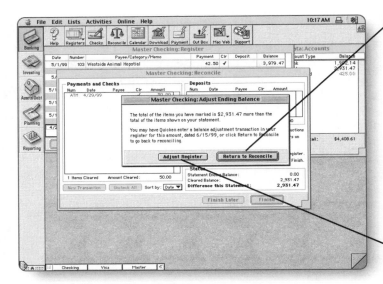

2a. Click on **Return to Reconcile** to return to the Reconcile dialog box and to make changes. The Reconcile dialog box will appear. If necessary, refer to the preceding set of instructions in this chapter for information on how to make the necessary changes.

OR

2b. Click on **Adjust Register** to ask Quicken to adjust the checking account register to match the statement. Quicken will add an adjustment transaction to the account and notify you by displaying an alert.

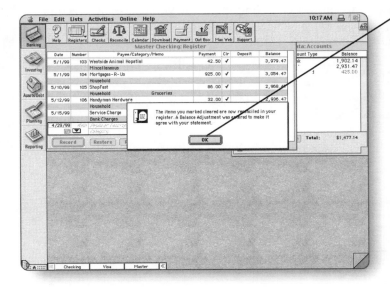

3. Click on **OK**. The Alert will disappear and you can continue with your next task.

12

Exploring the iMac's Recreational Software

Just to be sure that you have something the play with, the iMac includes a game called Nanosaur and Kai's Photo Soap, which you can use to modify photos. It is especially useful if you happen to have a digital camera or a scanner. In this chapter, you'll learn how to:

- Play the Nanosaur game
- Perform basic photo retouching with Kai's Photo Soap

Playing Nanosaur

Nanosaur is a short game that demonstrates the speed and capability of the iMac as a gaming platform. The premise behind Nanosaur is that you are a human engineered dinosaur from the future, a member of the only breed left after human-kind died out. Nanosaur society wants to go back in time to grab eggs from some other breeds of dinosaurs before the big meteor hits. You are the intrepid time-traveling egg stealer. Your goals are to gather five different kinds of eggs and deliver them into a time vortex before time (20 minutes) runs out, kill anything that moves, and survive the various dangers.

Using Adobe Acrobat Reader to View the Instructions

Nanosaur is accompanied by an instruction manual stored on your hard disk. It is in *portable document format* (PDF), a way of storing a document so that it can be viewed on the screen using Adobe Acrobat Reader software, which is already installed on your iMac. There are two great things about Acrobat Reader: The document looks exactly like it would if it was printed and Acrobat Reader is free. (Although you do need to purchase commercial software to *create* PDF files.)

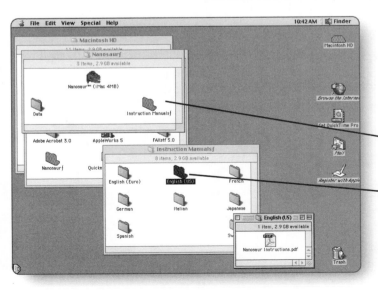

1. **Open** the **Nanosaur folder**.

2. **Open** the **Instructions folder**.

3. **Open** the **English (US) folder** (or the folder for any other language you want). A PDF file containing the instructions will appear.

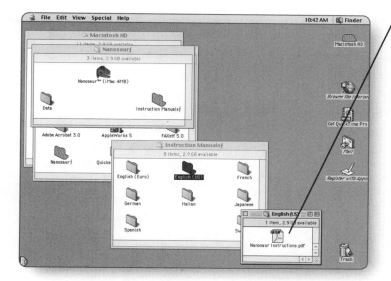

4. Double-click on the **Nanosaur Instructions file**. The Acrobat Reader will launch and display the first page of the instructions.

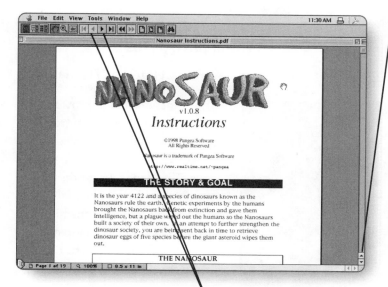

5a. Read the **instructions** by scrolling as necessary to bring the entire page into view.

5b. Alternately, **click** on the **right** or **left arrows** above the instruction window to scan through the pages.

6. Quit Adobe Acrobat Reader from the **File menu**. You will return to the Finder.

Starting Nanosaur

1. Double-click on the **Nanosaur application icon**. Nanosaur will launch.

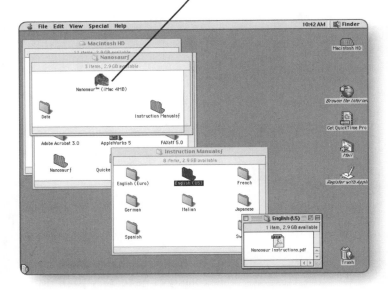

2. Press any key once to dismiss each of the two credit screens. A very short animated segment with the logo of the developer will begin to play. When the segment ends an animated introductory screen will appear.

3. Press any key to dismiss the introductory screen. The Selection screen will appear.

Using the Selection Screen

The Selection screen provides access to the game's controls. Switch between five choices by pressing the right and left arrow keys. The Nanosaur represents starting the game, a medal shows high scores, a question mark shows control mappings, an Exit sign allows you to quit, and a check mark allows you to select configuration options. Once you have the Nanosaur in front of you, press the spacebar to take you into that area to start the game and enter the past.

Playing the Game

The Nanosaur playing field is a game console that surrounds the view and movement of the Nanosaur. As the game begins, you (the Nanosaur) appear in the past, with a limited time to gather the eggs. Your view of the game is from above and behind the Nanosaur. From the normal camera view, you can use the 1 and 2 number keys to move the camera in or out, and the <> keys to move the camera around the Nanosaur.

NOTE

You can change your view of the game by pressing the Tab key to go to head cam view, where you see through the dinosaur's eyes. This makes the game more difficult!

The initial game console provides you with the following information:

❶ **Countdown timer.**

❷ **GPS map.** You are always at the center of the crosshairs.

❸ **Current weapon mode (ammunition being used).**

❹ **Amount of current ammo remaining.**

❺ **Fuel gauge for jet pack.**

❻ **You!**

❼ **Number of lives remaining.**

❽ **Score.**

❾ **Strength remaining (the Health bar).** When the length of this bar drops to zero, the Nanosaur dies.

At various places in the playing field, you will encounter a temporal vortex. That is where you toss an egg that you have recovered.

❶ Temporal vortex

❷ Pointer to a temporal vortex

❸ Eggs recovered

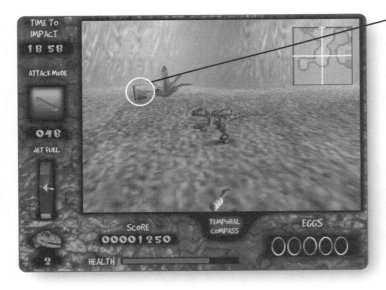

You can gain additional ammunition and power by running through ammunition or power-up drops. You will stay alive as long as you have ammo, fuel, and can avoid being stomped on by larger dinosaurs.

Exiting the Game

When you are through playing Nanosaur, you can quit by pressing ⌘-Q.

Using Kai's Photo Soap

Photo Soap is a program intended to "clean up" scanned photos. You can get rid of red-eye, touch up scratches and film flaws, bring back some of the sharpness to faded photos, put a frame or background behind a picture, add text, and crop a picture. In addition, you can use Photo Soap to create catalogs of the photos you have stored on disk.

NOTE

Photo Soap needs to be installed from the CD. The instructions that follow assume that you have installed it in the Applications folder on the iMac's hard disk. The first time you run the program, you will also be asked to insert the CD so that the program can copy additional files. See Appendix D, "Adding Software," for installation details.

Launching Photo Soap

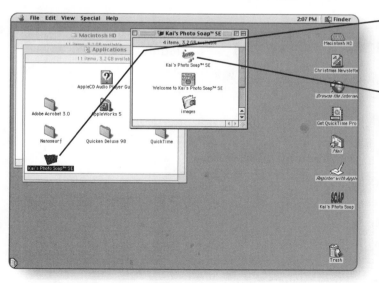

1. Open the **Kai's Photo Soap** folder from the Applications folder on the iMac's hard disk.

2. Double-click on the **Kai's Photo Soap™ SE icon**. Photo Soap will launch.

Moving Between Photo Soap Rooms

In Photo Soap there is no menu bar. Instead, you have a control palette at the left side of the screen. The screen contains some photo *thumbnails* (small representations of larger photos) and some rolled-up photo albums.

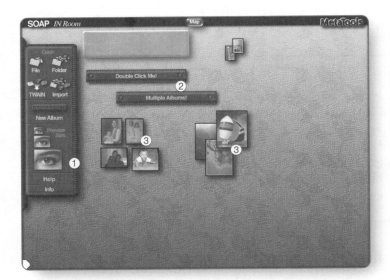

Photo Soap's functions are organized into a collection of "rooms." When you launch the program, you are automatically taken to the In Room, a place where you can bring photos and graphics into the program to work on them. Here you will be able to navigate through your collection of albums.

❶ Control palette

❷ Rolled-up photo albums

❸ Photo thumbnails

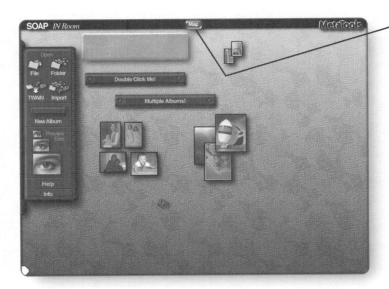

1. Double-click on the **Map button** at the top-center of the screen. The Map Room will appear.

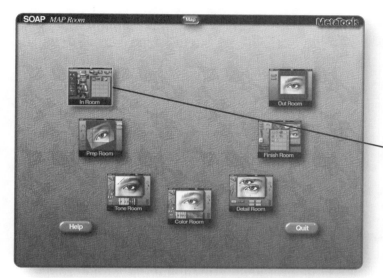

There are different rooms available for you for performing various enhancements to your photos. You can click on the room you want to enter. You will be taken to that room.

2. **Click** on the **In Room** icon to return to the In Room.

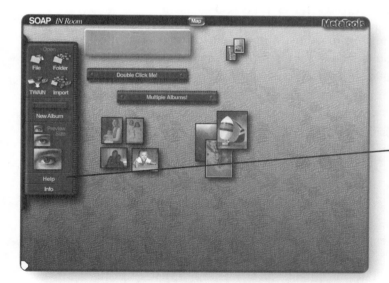

Getting Help

Photo Soap provides online help that describes how to interact with the program and how to use its tools.

1. **Click** on **Help** on the In Room control palette. The Help window appears.

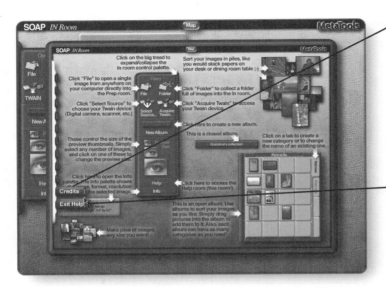

2. Move the **mouse pointer** up and down the left side of the Help window to display all the menu options.

3. Click on an **option** to display the Help page associated with it.

4. Click on **Exit Help.** You will be returned to the Map Room. Click on the In Room icon to return to the In Room.

Bringing in a Photo

Photo Soap comes with sample photos that you can use while you're learning the program, some of which appear on the In Room's Desktop when the program is launched. You can also open a graphics file, open a folder of graphics, or bring in (*import*) an image from a scanner or digital camera. In the example that follows, you'll use one of the photos that Photo Soap provides.

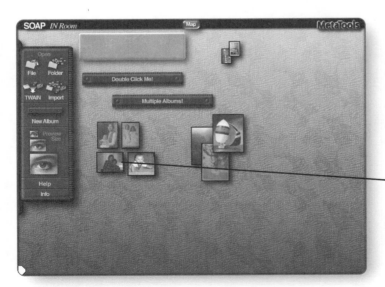

Preparing Your Image

1. Double-click on a **photo.** Photo Shop will open the photo and switch you to the Prep Room. The Prep Room has tools for cropping, enhancing, and rotating an image.

Cropping Your Picture

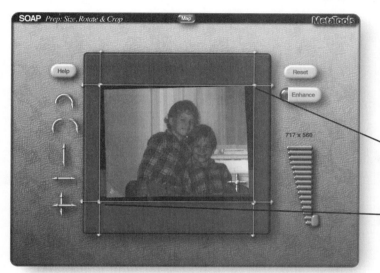

To crop the image, move the sliding white bars to frame the image. If you click on a bar, only that bar will move. Click on one of the corners to adjust both bars.

2. **Click and drag** a **corner** to frame adjacent sides of the subjects.

3. **Click and drag** the **opposite corner** to finish the cropping size and shape of your selection.

Enhancing Your Photo

The enhancing tool automatically brightens and sharpens the photo. Clicking on the Enhance button lets you see the result of the change. (Varying the cropping may also vary the enhancement.) Once you get the effect you like, lock it in place with the lock tool, which appears when the Enhance tool is turned on.

1. **Click** on **Enhance**. The light on the Enhance button will come on, and the photo will show the enhancement. The Lock button will also appear.

2. Click on **Lock** to lock in the enhancement. The Lock light will come on.

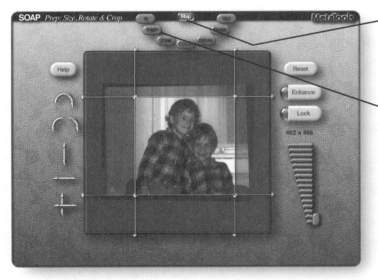

3. Move the **mouse pointer** over the Map button at the top of your screen. A button for each room will appear.

4. Click on **Tone**. A dialog will pop up, asking if you want to apply the cropping transformations that you made earlier.

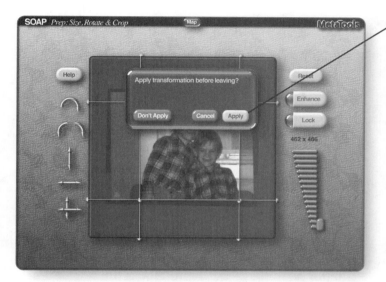

5. Click on **Apply**. The cropping enhancements will be applied to the photo and you will go to the Tone Room.

Adjusting Tone and Color

The Tone Room has controls for adjusting brightness and contrast.

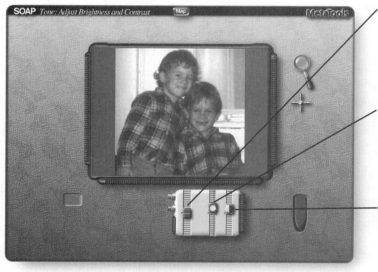

- **Global intensity slider**. Drag the overall intensity slider up and down to increase and decrease the overall intensity of the effects on the image.

- **Brightness slider**. Drag the brightness slider up and down to increase and decrease the overall brightness of the image.

- **Contrast slider**. Drag the contrast slider up and down to increase and decrease the contrast of the image.

● **Zoom slider**: Drag the zoom slider on the right side of the image up and down to zoom in and out.

When you have finished working with the controls in the Tone Room, you can move on to detail the photo. But first you must apply your tone enhancements if desired.

1. Move the **mouse pointer** over the Map button at the top of your screen. A button for each room will appear.

2. Click on the **Detail** icon. A dialog box will appear asking if you would like to apply the tone effects you made before leaving the Tone Room.

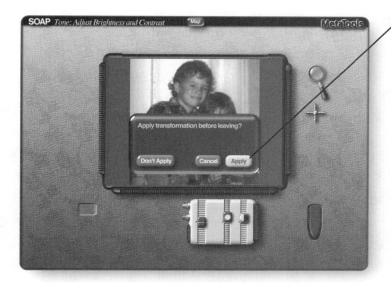

3. Click on **Apply.** The tone enhancements you made will be applied.

Detailing Your Photo

The Detail Room has controls for the following:

- **Sharpen**. The Sharpen control enhances edges.

- **Smooth**. The Smooth control softens edges.

- **Red Eye**. The Red Eyes control gets rid of the demonic effect caused by eyes reflecting a flash.

- **Heal**. Heal mixes and blurs an area, which can be used to cover spots or scratches on a photo.

- **Clone**. Clone copies an area from the photo and lets you blend it in elsewhere. You could, for example, clone sky to get rid of an ugly power line or billboard.

1. **Click** on **Heal**. The mouse pointer changes to a crosshair.

2. **Double-click** on the **image** in the area you would like to heal. The image will zoom to that area and the mouse pointer turns into a paintbrush.

3. **Click** on a **scratch or flake** in the image. The mark will fade to match the colors around it.

Adding the Finishing Touches

After detailing the photo, you can move on to finishing it.

1. **Move** the **mouse pointer** over the Map button at the top-center of the screen. The Room buttons will appear.

2. **Click** on **Finish**. The Finish Room will appear.

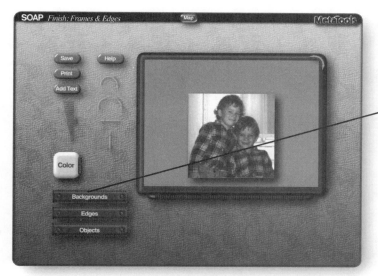

The Finish Room allows you to add a frame and background for the photo. You can also add text, ornaments, or graphics.

1. Click the **Backgrounds bar**. The Backgrounds album will appear.

2. Double-click on a **background image**. The chosen background will appear behind the photo.

3. Double-click the **left edge** of the backgrounds album. The album will close.

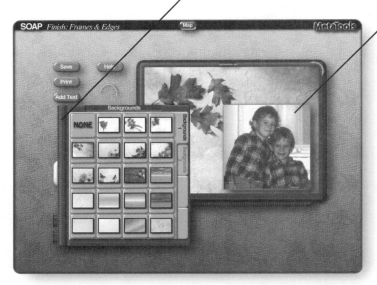

4. Click and drag the **photo** to any position on the background

Saving Your Masterpiece

When you modified the photo to look exactly the way you want, you can save the completed image, including all the additions you have made to it, on your disk.

1. Click on **Save**. The Save File dialog box will appear.

2. **Click** on a **destination folder** for the image file.

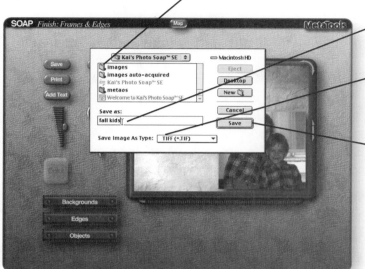

3. **Type** a **file name** for the photo.

4. **Click** on a **file type** from the pop-up menu at the bottom of the dialog box.

5. **Click** on **Save**. Your work will be saved.

TIP

If you are planning to include the photo in a Web site, select either JPEG or GIF as the file type. If you will be printing the photo, TIFF is probably the best choice. If you want to modify the photo using AppleWorks, use PICT. (AppleWorks can import JPEG, GIF, and TIFF images for display only.)

Using the Out Room

The Out Room allows you to save the photo you modified without any of the finishings such as background and border. Also, you can apply filters to the image or print it. You reach the Out Room just like any of the other Photo Soap rooms.

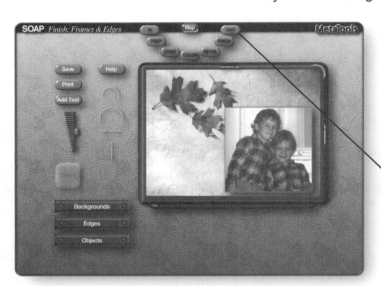

1. Move the **mouse pointer** over the Map button. The room buttons will appear.

2. Click on **Out**. You will be taken to the Out Room.

You can do any of the following in the Out Room.

• **Click** on **Save** to save just the photo without any backgrounds or border. This process is the same as that described in the preceding section of this chapter.

• **Click** on **Print** to print the photo.

• **Click** on **Quit** to exit the program. You can also press ⌘-Q to exit at any time.

13

Exploring the iMac's Reference Software

The iMac is accompanied by two programs that can be considered reference works: The World Book Encyclopedia and the Williams-Sonoma Guide to Good Cooking. In this chapter, you'll learn how to:

- Search for articles in the World Book Encyclopedia
- Find and use a recipe from the Williams-Sonoma Guide to Good Cooking

Starting the World Book Encyclopedia

The World Book Encyclopedia, a set of two CD-ROMs, provides not only an encyclopedia with articles that can be understood by sixth-grade students and up, but a dictionary and an atlas as well. The package includes text articles, illustrations, sound, and video.

After you install the World Book files in the Application folder on your iMac's hard disk, you can start the program.

TIP

See Appendix D, "Adding Software," if you need help installing new software.

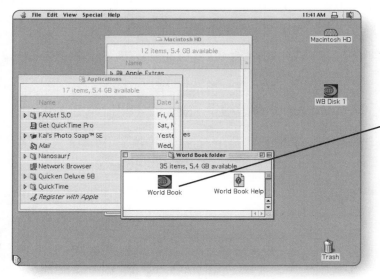

1. Insert World Book Disc 1 into the iMac's CD-ROM drive. The iMac will mount the CD and its icon will appear on the Desktop.

2. Double-click on the **World Book program icon,** located inside the World Book Folder, which is inside the Application folder on the iMac hard disk. The World Book program will launch. An opening screen will appear briefly and be replaced by the main menu screen.

Sampling the World Book's Features

The World Book discs actually contain four reference works, all of which are accessible from the program's main menu screen.

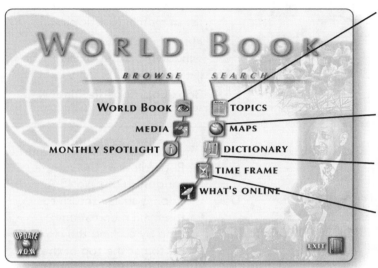

- **Topics icon.** This icon provides access to the World Book's search features and allows you to search the encyclopedia for articles.

- **Maps icon.** The Maps icon allows you to search the atlas.

- **Dictionary.** This icon lets you search the dictionary.

- **Time Frame.** To search for events that occurred on a specific date, use this icon.

The What's Online icon doesn't lead to a reference work, but provides a gateway to additional material from the Internet.

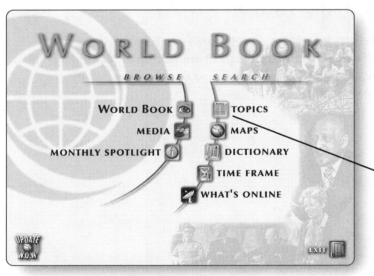

Searching for a Topic

Research in the encyclopedia begins in the traditional way—search for a specific topic. However, there are some distinct advantages to using a computer-based tool.

1. Click the **Topics icon**. The Search by Topic window will appear on top of the World Book Encyclopedia window, displaying an article about the current month.

2. **Type** a **search term** or **phrase** in the Enter search words text box.

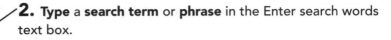

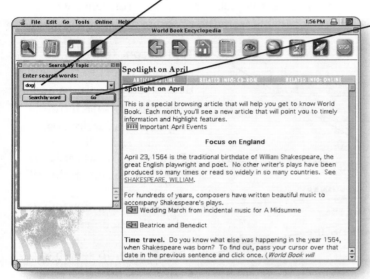

3. **Click** on **Go**. The World Book will perform the search. A list of matching articles will appear in the Search by Topic window. The first article in the list will appear in the World Book Encyclopedia window.

TIP

Regardless of the current window in the World Book, you can return to the main menu at any time by clicking the Home button at the top of the window.

Working with an Article

The articles in an electronic encyclopedia are somewhat different from those in a print encyclopedia. When you have an article that you want to read on the screen, there are a number of things you can do.

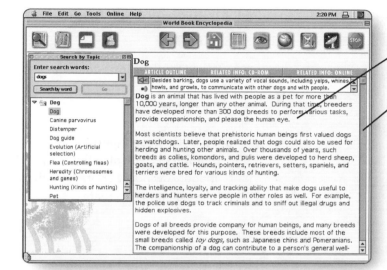

Reading the Text

1. Read the **viewable text** of the article.

2. Scroll the **text** as necessary to bring more of the article into view.

At the end of each article, you'll find a bibliography that describes additional print resources about the article's topic.

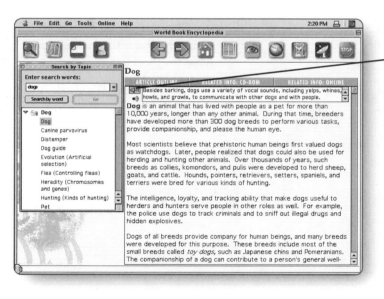

Playing Sounds

1. Click on the **speaker icon** at the top of the text box. The sound will play through the iMac's speaker.

NOTE

Because the sound in the preceding illustration is at the beginning of the article, it will play automatically when the article appears.

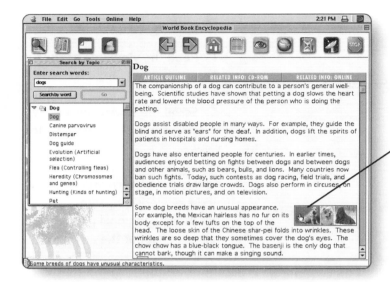

Viewing Full-Size Images

World Book articles contain thumbnails of images related to the article.

1. **Click** on an **image thumbnail** to display the entire image. A window containing the full-size image appears.

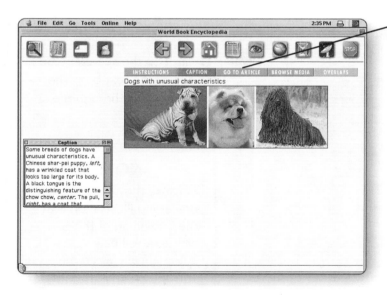

2. **Click** on **Go To Article** to return to the article when you have finished viewing the image and reading its caption. The article will appear again.

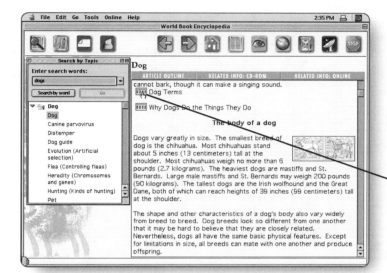

Viewing Tables

World Book articles often contain tables of useful information. The tables are not visible in the article text, but appear in their own window, just like full-size images.

1. Click on a **table icon** in an article. The table window will appear.

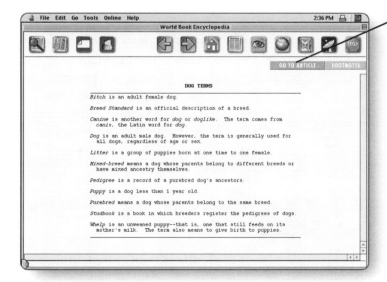

2. Click on **Go To Article** to return to the article. The article will replace the table window.

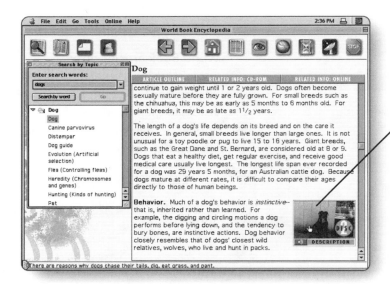

Watching a Video

Some World Book articles are accompanied by video clips stored on the second disc.

1. Click on the **video image**. You can recognize such an image by the Disc 2 displayed in its lower-right corner.

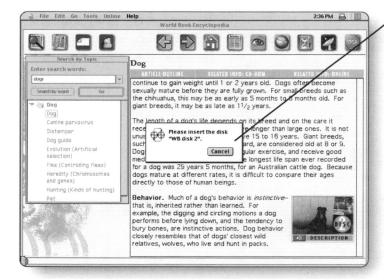

2. Remove Disc 1 from the CD-ROM drive's tray. If Disc 2 is already in the CD-ROM drive, the World Book will play the video. However, if Disc 1 is in the drive, the iMac will open the tray of the CD-ROM drive and display an alert asking you to insert Disc 2.

3. Place Disc 2 in the CD-ROM drive's tray.

4. Close the CD-ROM drive's **tray**. The iMac will mount the CD-ROM automatically. The alert will disappear from the screen and the video window will appear. The video will begin playing.

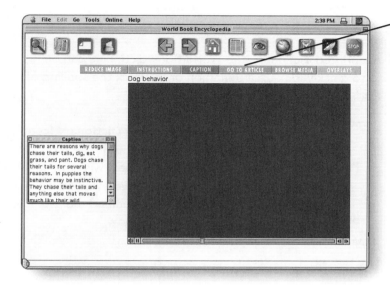

5. Click on **Go To Article** to return to the article when you have finished viewing the video.

Switching to Another Article

You can switch to and view another article at any time.

1. Double-click on an **article name** in the list in the Search by Topic window. The new article will appear in the World Book Encyclopedia window, replacing the article you were viewing previously. You will probably need to switch to Disc 1 again.

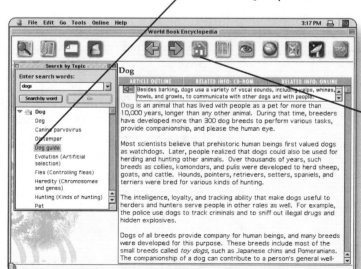

2. Click on the **Home button** to exit and go back to the main menu.

Using the Dictionary

Like a printed dictionary, the World Book dictionary can be used to quickly look up a definition or to check the spelling of a word.

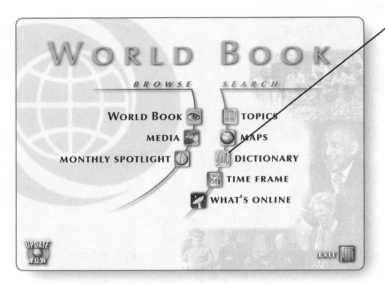

1. Click on the **Dictionary icon** in the main menu. The Dictionary window will appear. The last article you viewed will also be visible behind the Dictionary window.

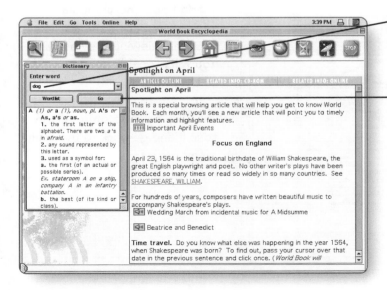

2. Type the **word** for the search in the Enter word text box.

3. Click on **Go**. The World Book scrolls the contents of the Dictionary window and shows the definition of the word.

You can also browse through the dictionary.

1. **Scroll up or down** to view the alphabetical listing.

2. **Click** on the **Home button** to exit.

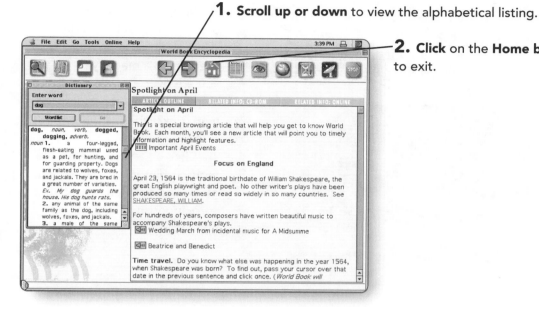

Using the Atlas

Electronic atlases have many advantages over paper atlases. In particular, rather than using insets to show detail, electronic atlases allow you to click on an area of a map and zoom to a detailed view.

Viewing Maps

1. **Click** on the **Maps icon** on the main menu screen. The World Book Encyclopedia window shows a map of the entire world.

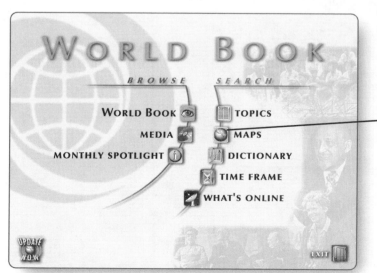

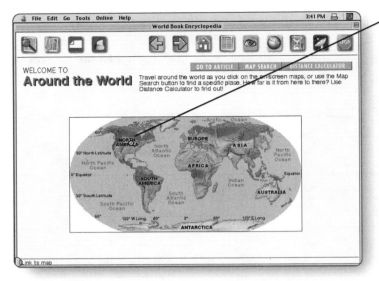

2. Move the **mouse pointer** over the map of the world. When the mouse pointer changes to a magnifying glass you are over a portion of the map for which a more detailed map is available.

3. Click on an **area** where the mouse pointer is a magnifying glass. The detailed map that corresponds to the area will appear.

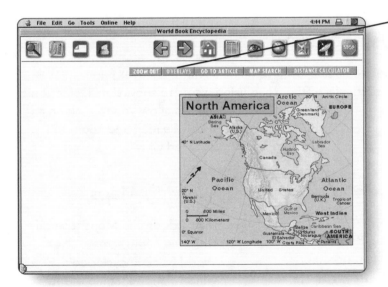

4. Click on **Overlays** to display the window that provides access to different types of maps. The Around the World Window will appear.

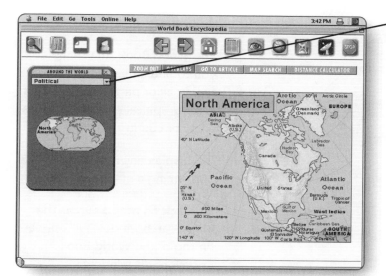

5. **Click** on the **down arrow** next to Political in the Around the World window to see a list of available menu types. The map types list will appear.

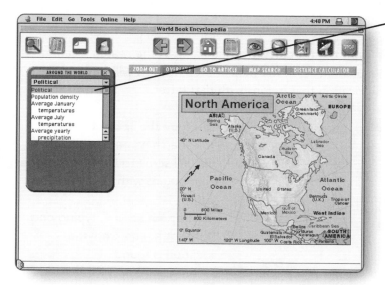

6. **Double-click** on a **map type** to display that type of map. The new map will appear.

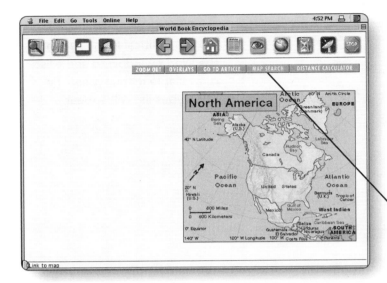

Finding a Map

The World Book Atlas enables you to find a map quickly by typing all or part of the name of a geographical element, such as a city or country.

1. Display any **map** before performing a map search.

2. Click on **Map Search**. The Map Search window will appear on top of the World Book Encyclopedia window.

3. Click on the **Enter location: text box** to get an insertion point, if necessary.

4. Type the **first letter** of the name of the search location. The location list in the Map Search window will scroll to the first location that begins with that letter.

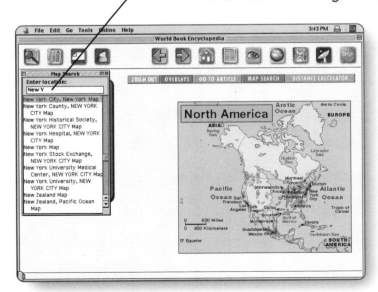

5. Type the **second letter** of the search name. The location list will scroll to the first location that begins with the two letters.

6. Repeat step 4, typing one letter at a time, until the location is found.

7. Press Enter. A map showing the chosen area will appear. The chosen location will be in a box.

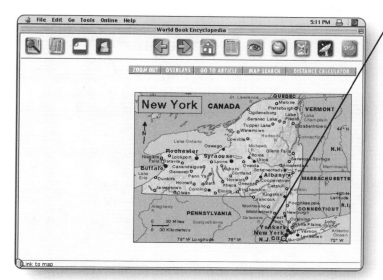

8. Click in the **boxed location** to see a more detailed map. The new map will appear. If even more detailed maps are available, the areas shown by those maps will be boxed.

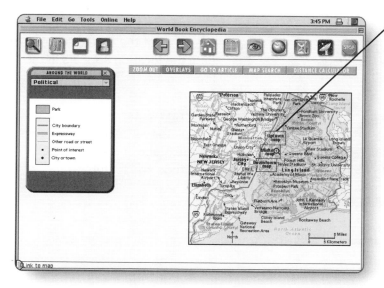

9. Click in a **boxed location** to display a more detailed map, if a boxed area is available. The more detailed map will appear.

10. Repeat step 9 until there are no boxed areas on the map, or until you reach the level of detail you desire.

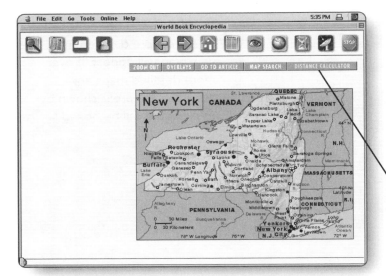

Using the Distance Calculator

The Distance Calculator makes it easy to find out the distance between two locations.

1. Display any **map**.

2. Click on **Distance Calculator**. The Distance Calculator window will appear.

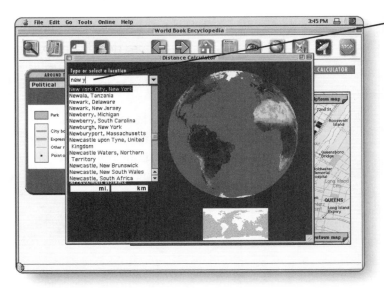

3. Type one letter at a time of the name of the first location until the location appears in the location list.

4. Press Enter. The Distance Calculator will mark the location on the globe and display the longitude and latitude.

5. Click in the **text box** for the second location.

6. Type one letter at a time of the name of the second location until the location appears in the location list.

7. Press Enter. The Distance Calculator will mark the location on the globe, display the latitude and longitude, and display the distance between the two locations.

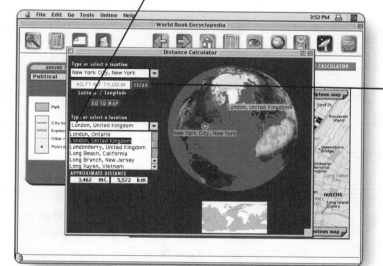

TIP

You can click the Clear button next to the location at any time to remove and select a different location.

8. Click on the **Home button** to exit.

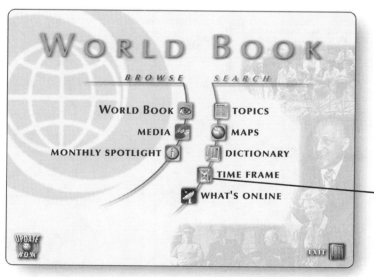

Using the Timeline

The World Book's Time Frame features let you display articles, graphics, sounds, and videos in chronological order. The Time Frame provides a timeline of events based on a variety of intervals.

1. Click on the **Time Frame icon** on the main menu window. The World Book Encyclopedia window will appear, displaying the New Time Frame Window.

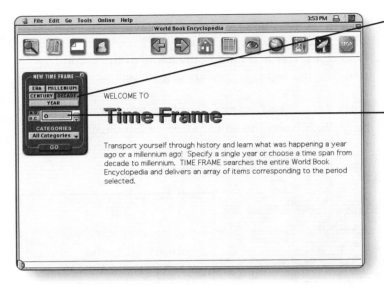

2. Click on a **button** to select the size of the time frame (an era, millennium, century, decade, or year).

3. Type a **year** in the time frame.

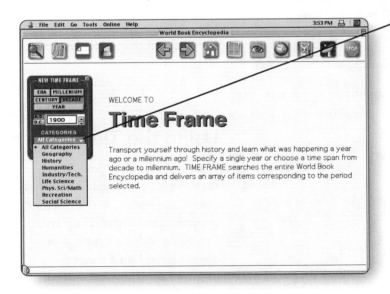

4. Click on a **category** for articles to be included in the search from the pop-up menu on the New Time Frame Window.

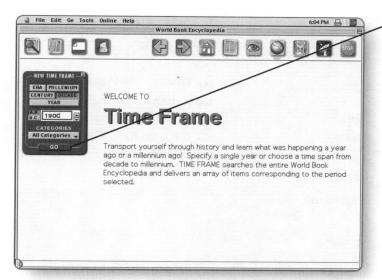

5. **Click** the **Go button** on the New Time Frame window to generate the timeline of articles. The World Book will perform the search and display thumbnails of related articles in chronological order.

6. **Click** on any **thumbnail** to expand it to full size.

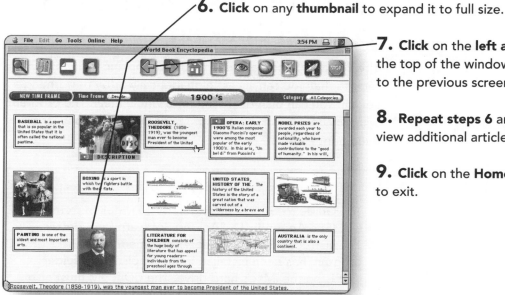

7. **Click** on the **left arrow** at the top of the window to return to the previous screen.

8. **Repeat steps 6** and **7** to view additional articles.

9. **Click** on the **Home button** to exit.

Exiting the World Book

1. Display the **World Book's main menu screen**.

2. Click on **Exit**. The program will stop running.

The Williams-Sonoma Guide to Good Cooking

The Williams-Sonoma Guide to Good Cooking includes 1000 recipes that you can access alphabetically or by performing a search. You can plan the menu for a whole meal. The program will provide a list of ingredients, print out the recipes, and even print a menu.

NOTE

The Guide to Good Cooking must be installed from the CD. (See Appendix D, "Adding Software," for details.) The instructions in this chapter assume that the program has been installed in the Applications folder that is on the iMac's hard drive. The CD-ROM must also be in the CD-ROM drive and mounted on the iMac's Desktop when the program is running.

Starting the Cookbook

1. Insert the **Williams-Sonoma CD-ROM** into the CD-ROM drive. The iMac will mount the disc on the Desktop.

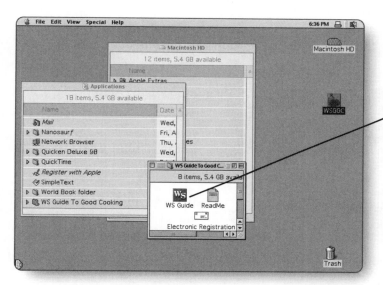

2. Double-click on the **Williams-Sonoma folder** in the Applications folder, which is stored on the iMac's hard disk.

3. Double-click on the **WS Guide icon**. The program will launch. Depending on the number of colors your monitor is set to display, an alert asking if the program can reset the number of colors may appear.

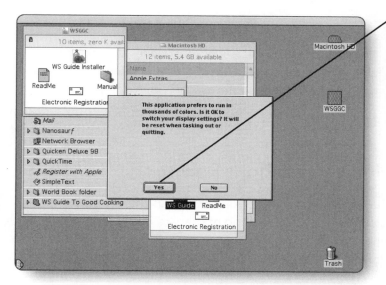

4. Click on **Yes** to remove the alert from the screen. There will be a short movie intro and then the main menu screen (the "kitchen") will appear.

Sampling the Cookbook's Features

The cookbook's main menu is a photo. Each labeled image in the photo is actually a button you can click to reach one of the program's features.

- **Glossary**. The glossary contains definitions of cooking terms.

- **Favorite Recipes**. Favorite recipes is an empty book for you to store your favorites from the 1000 recipes on the CD-ROM.

- **Recipe Finder**. The Recipe Finder searches through the program's recipe collection.

- **Menu Planner**. The Menu Planner selects up to six courses for a meal and prints out ingredient lists, recipes, and a menu for your guests.

- **Recipe Index**. The Recipe Index provides the recipes in alphabetical order. You can either search through the index or use it to browse the recipes.

- **Quit**. The Quit button exits the program.

Finding the Right Recipe

The Recipe Finder helps you find menus that meet your selection of course, method of preparation, season of year, time to cook, region of origin, ingredients, and dietary preferences.

1. **Click** on **Recipe Finder** on the main menu screen. The Recipe Finder screen will appear.

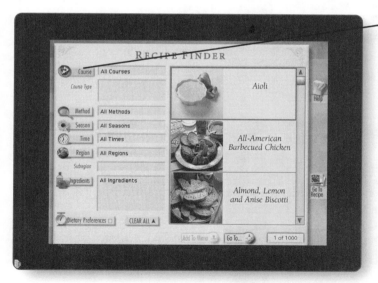

2. **Click** on **Course** to specify the course for which you want a recipe. The Course selection screen will appear.

3. Click on the **dish** that represents the course you want. A list of recipes available for the course will appear in a list at the right of the window. The number of recipes appears below the list.

4. Click a **course type** in the list. The course type will be highlighted.

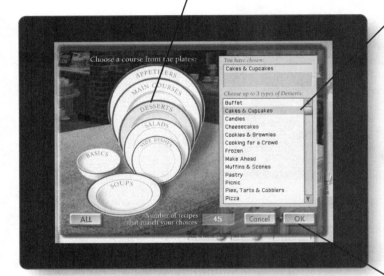

TIP

You can choose up to three course types. Just click on three items in the list, one at a time. If you change your mind about a selection, click on it again to remove the highlighting.

5. Click on **OK**. You will be returned to the Recipe Finder screen.

6. Click on **Time** to select the maximum cooking time you will accept. The Cooking Time screen will appear.

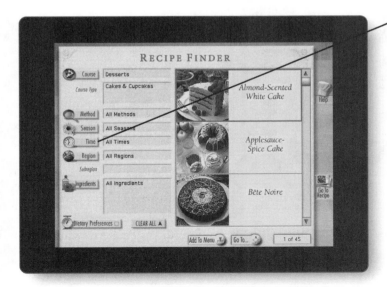

7. Click on the **bar** that represents the maximum cooking time you will accept. The program displays the number of recipes that match the criteria at the bottom of the screen. If the number of recipes is too low, choose a longer maximum cooking time.

8. Click on **OK** to return to the Recipe Finder screen. The recipes that meet the specified criteria appear in a list on the right of the screen.

9. Scroll through the **list** of recipes to view them.

10. Double-click on a **recipe**. A recipe description screen will appear.

11. **Click** on **See Recipe**. The recipe will appear.

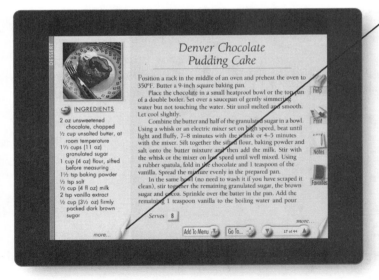

12. **Click** on the **corner** of the ingredients page if all of the ingredients for the recipe are not displayed. The rest of the ingredients will appear.

13. **Click** on **Go To**. A pop-up menu of the major program sections will appear.

14. **Click** on **Recipe Finder**. The Recipe Finder screen will reappear.

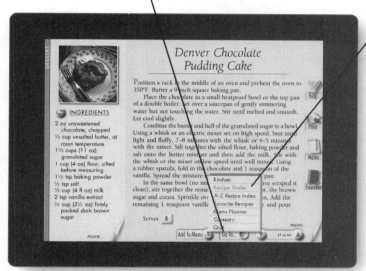

Adding a Recipe to the Menu

Once you have selected a recipe, you can add it to the menu for the meal you are planning.

1. Display the **Recipe Finder screen.**

2. Click on a **recipe** to select it. It will be highlighted.

3. Click on **Add To Menu**. An alert will appear confirming that the recipe has been added.

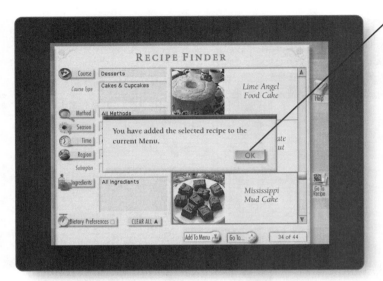

4. **Click** on **OK**. The alert will close and you will return to the Recipe Finder screen.

Viewing a Menu

When one recipe for each course is complete, you can view, save, and print the menu from the Menu Planner screen.

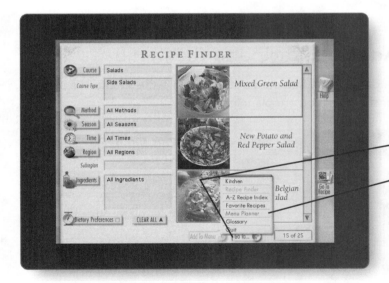

1. **Click** on **Go To**.

2. **Click** on **Menu Planner**. The Menu Planner screen will appear, showing the recipes that were added to the current menu.

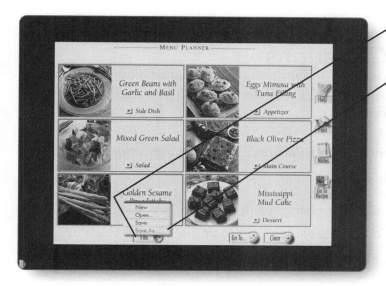

3. Click on **File**. The pop-up menu of actions will appear.

3. Click on **Save As**. A dialog box will appear. All menus are automatically saved in the WS Guide folder.

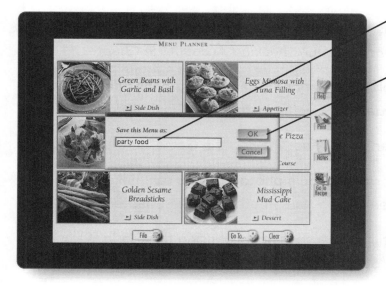

4. Type a **name** for the menu in the Save this Menu as: text box.

5. Click on **OK**. The program will save the menu for future use.

NOTE

One of the limitations to this program is that you can have no more than six dishes in a menu, although you can have more than one from a single category.

Exiting the Cooking

To exit the WS Guide, press ⌘-Q at any time.

Part III Review Questions

1. How do you use an AppleWorks Assistant? *See "Creating a Document with an Assistant" in Chapter 10*

2. What modules are part of AppleWorks? *See "The AppleWorks Modules" in Chapter 10*

3. How do you place an image from an AppleWorks graphics library into an AppleWorks document? *See "Choosing a Library Graphic" in Chapter 10*

4. How do you set up a new Quicken bank account? *See "Creating Bank Accounts" in Chapter 11*

5. Describe the process for reconciling a checking account using Quicken. *See "Reconciling Your Checking Account" in Chapter 11*

6. What is Adobe Acrobat Reader and what is its purpose? *See "Using Adobe Acrobat Reader to View the Instructions" in Chapter 12*

7. How do you play Nanosaur? *See "Playing the Game" in Chapter 12*

8. Describe the transformations to a photo that you can make using Kai's Photo Soap. *See "Using Kai's Photo Soap" in Chapter 12*

9. How do you find articles on a specific topic using the World Book Encyclopedia? *See "Searching for a Topic" in Chapter 13*

10. How do you find a specific recipe in the Williams-Sonoma Guide to Good Cooking? *See "Finding the Right Recipe" in Chapter 13*

PART IV

Communicating with Other Computers

14

Setting Up a Connection

The *i* in iMac stands for Internet, the global network of computers that provides you with e-mail and Web access. Your iMac is already equipped with the hardware and software to connect to the Internet and to communicate with other computer users around the world. In this chapter, you'll learn how to:

- Connect to the Internet using America Online (AOL).
- Connect to the Internet using Earthlink's Total Access 2.01.

Setting Up AOL

AOL is the world's largest service provider. It is a local call from most cities in the United States and has access numbers throughout the world. Once you connect to AOL, you can use any Internet software you have, though AOL's software provides everything you need.

Like most service providers, AOL has its good points and bad points. AOL's software is very easy to set up and use. AOL also provides a wealth of content and excellent technical support for Macintosh users. However, because AOL is so popular, you may experience trouble getting connected during peak usage periods. For information on how to pick the service provider that's right for you, see Appendix C, "Choosing a Communications Service Provider."

Launching AOL

The AOL software comes preinstalled on your iMac's hard drive. Launching the program is simple.

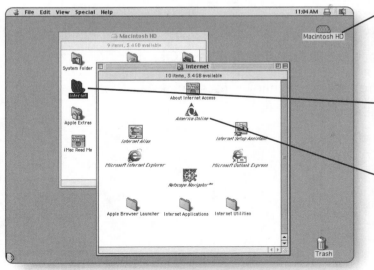

1. Double-click on the **Macintosh hard disk folder icon**. The Macintosh HD window will open.

2. Double-click on the **Internet folder icon**. The Internet window will open.

3. Double-click on the **Internet Applications folder icon**. The Internet Applications window will open.

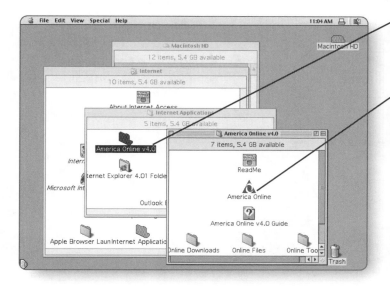

4. Double-click on the **America Online folder icon**. The America Online window will open.

5. Double-click on the **American Online icon**. The AOL software will launch and the first setup window will appear.

Setting Up AOL

The first time you run the AOL software, you will need to go through a setup process that includes entering personal information (including a credit card number to which account fees will be charged), finding a local access number, and discovering the correct modem settings.

1. Read the **setup information** in the AOL Setup window. Leave the Begin automatic setup radio button selected.

2. Click on **Next**. The program will search for your modem. When the search is complete, the second AOL Setup window will appear, displaying the type of modem it found.

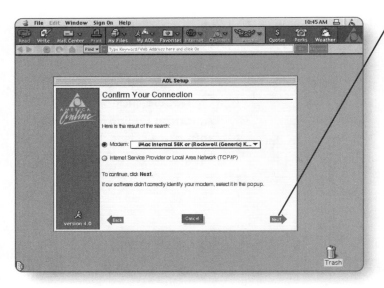

3. Click on **Next**. The third AOL setup window will appear, asking you to confirm your communications settings.

4. Click on the **check box** next to Use touch-tone service to remove the check mark if you do not have a touch-tone phone.

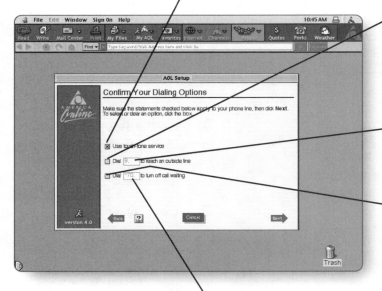

5. Click on the **check box** next to Dial 9 to reach an outside line if your phone is part of a system that requires a special number or numbers to dial out.

6. Type the **dialing sequence** to reach an outside line in the text box, if different.

7. Click on the **check box** next to Dial *70 to disable call waiting if your phone has this capability.

8. Type the **dialing sequence** needed to disable call waiting in the text box, if different.

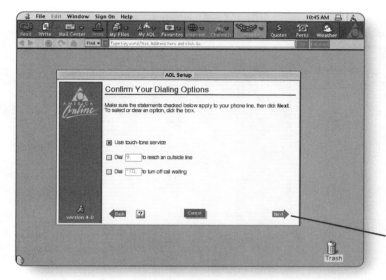

NOTE

Call waiting is a problem in data communications because an incoming call that arrives while you are connected to a service provider will disrupt the signal and terminate the connection abruptly.

9. Click on **Next**. The fourth AOL Setup window will appear.

Finding Local Access Numbers

The next part of this process is to allow the AOL software to find access numbers in your area code so that you can choose the local numbers you want to use.

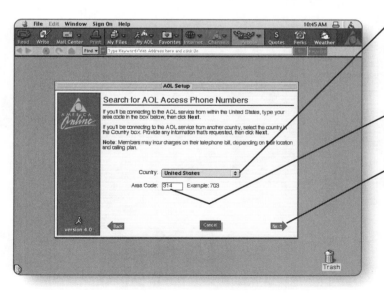

1. Click on the **country** in which you are located from the pop-up menu, if you are not in the United States.

2. Enter the **area code** from which you will be accessing AOL.

3. Click on **Next**. The next AOL Setup window will appear.

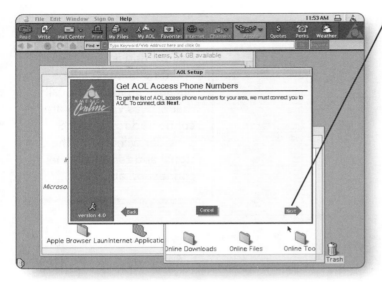

4. Click on **Next**. The AOL software will instruct your modem to dial a toll-free number so that the software can search for access numbers in your area code.

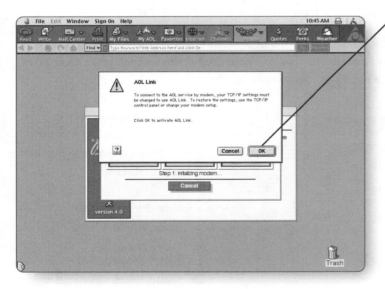

5. Click on **OK**. The AOL software will dial the toll-free number and download the list of local access numbers. A window will open, listing the numbers.

6. Scroll through the **list** to find a local number. Give priority to the V90 numbers, as these provide the fastest connections.

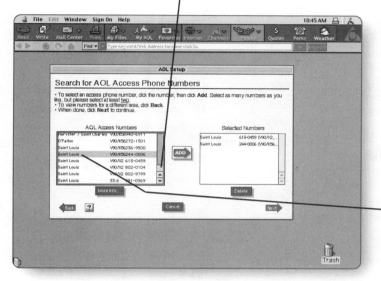

TIP

If there are no numbers that are local calls you can either use a toll call number in your area code, or you can use a local ISP along with the Bring Your Own Access pricing option.

7. Double-click on the **number** you want to use. An AOL Setup window for that number will appear.

8. Click on the **Use touch-tone service check box** to remove the check mark if you want to use pulse dialing.

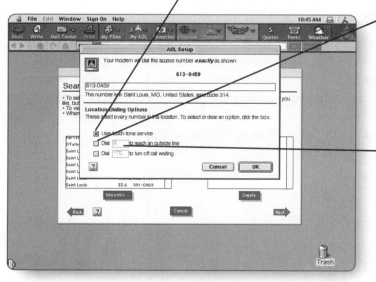

9. Click on the **Dial 9 to reach an outside line check box** if your phone is part of a system that requires a special number or numbers to get an outside line.

10. Type the **dialing sequence** to reach an outside line in the text box, if different.

11. **Click** on the **check box** next to Dial *70 to disable call waiting, if you have call waiting.

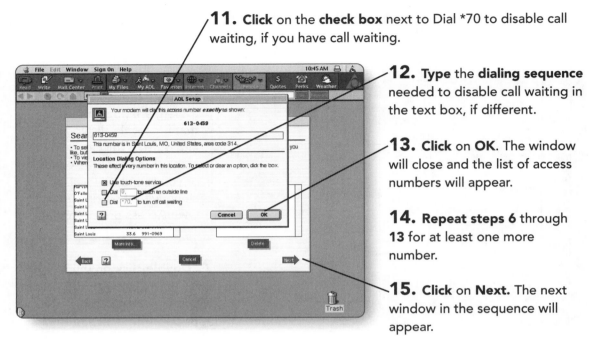

12. **Type** the **dialing sequence** needed to disable call waiting in the text box, if different.

13. **Click** on **OK**. The window will close and the list of access numbers will appear.

14. **Repeat steps 6** through **13** for at least one more number.

15. **Click** on **Next.** The next window in the sequence will appear.

16. **Click** on **Next**. The Information About You window will appear.

Registering the Account

Even if you only plan to use AOL for the first free month, you still need to supply personal information and a credit card number. If you decide to keep the service you don't need to do anything; your credit card will be billed automatically. To cancel the service before the free month is up, call AOL's Customer Service line at 888-265-8008.

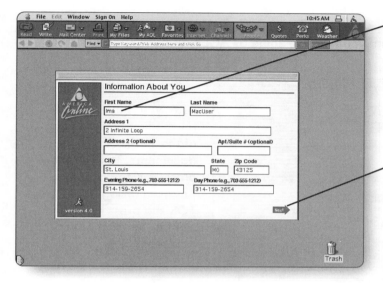

1. Type your personal **information** in the Information About You window. Use the Tab key to move between text boxes, or click in the text box in which you want to type to move the insertion point there.

2. Click on **Next.** The next window in the sequence will appear.

3. Click on **Next.** The Billing Information window will appear.

4. Read the billing **information** at the top of the window.

5. Type your **credit card number** and its **expiration date**.

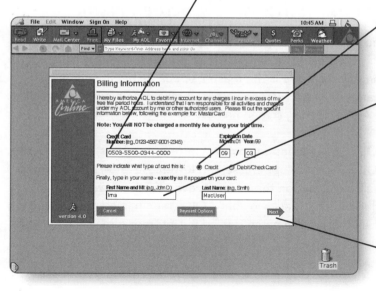

6a. Click on the **Credit radio button** if it is a charge card.

OR

6b. Click on the **Debit Check Card radio button** if it is a debit card.

7. Type your **first and last name**, exactly as they appear on the credit card.

8. Click on **Next.** The Conditions of AOL Membership window will appear.

9. **Leave** the **Agree radio button** checked. This indicates that you agree to abide by AOL's Terms of Service.

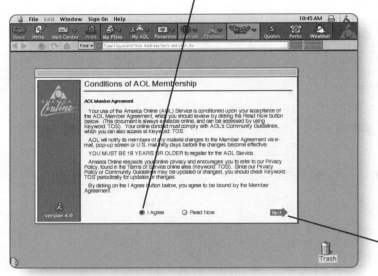

TIP

After you sign on to AOL for the first time, read all of the Terms of Service documents. To find them, press ⌘-K to display the Keyword dialog box. Type TOS and press Enter to see the Terms of Service documents.

10. **Click** on **Next**. The Choosing Your Screen Name window appears.

Choosing the Master Screen Name

Each AOL account can have up to five screen names, each of which represents a unique e-mail address. The first screen name you choose is the *master screen name*. It cannot be changed. Like all screen names, it must be unique among all of AOL's existing screen names.

AOL screen names can contain letters, numbers, and spaces. AOL will display uppercase and lowercase letters as different characters, but on the Internet, everything is lowercase. In addition, any spaces in your AOL screen name are removed when that screen name is used for Internet e-mail.

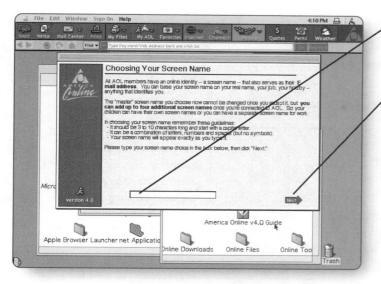

1. **Type** a **master screen name** in the text box at the bottom of the window.

2. **Click** on **Next**. The AOL software will ask you to choose a password.

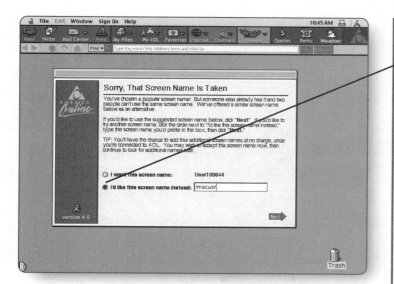

TIP

If the screen name you entered is already in use, the AOL software displays the Sorry, That Screen Name is Taken window. Type a new choice text box next to the I'd like this screen name instead radio button and click on Next. Or, click on the I want this screen name radio button to accept the screen name AOL suggests for you, then click on Next.

3. Type your **password twice**, once in each box at the bottom of the window. You won't see the characters as you type; only dots will appear.

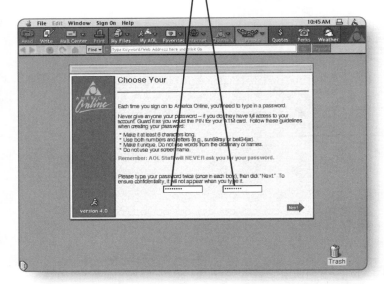

TIP

The security of your AOL account rests with the secrecy of your password. There are many unethical people lurking on the Internet who will try to guess your password or trick you into revealing it. Remember, the AOL staff will *never* ask you for your password. The only time you need to enter your password is when you sign on. Any other request for your password is a scam and an attempt to steal your account.

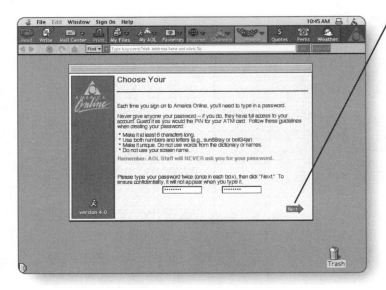

4. Click on **Next**. The AOL software will sign you on to the AOL service. The AOL QuickStart window will appear.

Getting Started with AOL

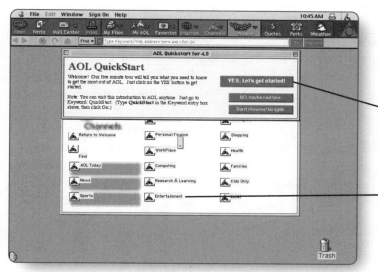

AOL has a lot to offer. The best way to become acquainted with it is to take advantage of the AOL QuickStart.

1. **Click** on **Yes, Let's get started** to begin the QuickStart tour. The QuickStart Tour window will open.

2. **Click** on the **channel buttons** in the window to view information about using AOL.

Signing Off AOL

When you have finished exploring AOL, choose Sign Off from the Sign Off menu. The AOL software will disconnect you from the service and hang up the telephone.

Setting Up EarthLink's Total Access 2.01

If you prefer a more traditional ISP, consider Earthlink, a national ISP that has access numbers across the United States. The software to access EarthLink is preinstalled on your iMac.

Once you have an EarthLink account, your iMac calls EarthLink and connects to the Internet. That's all a standard ISP does: It provides the Internet connection. You can use any Internet software you choose; for example, you can use Microsoft Outlook for e-mail and either Microsoft Internet Explorer or Netscape Navigator for the Web.

Starting the Internet Configuration Process

To connect to EarthLink, you need to configure your iMac for Internet access. The first time you access the iMac's Internet software, you will be taken through the setup process.

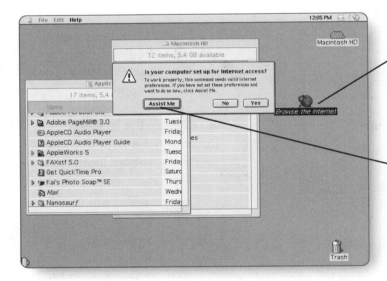

1. Double-click on the **Browse the Internet alias icon** on the iMac Desktop. An alert box will appear asking if your computer is set up for Internet access.

2. Click on **Assist Me**. The Internet Setup Assistant will launch and ask if you want to connect to the Internet.

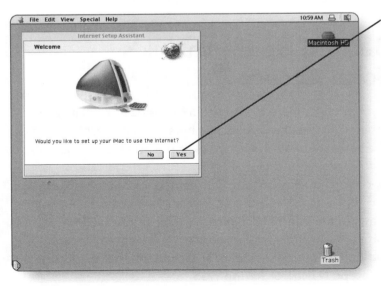

3. Click on **Yes**. The Internet Account Screen will appear and ask whether you already have an Internet account.

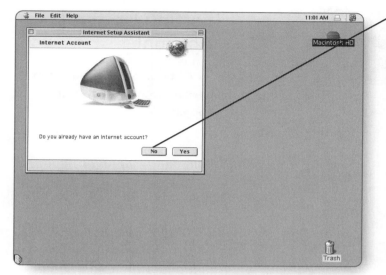

4. Click on **No**. The TotalAccess Agreement window will appear and a voice will begin reading directions aloud to you.

Understanding the Subscription Agreement

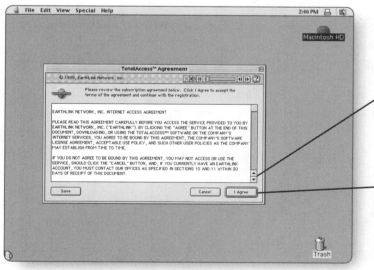

The rules that govern the use of an EarthLink account are contained in the scrolling Agreement window.

1. Scroll down through the **window** to read the entire contents of the Agreement document.

2. Click on **I Agree** to accept the agreement. The Welcome to TotalAccess window will appear and a voice will begin reading directions to you.

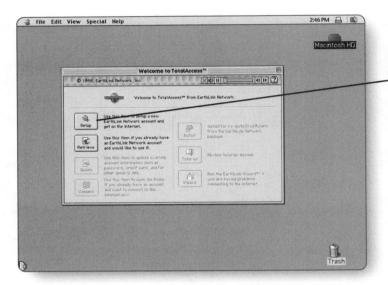

Setting Up the Account

1. Click on **Setup**. The Setup New Account window will appear.

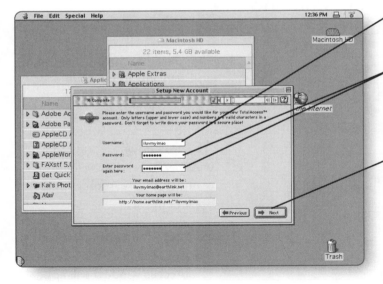

2. Type an **account name** in the User Name: text box.

3. Type your **password** in each password text box. The characters in the password will appear as dots as you type.

4. Click on **Next**. The General Information window will appear.

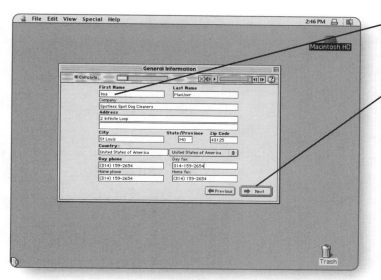

5. Type your **information**. Use the Tab key to move from one text box to the next.

6. Click on **Next**. The Phone Setup window will appear.

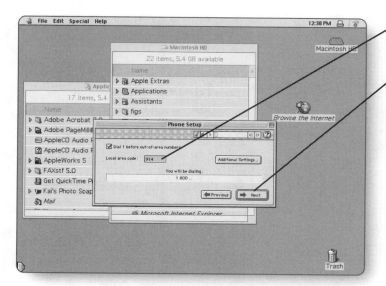

7. Type your **area code** in the Local area code: text box.

8. Click on **Next**. A dialog box will open, telling you that EarthLink Setup is dialing an 800 number to obtain access numbers in your area code.

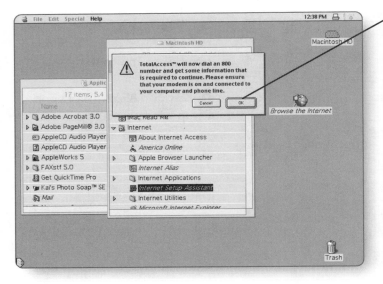

9. Click on **OK**. The dialog box will close and another dialog box will open showing the progress of the call. When the call is complete, a list of account options will appear.

Choosing an Account Type

EarthLink provides three types of accounts. The first is for unlimited access through a local access number. The second provides the same local access, but adds five hours of access through a toll-free 800 number. This is a good choice if you travel frequently. The third account is for those who have ISDN access, a high-speed connection that does not use standard telephone lines.

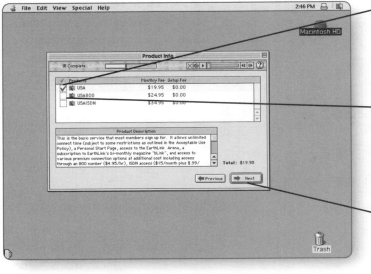

1a. Leave the **check** in the USA check box if you want the local access service.

OR

1b. Click on the **check box** next to the USA800 account type if you want to add the five hours of toll-free access. A check mark will appear in the box.

2. Click on **Next**. The Credit Card Information window will appear.

Entering Credit Card Information

As with AOL, you must provide EarthLink with credit card information, even if you are only planning to try the service for the free month. You will be charged at the beginning of the second month if you don't cancel the account before the free month is up.

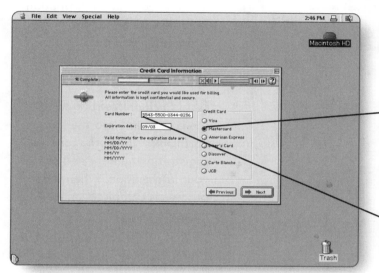

1. Click on the **radio button** next to the type of credit card you will be using. The button will appear darkened to indicate that it has been selected.

2. Type the **credit card number** in the Card Number: text box.

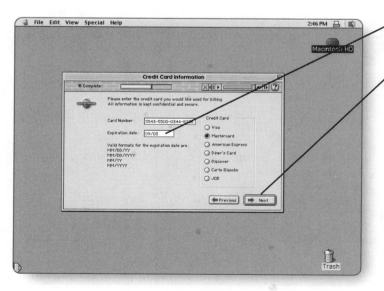

3. Type the **expiration date** in the Expiration Date: text box.

4. Click on **Next**. The Account Verification window will appear.

5. Read the **information** in the window and verify that it is correct.

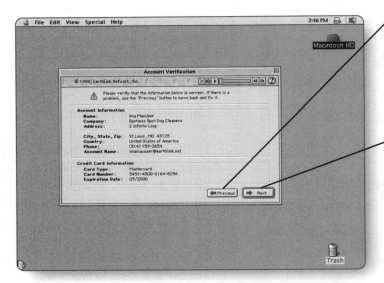

6a. Click on **Previous** to return to the Credit Card Information window to change any information you entered.

OR

6b. Click on **Next** to accept the credit card information. EarthLink will dial the toll-free registration number and send your information. When the process is complete, an alert will appear.

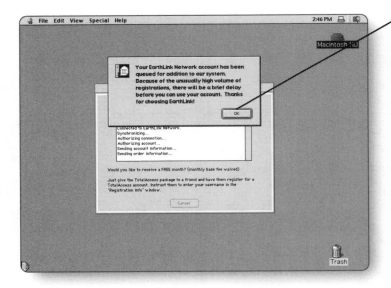

7. Click on **OK**. The alert and the registration window will close and the software Installation window will appear.

TIP

At this point, you must decide which software you will use to guide you through the Internet. The Installation window shows you the software that you can install. EarthLink's New Users Guide is an excellent audio/visual introduction to using the Internet. Internet Explorer is already on your iMac's hard drive.

8. Click on the software you want to install. It will be highlighted.

9. Click on **Install**. The EarthLink software will install the software and a dialog box will open recommending that you restart the system.

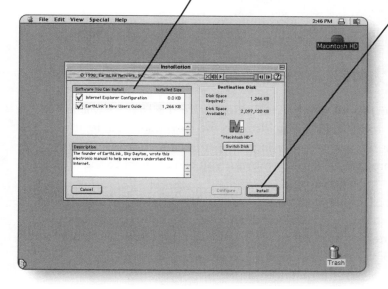

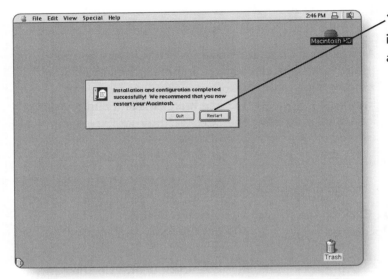

10. **Click** on **Restart**. Your iMac will close down all open applications and reboot.

Connecting for the First Time

On reboot, the EarthLink Registration & Utilities will launch automatically. If you installed the New Users Guide, it will launch and start playing the instructional movies. When you're through viewing the movies, you can connect to the Internet.

1. **Double-click** on the **Browse the Internet alias**. Internet Explorer will launch and automatically connect you to the Internet via EarthLink. (For more information on using Internet Explorer, see Chapter 15 "Wandering the World Wide Web").

15

Wandering the World Wide Web

The Web was originally created as a means of delivering text and graphics over the Internet. Today the Web has evolved far beyond simple document transfer. Not only does it span the entire globe, but it contains a wealth of information, lets us shop for just about anything that can be delivered, and supports real-time audio and video as well as text and graphics. In this chapter, you'll learn how to:

- Launch a Web browser
- Search for information the Web
- Follow hyperlinks
- Save the location of favorite Web pages
- Register your iMac with Apple using a Web browser

Introducing the Web

When people talk about the information superhighway, they typically mean the Internet, and the bulk of the Internet's information content is provided over the Web. When a company or individual wants to make Web content available to the world, they create what's known as a *Web site*, a collection of documents that can be viewed using a Web browser. Web documents are formatted using a language called *HyperText Markup Language* (HTML). Each document is known as a *Web page*; the first page that you see when you reach a Web site is usually called the *home page*.

Looking at Web Activities

An enormous amount of content is on the Web. Among the many things you can do on the Web are:

- Research a product.
- Make a purchase.
- Look up information for a school paper, using one of the many homework helper sites.
- Get technical support for hardware and software by sending a question to the manufacturer.
- Track a package that has been sent by a major courier such as UPS or Federal Express.
- Find the lowest airplane fare and book a flight.
- Get updates to software, such as the updates that are available for the World Book Encyclopedia that came with your iMac.
- Play games.
- Read information about your hobby, a favorite entertainment, or your favorite entertainer.
- Listen to music.
- Obtain tax forms.
- Find a weather forecast and weather maps.

This list could go on for pages! The Web is an excellent source of information on many subjects, but you should be aware that there is no guarantee that precisely what you need will be available.

Understanding URLs

Each Web page has an address called a *Uniform Resource Locator*, or URL. (This is pronounced by saying the letters in the acronym, not by saying "earl.") Assuming that you are connected to the Internet, you can reach a Web page by giving your browser the URL of the page you want to view.

URLs for Web pages begin with *http://*. The characters that follow specify exactly which page you want. In most browsers, it is no longer necessary to type in http:// anymore. Some Web sites you might want to explore are:

- Macintosh hardware and software sellers: **www.microwarehouse.com**, **www.maczone.com**, **www.macmall.com**, **www.macconnection.com**
- Homework helper site: **www.homeworkcentral.com**
- Apple Computer: **www.apple.com**

Making the Internet Connection

Web browsers assume that your computer is already connected to the Internet. If you're using AOL as your ISP, you need to sign on to AOL before launching a browser. If you are using EarthLink, the first Internet application you use, such as a Web browser, will make the connection for you.

Launching Your Browser

The iMac comes with two Web browsers: Microsoft Internet Explorer and Netscape Navigator. Both are very similar and you'll see each of them in this chapter. You may therefore want to experiment with both before deciding which one you like best.

NOTE

If you have chosen a local ISP, you may need to make the connection manually. Check with the ISP's tech support personnel to be sure.

NOTE

AOL's software also includes its own browser, which is based on Internet Explorer. However, the AOL browser is clumsier to use than either of the stand-alone programs and has some compatibility problems with some Web sites. Therefore, you may want to use a separate browser rather than relying on AOL's implementation.

Browsing the Web with EarthLink

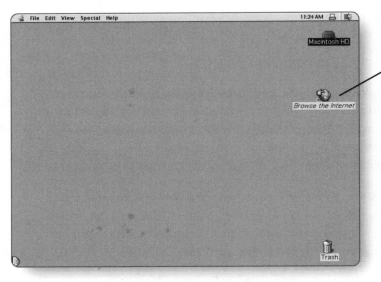

To launch a browser if you are using EarthLink as your ISP:

1. Double-click on the **Browse the Internet alias** on the Desktop. Internet Explorer will launch. The iMac will connect to EarthLink and then display the Web page that is stored in your software as your home page.

Browsing the Web with AOL

To launch a browser if you are using AOL as your ISP:

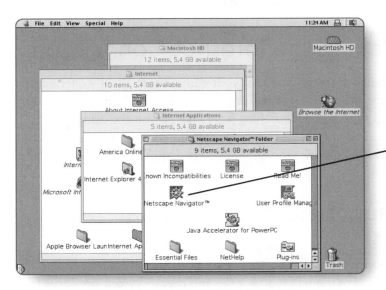

1. Open America Online in the Internet Applications folder.

2. Sign on to **AOL** by typing in your password in the Welcome window and clicking Sign on.

3a. Open the **Netscape Navigator folder** in the Internet folder on the iMac's hard disk, then **double-click** on the **browser icon**. The browser will launch and display the browser's home page.

OR

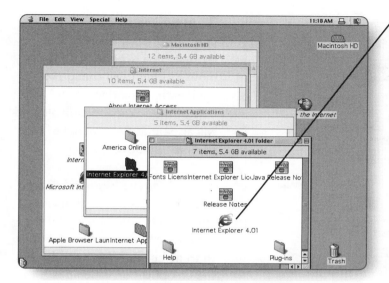

3b. **Open** the **Microsoft Internet Explorer folder** in the Internet folder on the iMac's hard disk, then **double-click** on the **browser icon**. The browser will launch and display the browser's home page.

NOTE

This section will use Netscape Navigator for the examples. You will see Internet Explorer at the end of this chapter.

Navigating the Web

The Web is made up of literally millions of Web sites. After your browser launches, you are taken to the page that has been designated as your browser's home page. From there, you'll move from page to page, following trails of information. To navigate the Web, you have many choices. Six of them will be covered in this section.

Following a Hyperlink

The most common way to move from one Web page to another is to click on a text hyperlink. The hyperlinks used in Web pages function exactly like those in the Apple Guide: you click on underlined text and are transported to whatever location is linked to that text.

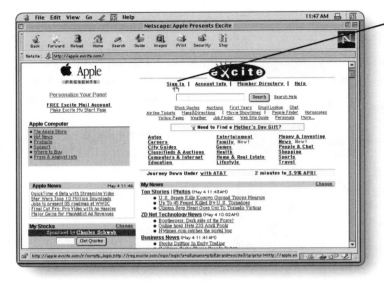

1. Move the **mouse pointer** over the underlined text that represents a hyperlink. The mouse pointer will change to a hand with a pointing finger. The URL of the linked location also will appear at the bottom of the browser window.

2. Click on the **hyperlink.** The URL of the linked location will appear in the Netsite line of the browser and the browser begins to transfer that Web page from the computer on which it is stored. This process is called *downloading* (transferring a file from some other computer to yours).

Searching a Site

Many Web sites, especially corporate Web sites, are made up of hundreds of pages. If you go to a site looking for some specific information, following the hyperlinks through the entire site can be tedious. Fortunately, most large sites make it possible for you to search through the site by supplying a search term that represents what you want to see.

1. Find a **button** that says Search. There should be a text box near it for you to enter a search term.

2. Type the **search term** in the text box.

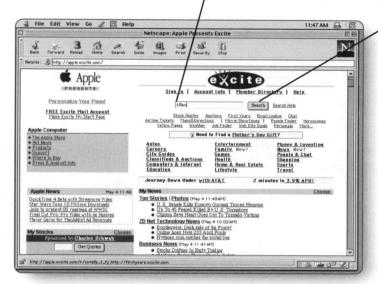

3. Click on **Search**. The Web site will search through its documents and present you with a hyperlinked list of all the relevant documents it found.

TIP

There is no official standard for the design of Web sites or Web pages. Therefore, you may discover that instead of a Search button, there is a Go button.

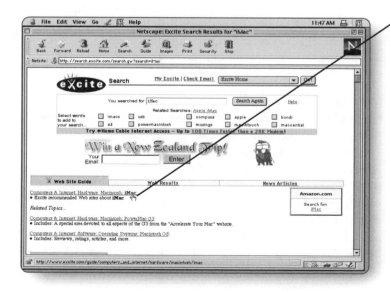

4. Click on a **hyperlink** to reach a Web page you want to see.

Submitting a Form

Some Web pages are designed to gather information from you and send that information to the person or company who owns the Web site. Such pages contain *forms*. Fill out the information and use a Submit button to send the information over the Internet to its destination.

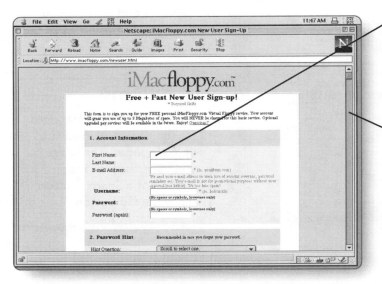

1. Fill in the **text boxes** with the requested information. Some pieces of information may be required in order to submit the form.

2. Scroll the **window,** if necessary, to find the Submit button at the bottom of the form.

3. Click on **Submit**. Your data will be sent to the computer from which the Web page came. Usually, you'll see a page confirming that your data have been sent.

NOTE

Many Web sites, especially those from which you can make purchases, have implemented security measures to protect your credit card number and other sensitive information while it is traveling over the Internet and when it is stored on a Web server. When you submit a form to a secure site, your browser may display an alert telling you what security is being used. If you don't see anything about security, either on a Web page or in an alert, be wary about transmitting sensitive data. It's better to place an order using the telephone than risk sending your private information to an unsecured site.

Using Bookmarks

As you navigate the Web, you will come across Web sites that you want to visit again. The easiest way to keep track of these sites is to *bookmark* them.

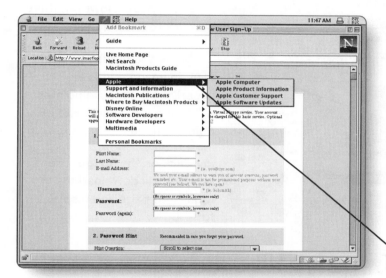

NOTE

Bookmark is a Netscape Navigator term. Internet Explorer refers to bookmarks as Favorites.

Bookmarks are listed in the bookmark menu (the menu with a picture of a bookmark as its name).

1. Choose a **bookmark** from the **Bookmarks menu**. The browser will download the chosen site and display it.

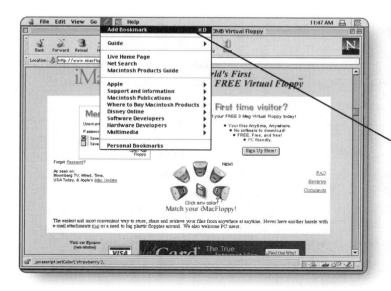

Adding Your Own Bookmark

1. Display the **page** you want to bookmark.

2. Choose Add Bookmark from the **Bookmarks menu** or press ⌘-D. The new bookmark will be added to the bottom of the Bookmarks menu.

Clicking on Image Hyperlinks

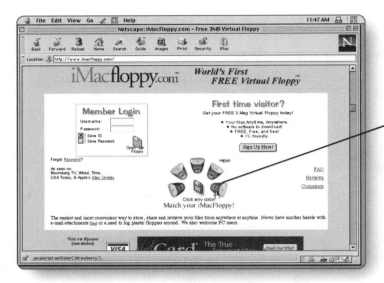

Not all hyperlinks are text; many of them are images. At first, this may make it hard for you to find links on a page. However, there is a trick to finding them.

1. Move the **mouse pointer** over an image that is a hyperlink. The mouse pointer will change to a hand with a pointing finger.

2. Click on the **image**. The browser will download the requested page and display it for you.

Typing in a URL

Another method for reaching a Web page is to simply type the URL.

1. Select the **text** in the text box directly above the Web page. The label to the left of the text box will say Location.

2. Type the **URL** of the site you want to view. The label to the left of the text box will change to Go To.

3. Press Enter. The browser will download the Web page and display it for you.

Searching the Entire Web

Probably the biggest problem with the lack of regulation over the Web is that it can be difficult to find exactly what you need. *Search engines*, Web sites that index other Web sites, have developed to provide some global search capabilities.

One of the first search sites was **www.yahoo.com**. It is still a good site for finding commercial information, especially information that is organized into business categories.

1. **Go** to **www.yahoo.com**.

2. **Type** a **search term** in the text box at the top of the page.

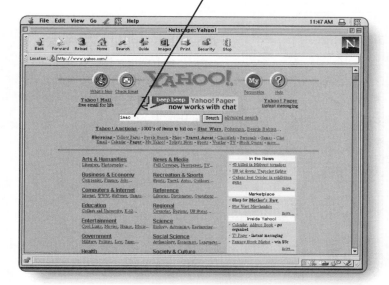

TIP

If you have more than one search term, put a plus sign (+) in front of each term. That will instruct Yahoo to retrieve only those sites that contain *all* your search terms.

---

3. **Click** on **Search**. Yahoo will search its database to find Web sites and categories of Web sites that include your search term. It will then display the results of the search on a new Web page. Yahoo results include hyperlinks to categories and individual Web sites.

TIP

Don't bother bookmarking pages that contain results produced by a search engine. Those pages are temporary, generated by your search, and then discarded when you are finished with them. If you try to return to one via a bookmark, you will get an error message indicating that the URL doesn't exist.

4a. Click on the **hyperlink** to an individual site to go directly to a Web page. The browser will download the page and display it.

OR

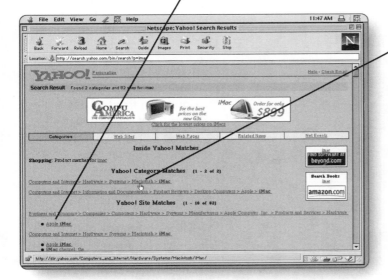

4b. Click on the **hyperlink** to a category to view the Web sites in that category. Yahoo will display a list of individual sites on a new page.

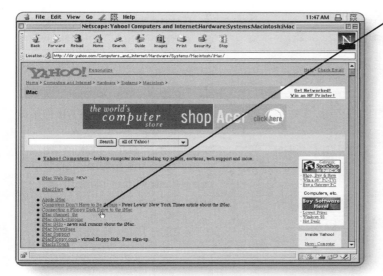

5. Click on a **hyperlink** to go to that page. The browser will download the page and display it for you.

TIP

For serious research on the Internet, you may want to consider using a *metasearch engine*, a search engine that searches many other search engines for you. Two of the best are **www.dogpile.com** and **www.savvysearch.com**.

Registering Your iMac with Apple

The Web can save you the cost of sending in product registration cards because many companies allow you to register your purchases through their Web sites. As an example of the process, you will see how to go about registering your iMac with Apple.

NOTE

Registering your hardware and software is usually a good idea. It gets you on the companies' mailing lists so that you can be notified of upgrades and special offers. Registration is also essential if you want technical support.

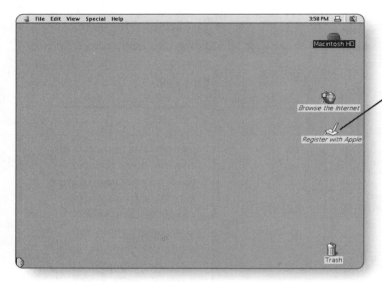

1. **Connect** to the **Internet**, either through AOL, EarthLink, or your local ISP.

2. **Double-click** on the **Register with Apple alias** on the Desktop. An alert will appear asking if you want to connect to the Internet so you can register your computer, even though you are already connected.

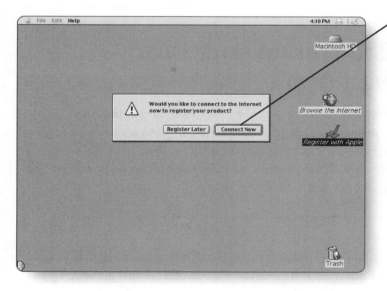

3. **Click** on **Connect Now**. A new alert will appear asking if your computer is configured for the Internet.

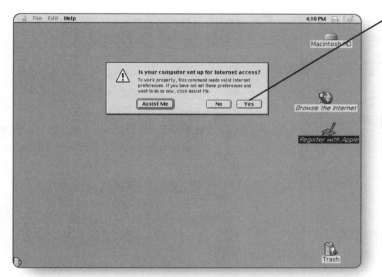

4. **Click** on **Yes**. The alert will disappear and the registration program will launch Internet Explorer. You will be taken to the first of the registration pages. The Register with Apple alias will disappear from your Desktop and reappear in the Trash.

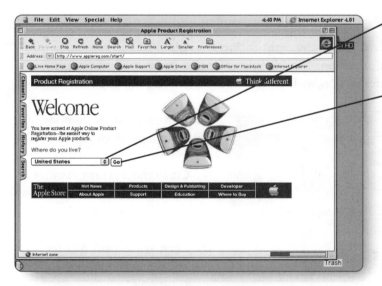

5. **Choose** a **location** from the Where do you live? pop-up menu.

6. **Click** on **Go**. The next registration page will appear.

7. **Fill out** and **submit** the three pages of information.

The only information you may have trouble finding are the model and serial number of your iMac.

Finding the Serial Number

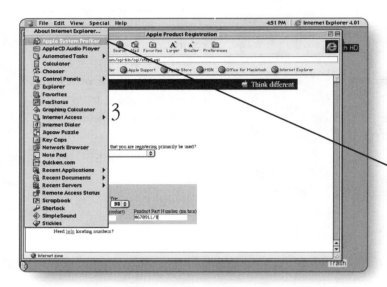

Although the serial number is on the bottom of the computer, it's *not* a good idea to turn it over while it's on! Fortunately, however, the Apple System Profiler can get the information for you.

1. **Choose Apple System Profiler** from the **Apple menu**. The Profiler window will appear.

2. **Click** on the **right-facing triangle** next to Production Information. The triangle will point downward and more information, including the serial number, will appear.

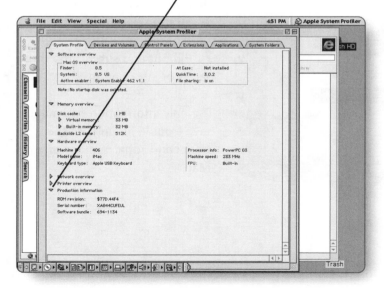

3. **Write** the **serial number** down on a piece of paper.

4. **Close** the **System Profiler window**. You will be able to see the entire browser window.

5. **Click** in the **text box** for the serial number to get an insertion point.

6. **Type** the **serial number**.

Finding the Model Number

Apple puts the model numbers of its computers on the outside of the box. You do still have the box, right? If not, don't panic. This might help: The original US iMac that shipped with Mac OS 8.1 was M6709LL/A. The updated Bondi-blue iMac with Mac OS 8.5 was M6709LL/B. The original multi-flavored iMacs were M7391LL/A (Tangerine), M7392LL/A (Lime), M7389LL/A (Strawberry), M7390LL/A (Grape), and M7345LL/A (Blueberry).

If your model came out after this, and you threw away the box, your best bet is to check the Apple Store. To reach the Apple store, go to **www.apple.com** and look for a link that says "Apple Store."

Once you have found the model number:

1. **Type** the **model number**.

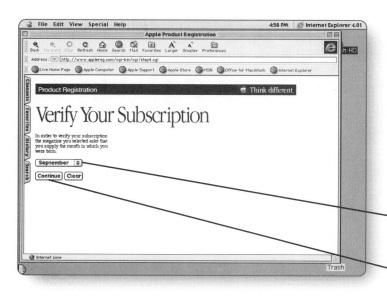

Finishing the Registration

At the end of the last registration page, you can choose a gift from Apple. If you choose one of the magazines, you will be asked for your birth month again.

1. **Choose** your **birth month** from the pop-up menu.

2. **Click** on **Continue**. You will see a page thanking you for your registration.

16

Using E-mail

E-mail (originally known as "electronic mail") is the main reason early users of the Internet connected to the network. E-mail is an essentially free way to send messages and files across the Internet to one or more recipients. It's fast, easy to use, and available at your convenience.

There are many e-mail programs available, including Outlook Express, which comes on your iMac. If you're using EarthLink or a local ISP, you would use Outlook to send and read e-mail. However, if your ISP is AOL, you would use AOL's to manage your e-mail.

Because it is so straightforward, this chapter will use AOL's software as an example of how e-mail works. You can then transfer what you have learned to just about any e-mail software. In this chapter, you'll learn how to:

- Create e-mail messages
- Send e-mail messages
- Read e-mail that has been sent to you
- Handle unwanted e-mail and e-mail attachments

E-mailing Messages

Nearly 15 years ago, people began talking about the paperless office, a world where business was conducted with a minimum of printer material. At the heart of the paperless office is e-mail, which can replace paper memos and, in some cases, meetings and phone calls. For many people, e-mail has also replaced personal letters. Miss Manners recently fielded a question about the propriety of e-mail thank you notes in her newspaper column!

The basic e-mail message is text that you type. All the skills that you've learned about working with text can be applied to the body of an e-mail message. You can also add graphics to e-mail. The way in which you do so depends somewhat on the e-mail software you are using, however.

Creating an E-mail Message

As noted earlier, an e-mail message is essentially a text document. It has two unique parts: the address of the recipient and a subject. Once you have entered those, you can work on the content of the message.

You can create e-mail either *online* (connected to your ISP) or *offline* (not connected to your ISP). If you create the message while you are online, you can send it immediately. If you create it offline, you can't send it until you connect to your ISP. Composing mail offline has a definite advantage if your home has only one telephone line—you don't tie up the phone line while you're typing. Offline message creation is also a good idea if you are sending a large number of messages. However, if you are just typing a fast reply to someone, it may be just as easy to create the reply online.

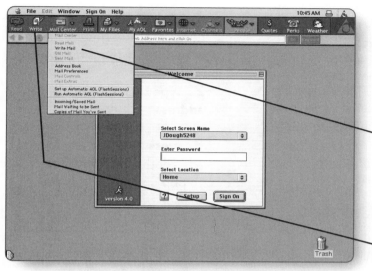

To create a new e-mail message:

1. Launch your **e-mail software**. Assuming that you are using AOL, you will launch the AOL software.

2a. Choose Write Mail from the **Mail Center** pull down menu. An untitled e-mail window will appear.

OR

2b. Click on **Write**. An untitled e-mail window will appear.

Understanding E-mail Addresses

Internet addresses have the form *user_name@location_name*. The *user_name* is your AOL screen name or the account name you gave your ISP. You get the *location_name* from your service provider. For example, AOL is aol.com. Therefore, JDough5248's Internet e-mail address is jdough5248@aol.com.

Where can you get e-mail addresses? If you know someone's AOL screen name, you can create his or her e-mail address by adding @aol.com to their screen name. However, if the person's e-mail uses a different service provider, you will either need to ask them for an address, reply to a message that was sent to you, or find the address by doing an Internet search. One of the best places to search for e-mail addresses is **www.infoseek.com**.

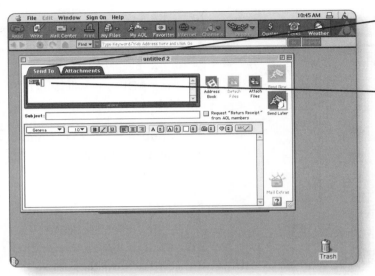

1. Click on the **Send To** tab if necessary. A To pop-up menu will appear in the text box.

2. Type the recipient's **e-mail address**.

3. Press Return if you want to add another recipient. A second To pop-up menu will appear on the line below.

TIP

Be careful to press the Return key rather than the Enter key. If you happen to be online, pressing Enter will send your e-mail before you are ready to do so. If you are offline, pressing Enter will have no effect.

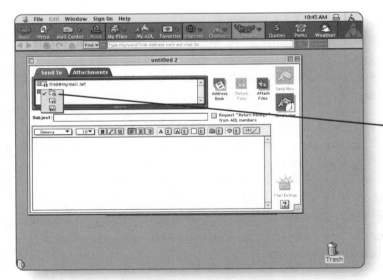

4. Choose the **type of recipient** from the To pop-up menu if necessary. If you choose CC (carbon copy, a holdover from the days when carbon paper was used), the person receiving the message on the To line will see the e-mail address of the person receiving the copy. However, if you choose BCC (blind carbon copy), the only address that will appear on all copies of the e-mail is the single person who is receiving it. BCC is a good choice when you are sending the same e-mail to many people and you don't want them to know to whom else you sent the mail.

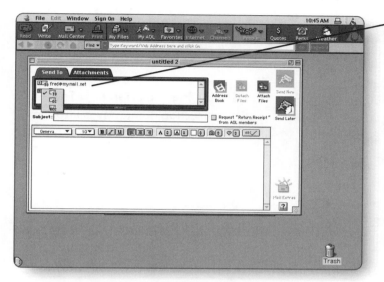

5. **Type** the recipient's **e-mail address**.

6. **Repeat steps 4** and **5** until the e-mail addresses of all recipients have been entered.

7. **Press** the **Tab key**. The insertion point will move to the Subject line.

Entering the Subject

When e-mail arrives at its destination, all the recipients see is the address of the sender and whatever has been entered on the subject line. There is a great deal of junk e-mail (*spam*) today, including advertisements for pornographic web sites, get-rich-quick schemes, and chain letters. Therefore, if you are sending e-mail to someone who won't recognize your e-mail address, you would do well to put something on the subject line that will let the recipient know that you have sent a legitimate message that should be read rather than deleted out of hand.

For example, if your e-mail is announcing a meeting, make sure the subject says exactly that ("Boys Club Meeting on 5-5-00"). When you are introducing yourself, steer away from subjects like "Hello" or "Greetings." Such subjects are often used by bulk e-mailers to disguise junk e-mail. Instead, use something like "Introduction of Jane Dough" or "Recommendation from John Doe" or "Application for Clerical Position." If at all possible, use something that will be personally meaningful to the recipient of the message.

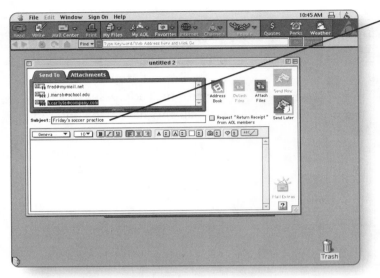

1. Type the **subject** of the e-mail message in the Subject: text box.

2. Press the **Tab key**. The insertion point moves into the text area for the body of the message.

Writing the Message

Writing the body of an e-mail message is generally like working with a text editor. You can use any of the text handling techniques you learned in Chapter 5, "Manipulating Files and Folders." The extent to which you can format the text depends on the e-mail software you are using. AOL's software, for example, lets you set the font, type size, and type style along with the alignment and text color. However, if the recipient of the e-mail is not another AOL subscriber, there is no guarantee that the recipient will see the formatting. The recipient's e-mail software may not support formatted text and will therefore present the message in plain text.

1. Type the **message**.

2. Format the **text** as desired.

As you can see from the preceding illustration, the AOL e-mail window has formatting menus and buttons just above the text entry area for the body of the message.

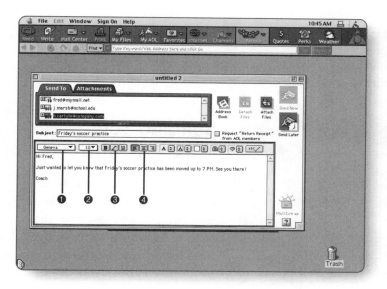

From left to right, these formatting controls are as follows:

❶ Font menu

❷ Font Size menu

❸ Style buttons. Click on **B** for boldface, *I* for italic, and U for underlining. To go back to plain text, click on the button again.

❹ Alignment buttons. Click on the left alignment button for text that is even on the left side but ragged on the right. Click on the middle alignment button for centered text (good for headings and titles). Click on the right alignment button for text that is even on the right side but ragged on the left (good for placing text up against the right margin).

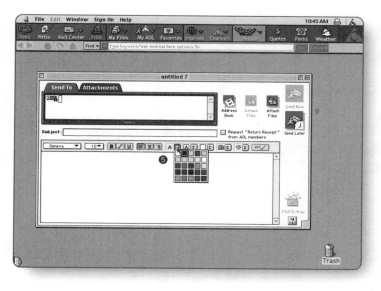

❺ Color menus. Each of the three color menus is a pop-up palette from which you can make a choice by dragging the mouse pointer to the desired color square. The left color menu controls the text color. The middle color menu controls the text background color. The right color menu sets the color for the entire message body. Note that if the text background color is set to white, the message body color will show through. Therefore, in most cases you will use only a text color and a message body color. Leave the text background color set to white.

Sending the Message

Now that you have finished composing the e-mail message, you can send it.

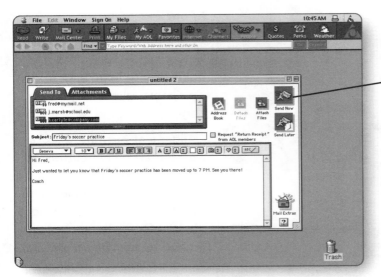

Sending Your Message Now

1. Click on **Send Now.** AOL sends the message and deletes the message window from the screen. AOL then displays an alert telling you that the message has been sent.

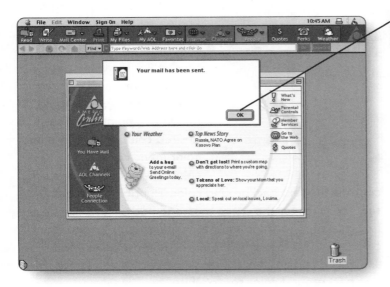

2. Click on **OK** to remove the alert from the screen.

Sending Your Message Later

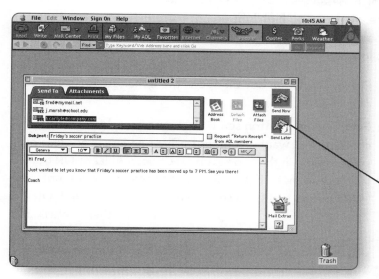

If you are not online or if you want to wait before sending a message, you can ask AOL to send the message at a later time. AOL will add the message to the "Mail Waiting to Be Sent" list and hold it until you tell AOL to send it.

1. Click on **Send Later**. AOL stores the message as Mail Waiting to be Sent and removes the message window from the screen. AOL displays an alert, asking you what you want to do.

2a. Click on **Auto AOL** to send all waiting mail automatically. If you are not online, AOL will initiate the sign on process.

OR

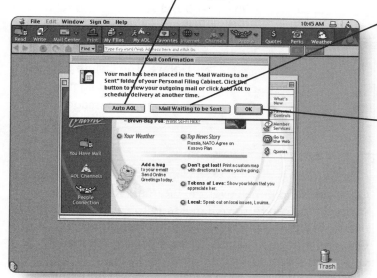

2b. Click on **Mail Waiting to be Sent** to view the Mail Waiting to be Sent window.

OR

2c. Click on **OK** to dismiss the alert and leave the message in the Mail Waiting to be Sent list. AOL removes the alert from the screen and you can continue working.

The Mail Waiting to be Sent window gives you control over which messages are to be sent. To work with the messages in the window, you highlight one or more messages and then use the buttons at the bottom of the window to do any of the following:

- **Open**. The Open button opens the e-mail so you can read or edit it.

- **Find**. The find button searches the name, address, and/or content of all waiting messages. Type an e-mail address or screen name in the top text box. Choose AND or OR from the pop-up menu if you also want to search for contents. (AND means that both search strings must be found; OR means that either one will do.) Type the text you want to search for in the subject line or body of the message in the lower text box. Click on Find to perform the search.

- **Send**. The Send button sends just the highlighted message or messages.

- **Send All**. The Send All button sends all the messages in the list.

- **Delete**. The Delete button deletes the highlighted message or messages.

NOTE

Once you send e-mail over the Internet, you cannot undo it. (You can retrieve a message to another AOL user only if the user has not read the message.) Queuing mail to send later is therefore a good idea if you aren't sure you want to send a message.

Working with E-mail Attachments

E-mail has become an important vehicle for the delivery of electronic files. You can attach any file to an e-mail message and have that file sent when the message is sent. Such *attachments* are often compressed so they will be as small as possible and therefore take the minimum amount of time to send. In addition, multiple files being sent at the same time can be combined into a single, compressed file called an *archive*. This further simplifies the transmission of multiple attachment files.

Attaching Files

To attach one or more files to an AOL e-mail message:

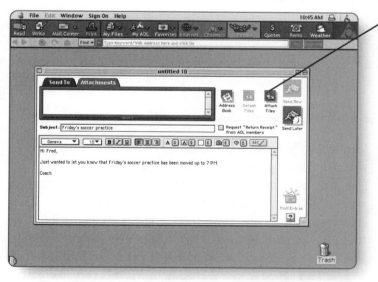

1. Click on **Attach Files**. An Open File dialog box will appear.

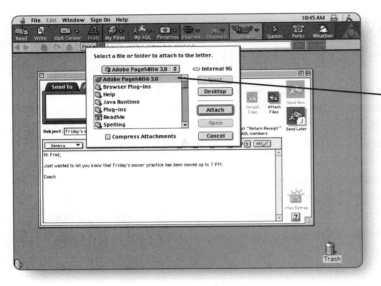

2. **Locate** the **file** you want to attach using the Open File dialog box.

3. **Double-click** on the **file name**. AOL will attach it to the e-mail. The file name and size of the attachment will appear at the top of the e-mail window when the Attachments tab is clicked.

Understanding Archives

When you send multiple attachment files, AOL automatically compresses them into an archive. This may not be what you want, especially if the files are going to a Windows user rather than a Mac OS user.

There are three major types of file archives currently in use:

NOTE

The full version of StuffIt Deluxe has translators that can remove files from almost every archiving and compression format in use.

- **StuffIt**. StuffIt Deluxe is a commercial archiving utility that was developed primarily for the Macintosh. UnStuffIt is a free program that will remove and decompress files from an archive. It is supplied with AOL and is used by AOL to create an archive when you send multiple attachments. Although UnStuffIt is available for Windows, most Windows users don't have it. Therefore, if AOL creates a StuffIt archive and sends it to a Windows users, it is very likely that they won't be able to extract the files from the archive.

- **Zip**. Zip is a primarily Windows archiving format produced by the *shareware* programs PKZip and PKWinZip. (Shareware is inexpensive—but often very helpful—software that you can try for free but must pay for if you intend to keep using it.)

Most Windows users will have PKUnzip or PKZip, so they can decode Zip archives. The Macintosh version is ZipIt. If you need to send multiple attachments to a Windows users, go to AOL's keyword SOFTWARE and search through the shareware library for ZipIt. You can then download the file and try it out. You can use it both to create Zip archives and to extract files from them. The latest version of StuffIt Expander for Macintosh will uncompress zipped files. It's free on Aladdin Systems' website, **www.aladdinsys.com**.

- **MIME**. MIME (often abbreviated MIM) is an Internet archive created by many e-mail programs when a user sends more than one attached file. To decode a MIME archive, you need the MIME Decoder shareware utility, which you can also find by searching the shareware library at AOL's keyword SOFTWARE. MIME decoder only removes files from archives; it does not create them because MIME archives are generally handled by e-mail software rather than users.

Reading E-mail

When you sign on to AOL, you will first hear a male voice say "Welcome." Then, if you have mail that has not been read,

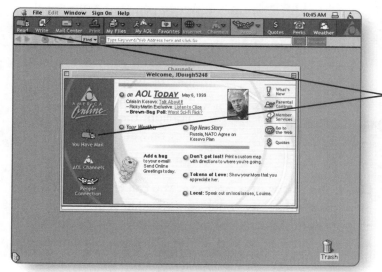

you will hear that famous phrase "You've got mail!" At that point, you can open your mailbox and read the messages.

1. Click on either **mailbox icon**. The Mailbox window will appear. You will see one line for each message, including the date it arrived, the source screen name, and the subject line.

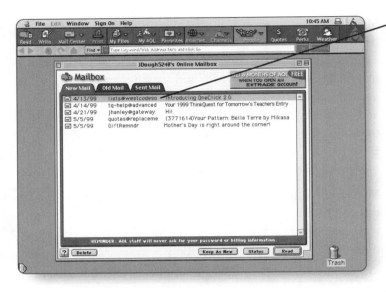

2. Double-click on the message you want to read. The message window will open so you can read it.

Handling Messages

The Mailbox window and windows containing e-mail messages provide tools for handling messages. You can do the following from the Mailbox window:

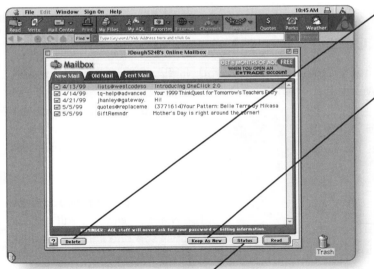

- **Delete a message**. Highlight one or more messages and click on Delete to delete the message or messages.

- **Leave a message as unread**. When you read a message, AOL automatically transfers it to the Old Mail section of the Mailbox. If you want to leave it in the New Mail section after you have read it, highlight the message and click on Keep as New.

- **Check the status of a message**. You can check the status of messages that have been sent to other AOL users. (You cannot check the status of Internet e-mail). Highlight the message and click on Status. You will then know whether the mail is unread, has been read, or has been deleted.

Replying to a Message

One of the most common actions you perform with an e-mail message is to reply to it, sending a new message back to the original sender.

1. **Open** the **e-mail message** to which you want to reply.

2. **Select text** that you want to include in the reply. This step is known as *quoting* and is optional. The advantage to quoting is that you can reply directly to something in the original message and have the original text available for the recipient of the reply to view.

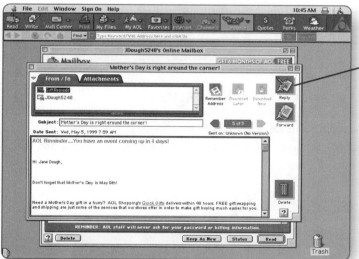

3. **Click** on **Reply**. An untitled e-mail window will open with the sender of the original message as the recipient. The subject of the reply will be RE: plus the subject of the original message. If you quoted any of the original message, it will appear in the body of the reply.

TIP

If a message was sent to other people as well as yourself, you can send your reply to all of them at once by clicking on Reply To All rather than Reply. However, use this very judiciously. Be certain that the reply will be of interest to everyone in the list. Otherwise you run the risk of people becoming annoyed with you for filling up their mailboxes with unnecessary e-mail.

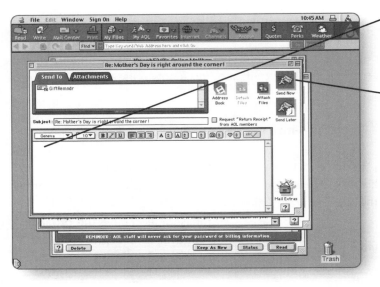

4. Type the **text** of the reply, integrating any quoted text into what you type.

5. Send the **message** in the same way you would send a message that you originated.

Forwarding a Message

Forwarding e-mail is very similar to replying to e-mail. However, forwarding copies the entire original messages to the end of your reply.

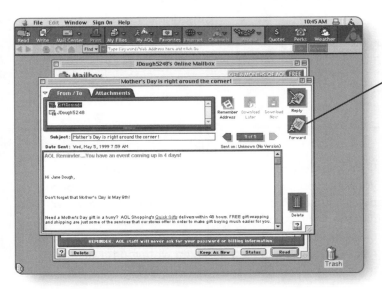

1. Open the **message** you want to forward.

2. Click on **Forward**. An untitled e-mail message will appear. The subject will be FWD: plus the subject of the original message. You will not see the original message.

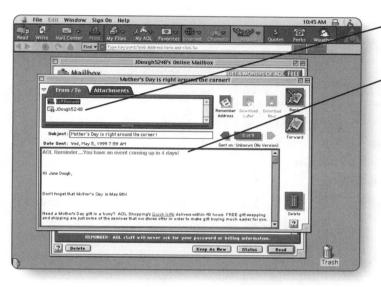

3. Enter the **recipient** of the forwarded message.

4. Type any **text** you would like to accompany the forwarded message. When the message is sent, your added text will appear *before* the forwarded original message.

5. Send the **message**.

Handling Attachments Safely

Just as you can send attached files to other people, they can send attachments to you. Be very careful with attachments. If you receive any attached files that are from someone you do not know and that you did not expect, don't download the attachment.

> ### NOTE
>
> On AOL, forward e-mail with suspicious attachments to TOSFiles. For other ISP's, check with the ISP to see what address they want you to use for reporting problematic attachments.

Why the caution? Because more often than not unexpected attachments from strangers are either password-stealing scams or *viruses*. A virus is a malicious program that causes damage to your computer, often by erasing all or part of your hard drive. You will read more about protecting your iMac from viruses in Appendix A, "Protecting Your iMAC." It is true that most password-stealing and virus programs are designed for the Windows operating system and therefore will not affect a Macintosh. However, there are enough Mac OS viruses on the Internet to make caution extremely important.

If you know the sender of an attachment or if the attachment is something that you expected to receive, you will want to download that attachment from your ISP's computer to yours. To download an attached file using AOL:

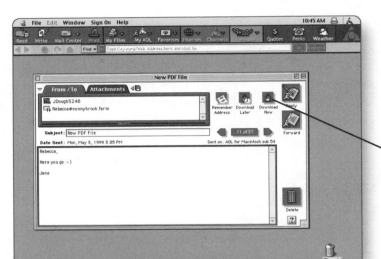

1. Open the **message** containing the attached file.

2. Click on **Download Now** to immediately begin the transfer of the file to your computer. A Save File dialog box will appear.

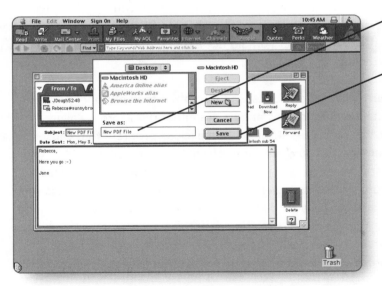

3. Choose a **location** to which to save the file.

4. Click on **Save**. The e-mail software will download the file.

5. When finished, sign off AOL to return to the iMac desktop.

17

Creating a Web Page with Adobe PageMill

In Chapter 15, "Wandering the World Wide Web," you learned how to look at Web pages. This chapter gives you a start at building your own. Your iMac package includes Adobe PageMill, a popular tool for building Web pages. With PageMill, you don't need to know HyperText Markup Language (HTML). Instead, you can work in an environment very much like the drawing portion of AppleWorks. In this chapter, you'll learn how to:

- Launch Adobe PageMill
- Build a personal Web Page
- Upload your Web page to an ISP

Understanding How a Web Site Is Organized

A Web site is a collection of files that are downloaded over the Internet to a remote user. Although there are no specific rules on how the files in a site are organized, files are typically named and organized in the following way:

- The first page that a user will see, the *home page*, usually has the name index.html. The .html portion of the name is known as a *file name extension*.

- Most Web page document files have an html or htm extension. Their names can be anything that makes sense to you. Keep in mind, however, that you should use only letters, numbers, and underscores (_) in Web page file names. Any other characters may cause problems with systems that are accessing your Web site.

- Graphics are usually stored in a folder called *images*, which is within the folder holding the Web pages.

- As a site becomes large, you may decide to create additional folders to help organize the documents.

Introducing Path Names

One of the problems that arises from the Web being platform-neutral (not tied to any specific operating system) is that the way in which the location of files is specified must adhere to the rules of the least capable operating system. When you double-click on a document to open it, the Mac OS automatically searches all mounted volumes to find the application that created it—you don't have to tell the operation system where to find the application. Unfortunately, most other operating systems can't do that. So you have to tell them exactly where something is located.

The path from the top of the disk directory hierarchy down to the location of a specific file is known as its *path name*.

When you specify a path name, you can start at the current folder (a *directory*) and work down the folder hierarchy. The folder names in a path name designed for Web use are separated by a forward slash (/). For example, a file named logo.gif stored in the images folder would have a path name of images/logo.gif. The computer assumes that the images folder is stored in the current folder and that logo.gif is within images. You will need to use path names of this sort when you are creating a Web page to indicate the location of any file that isn't in the same folder (directory) as the current Web page.

NOTE

PageMill was not preinstalled on your iMac, so you'll need to install it from the CD. Detailed instructions on how to install software can be found in Appendix D, "Adding Software."

Using a Web Server

Although you can create Web pages on your iMac, your Web pages need to be located on a computer that is running *Web server* software for people to be able to see them. This computer must be always turned on and always connected to the Internet. Normally your ISP will provide space on a Web server as part of your account service. For example, AOL gives you 2Mb of Web space per screen name for a total of 10Mb; EarthLink gives you 6Mb of Web space. The details of how you get the files onto their server can vary quite a bit.

Launching PageMill

Assuming that you have installed PageMill in the Applications folder on your iMac's hard disk, you'll first need to launch PageMill to create your first website.

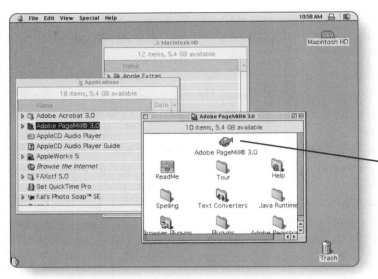

1. **Open** the **hard disk folder**.

2. **Open** the **Applications folder**.

3. **Open** the **Adobe PageMill folder**.

4. **Double-click** on the **Adobe PageMill icon**. An empty document named Untitled.html will open in the PageMill application.

Creating a Site

PageMill not only has tools for building individual Web pages, but also includes the functions for managing sites. When working with PageMill, you'll design your site (even if it's just a single Web page and some graphics) on your iMac, and then upload them to your ISP, or possibly to one of the companies that offer free Web page space such as **www.tripod.com/**, **www.xoom.com/webspace/**, or **www.geocities.com/**. In this section, you'll create the site on your hard disk.

1. **Choose New Site** from the **New** submenu of the **File menu**. The New Site dialog box will appear.

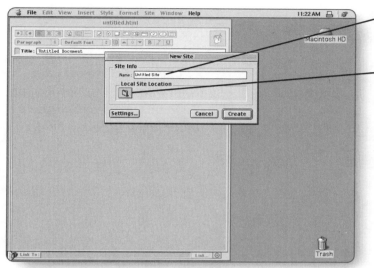

2. Type a **name** for your Web site in the Name: text box.

3. Click on the **folder icon** and choose a storage location on your hard disk for the site's files. An Open File dialog box with the title "Choose a Folder" will appear.

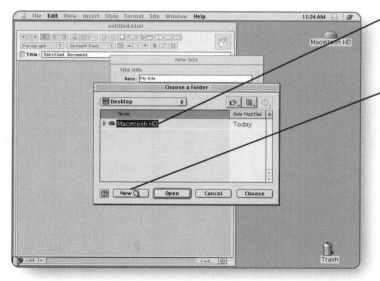

4. Locate the **folder** in which you want the site files to be stored.

5. Click on **New Folder** to create a new folder for the site. The New Folder dialog box will appear.

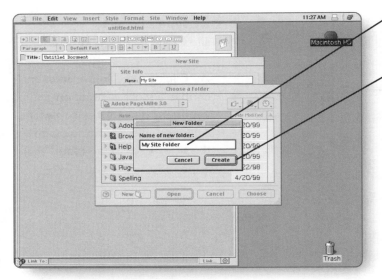

6. Type a **name** for the new folder.

7. Click on **Create** to create the new folder. The New Folder dialog box will close and you'll return to the Choose a Folder dialog box.

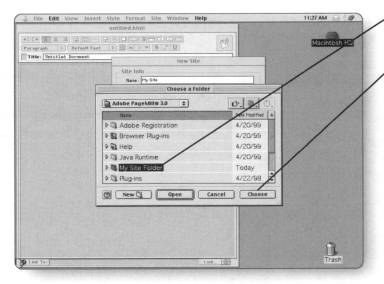

8. Click on the **new folder** to select it if necessary.

9. Click on **Choose** to select the folder as the storage location for the new site. The Choose a Folder dialog box will close and you'll return to the New Site dialog box.

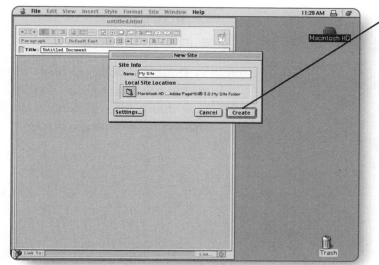

10. Click on **Create** to create the site. A window will open with the name of your site, containing the Site Overview area on the left, and areas on the right showing a list of files that are part of the site and how those files are interrelated. Initially you'll see only index.html in the list.

Creating a Page

As you read earlier, the file created with your site, index.html, is the default name most commonly used for the home page within a site. If you access a site with a URL such as **www.somesite.com/foldera/,** the Web page that will appear will be the one in foldera with the default name used by that server. The most popular default names are index.html, default.htm, and index.htm. You'll have to check with your ISP to see which they use, or try each and see. Index.html works for both EarthLink and AOL.

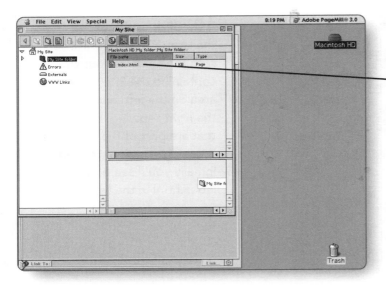

Building a Home Page

1. Double-click on the **name** of the file you want to open. In this case, double-click on index.html. The empty document will open.

2. Type a **heading** for the Web page in the body of the document.

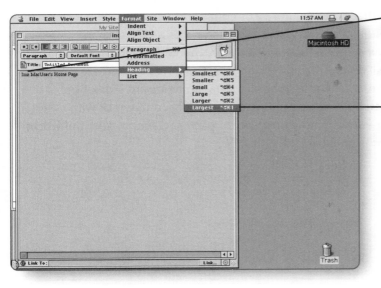

3. Triple-click anywhere in the heading to select the entire heading. The heading will be highlighted.

4. Choose Largest from the **Heading** submenu of the **Format menu**. The text line will change style and size.

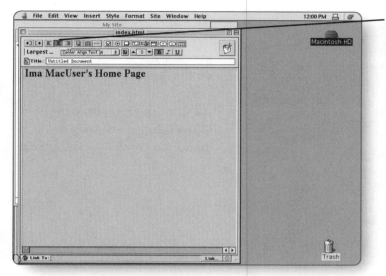

5. **Click** on the **Center Alignment button** to center the heading on the page.

Adding a Background Image

The PageMill CD has many sample files, sites, and styles that you can use, including several full sample sites and sample styles. The large collection of styles include complementary color schemes for the background, text, buttons, and banners.

Some of the images used by the sample pages on the CD are *background images*, graphics that the browser *tiles* (repeats as often as necessary until the background of the browser window is completely filled). You could create a single image that was the same size as your browser window, but smaller files download more quickly than larger files. You also cannot predict the size of a browser page, because windows can be resized and screen sizes differ. In PageMill it is quite easy to add a background image to your page.

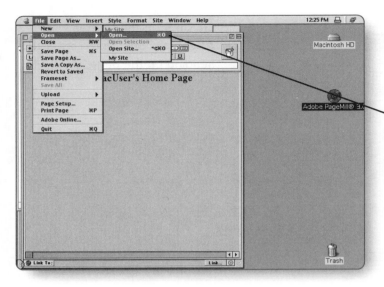

1. **Insert** the **PageMill CD** into the iMac's CD-ROM drive if necessary. The disc will mount on the Desktop.

2. **Choose Open** from the **Open** submenu of the **File menu**. An Open File dialog box will appear.

3. **Choose Desktop** from the pop-up menu at the top of the window. All files and mounted volumes on the Desktop will appear in the dialog box's file list.

4. **Double-click** on **Adobe PageMill 3.0**. The contents of the CD will appear in the dialog box's file list.

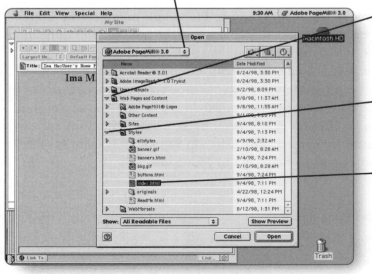

5. **Click** on the **triangle** next to Web Pages and Content. The contents of the folder will appear.

6. **Click** on the **triangle** next to Styles. The contents of the folder will appear.

7. **Double-click** on **index.html** in the list of the Styles folder's contents. An alert warning you that you cannot modify the file will appear. (This is because the file is on a CD.)

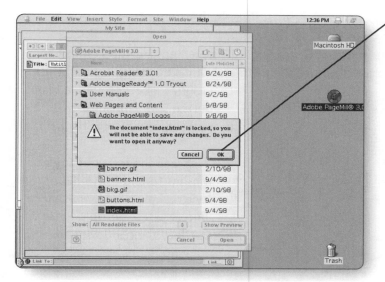

8. Click on **OK** to dismiss the alert. PageMill opens the page.

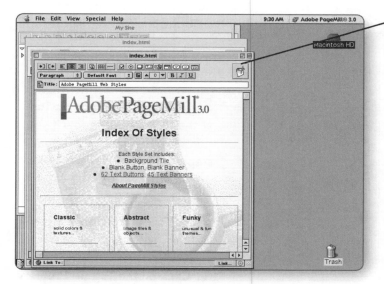

9. Click on the **Toggle Preview Mode icon**. The window switches from Edit mode into Preview mode, which allows you to view the page similar to how it will look in a browser. You can even follow links, as long as they are on your iMac. The icon will change to a globe.

Finding a Style

The Index of Styles PageMill document included on the PageMill CD includes three columns of styles, each of which includes a background, a blank button and banner, 62 text buttons, and 45 text banners.

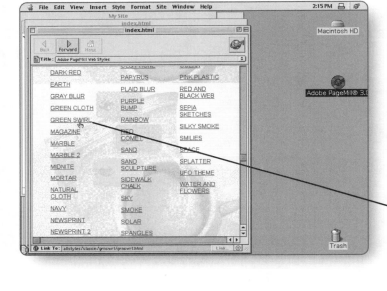

1. Scroll the **Index of Styles** window to find a style. Each style name is a hyperlink and therefore the mouse pointer will turn into the hand with a pointing finger as it passes over each link.

2. Click on a **style**. The style document will open in the window.

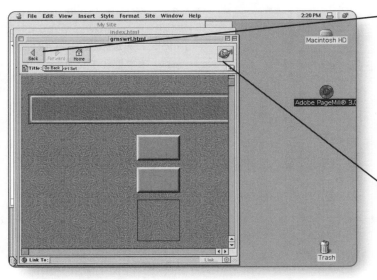

3a. Click on the **Back button** at the top of the window if you don't like the style and repeat steps 1 and 2.

OR

3b. Proceed to **step 4** if you like the style and want to use it.

4. Click on the **Toggle Preview Mode icon** again. The window will return to Edit mode and change the icon to a pen writing on a page.

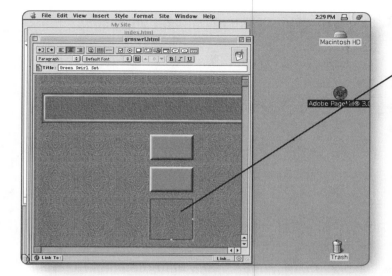

Copying the Background Graphic

1. Hold down the ⌘ **key** and **double-click** on the **background tile**. The tile will appear in an image window.

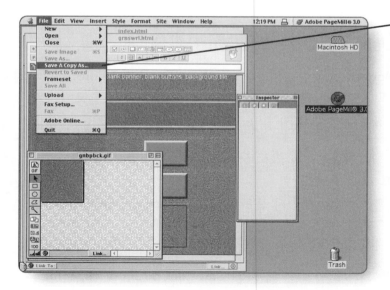

2. Click on **Save A Copy As** from the **File menu**. A Save File dialog box will open.

3. **Find** the **folder** in which your site is stored.

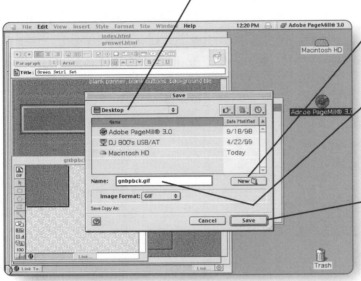

4. **Create** a new folder named **Resources or Images** within your site folder, if necessary.

5. **Change** the **name** of the file if you wish. You must not, however, change the .gif extension, as this will tell a Web server what type of graphic file it is.

6. **Save** the **file** in the Resources or Images folder. A copy of the background graphic file will be stored on your hard disk in the chosen folder.

Using the Background

Now that you have the background graphic in its own file, you can use it on your own page.

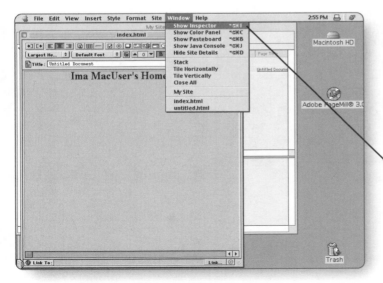

1. **Click** on the **Close boxes** of the background graphic and style windows to close them.

2. **Click** on **any part** of the index.html window to make it the active window if necessary.

3. **Click** on **Show Inspector** from the **Window menu** if the Inspector window is not visible. The Inspector window will appear.

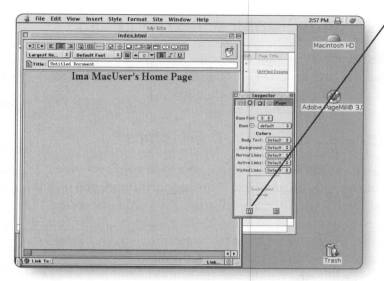

4. Click on the small **file icon** in the lower-left corner of the Inspector window. The Insert File dialog box will appear.

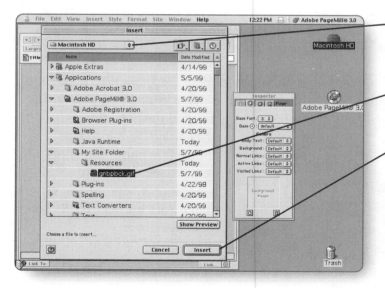

5. Locate the **folder** in which you stored the background image file.

6. Click on the **background image file** to select it.

7. Click on **Insert**. The dialog box will close and the background image will fill the index.html window. It will also appear at the bottom of the Inspector window.

Inserting Graphics, Text, and Links

Most simple Web pages are made up of three elements: text, graphics, and hyperlinks. In this section, you'll learn more about adding all three of these elements.

Understanding Web Graphics

When you add a graphic image to a Web page, you don't actually copy the graphic into the page. Instead, you give the Web page the path name to where the image is stored. A Web browser can then download the image from its file and display the content of that file inside the page that references it. A user won't be able to tell that the graphic actually isn't stored within the page.

This arrangement has two advantages. It keeps the size of the Web page to a minimum and you can change the graphic, substituting another file with the same name for the original, without having to modify the Web page.

There are two basic image formats used with Web pages: GIF and JPEG. Both compress the images so that file sizes are as small as possible, thus minimizing download time. Image files must have either a .gif or .jpeg extension, whichever is appropriate, so that a Web browser knows how to handle them.

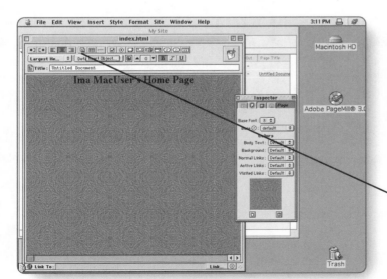

Inserting a Graphic

1. Click on the **Insert Object button**. An Insert File dialog box will appear.

2. **Find** the **graphic file** to insert.

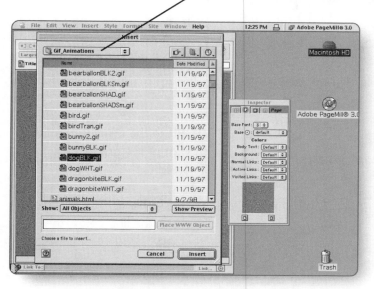

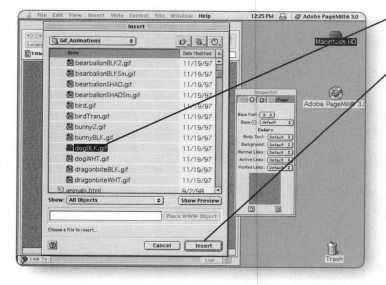

3. **Click** on the **file name** to select it.

4. **Click** on **Insert**. The dialog box will disappear and your image will appear in your Web page at the current insertion point.

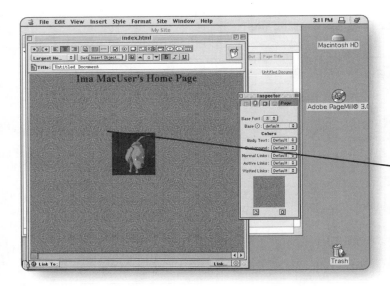

5. Place the **insertion point** to the left of the graphic you just inserted.

6. Press Enter. The graphic will move to the line below the heading.

Entering and Formatting Text

You type text in a Web page just like you would in any other Macintosh application. However, formatting options are restricted by the needs of the Web. When you choose a style, it affects an entire paragraph. However, you can add boldface, italics, and underlining to characters within a paragraph.

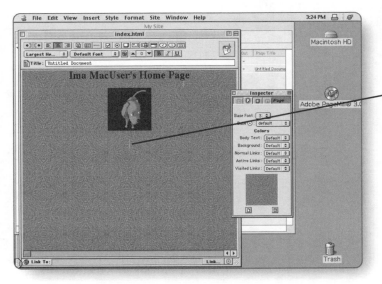

1. Move the **insertion point** to the place where you want text to appear if necessary.

2. Click on a **style**.

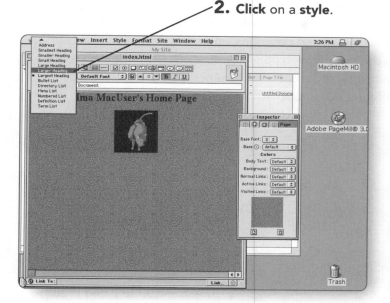

3. Type the **text**. The text will appear in your chosen paragraph style.

> ### TIP
>
> To add boldface, italics, or underlining, select the text to which you want to apply the style and click on the appropriate style button. To remove the style, select the text and click on the style button once more.

> ### TIP
>
> You can also apply paragraph styles to paragraphs already in the document by selecting the paragraph and then choosing the style from the paragraph styles menu.

Adding Hyperlinks

Clicking on a hyperlink while looking at a Web page in a browser will cause the browser to follow the link. Depending on the type of reference (the URL), that can mean several different things. If the URL begins with http://, it will go to another Web page at the address that follows.

Not all URLS begin with http:// however. For example, a URL that begins with ftp:// instructs the browser to download a file; a URL that begins with mailto: sends an e-mail address to your e-mail program and then opens an empty e-mail window for you to compose a message to send to that address.

Sometime URLs are just given as a file name or a path and file name. That means the link is to another document on the same server, and describes where the document is in relation to the current Web page. Other URLs, which contain the complete address of the document, can be located on different servers, anywhere in the world.

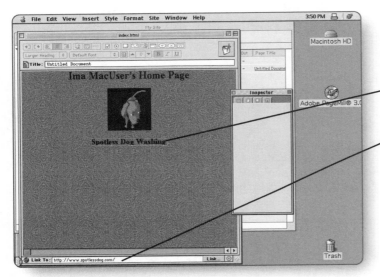

Follow these simple steps to turn text or a graphic image into a hyperlink.

1. Select the **text or graphic** that will be the link.

2. Click in the **Link To** text box at the bottom of the window. The item you selected in step 1 will be surrounded by a thin rectangle.

3. Type the **URL** of the link.

4. Press Enter. Selected text will appear as underlined blue text. A selected graphic will have a blue rectangle around it.

Pasting an Image

Another way to insert a graphic into a Web page is to paste it in from the Macintosh Clipboard, where you have copied it from some other application.

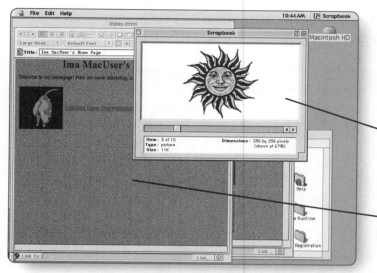

1. Open the **document** containing the original image. For this example, you'll use the Scrapbook. The Scrapbook is located under the Apple menu.

2. Select the **image**.

3. Press ⌘-**C** to copy the image to the Clipboard.

4. Click on the **Web page document** to make it the active window.

5. Press ⌘-**V** to paste the graphic into the page. An alert will appear with a message telling you that the Resources folder has been modified and ask if you want to reload the listing of the files in the site. What has actually happened is that PageMill has created a new GIF file for you containing the pasted graphic and stored it in the Resources folder.

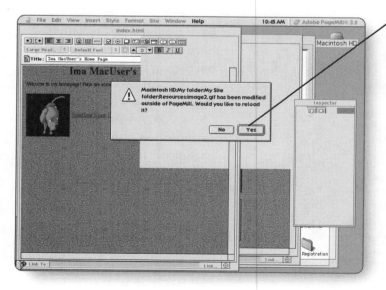

6. Click on **Yes**. PageMill will reload the site listing from your hard disk and display the new graphic in the Web page.

Making an Image's Background Transparent

One of the problems with the image pasted in from the Scrapbook is that it has a white background, while the background of the Web page is green. The image would look much better if its background was transparent so the page's background could show through.

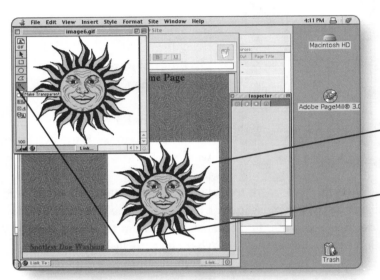

1. ⌘-**double-click** on the **image** to open it in an image window.

2. Click on the **transparency tool**. The mouse pointer will turn into the transparency tool.

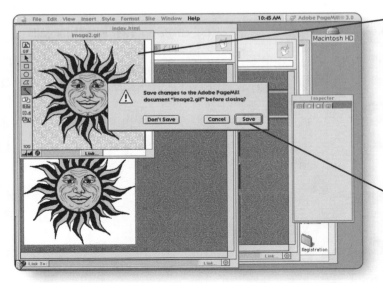

3. Click on the **image's background**. The areas that have been made transparent will become gray.

4. Click on the image window's **Close box**. An alert will appear asking if you want to save your changes.

5. Click on **Save**. The image window will close, PageMill will save your changes to the image file, and the image will appear with its transparent background in the Web page.

Resizing an Image

When you first bring an image into a Web page, it will appear in its original size. If that size is too large or too small for your needs, you can resize the image in much the same way you resized an image in the AppleWorks drawing module.

1. Click on the **image** you want to resize. A faint rectangle will appear around it to indicate that it is selected. There will also be a square handle in the lower-right corner, the middle of the right side, and the middle of the bottom. You drag these handles to resize the image.

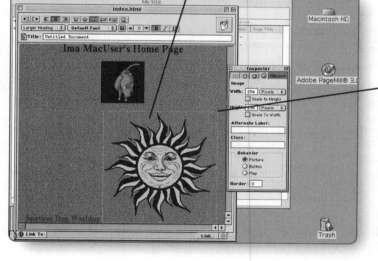

2. Drag a **handle** until the image is the size you want.

TIP

To maintain the original proportions of the graphic while you drag, hold down the Shift key.

NOTE

Resizing an image merely changes the size at which a user sees the image. It does not affect the size of the file in which the graphic is stored and therefore does not affect the time necessary to download the file to the user's computer. If you have a large graphics file, the best way to make the file smaller is to open the image in a graphics program, resize the image, and save it again. By the same token, one way to obtain a large image is to take a small image and enlarge it on the Web page.

Using a Table to Position Elements

One of the biggest problems with HTML is that it doesn't give you any control over the positioning of elements on the page. The length of a line changes as the width of the browser's window changes. All text and graphics flow onto a line until the edge of the browser window is reached, regardless of where you might have placed the elements when you were creating the page.

The traditional way to work around this problem is to place page elements in a table, which has a more rigid structure. The general process is to create a table with the necessary number of columns and rows, and then place page content inside the table cells.

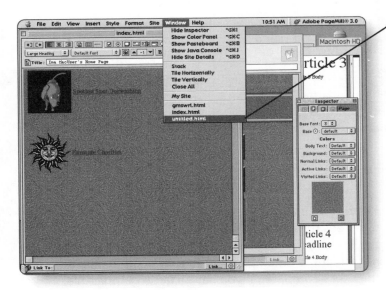

1. Click on the **name** of the page that will contain the table from the bottom of the **Window menu**. The page will become active.

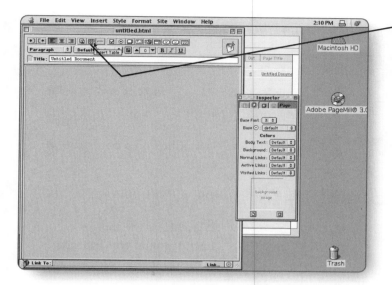

2. Click on the **Insert Table icon**. The Create Table dialog box will appear.

3. Type the **number of columns and rows**.

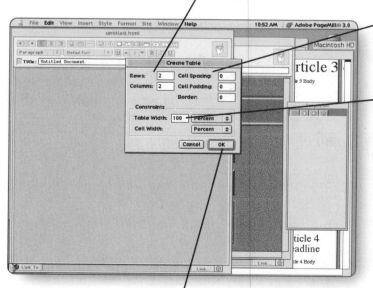

4. Type a **value** for the cell spacing, cell padding, and border. You should use "0."

5. Type a **value** for the width of the table. If you use "100" and "percent" for the table width, it will produce a table without visible borders on the finished Web page that uses the full width of the page, regardless of the size of the browser window in which it is displayed.

6. Click on **OK**. The table will appear with gray lines delineating the cells. These lines are for your use in editing the page only—they will not be visible when the page is viewed in a Web browser.

7a. **Paste images** into the table cells.

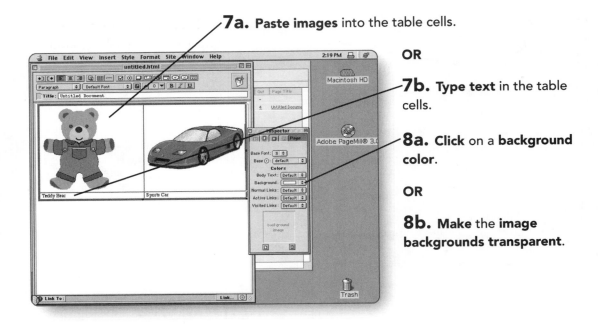

OR

7b. **Type text** in the table cells.

8a. **Click** on a **background color**.

OR

8b. **Make** the **image backgrounds transparent**.

9. **Select text**. It will be highlighted.

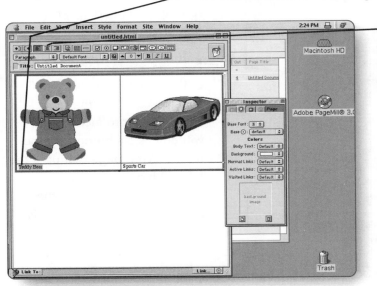

10. **Click** on the **center alignment button** to center the text between the right and left edges of a table cell.

11. Click on an **image** to select it.

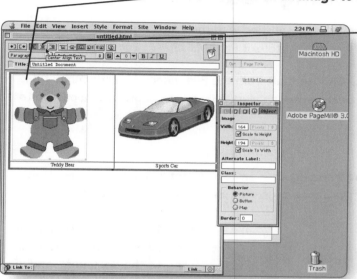

12. Click on the **center alignment button** to center the image between the right and left edges of a table cell.

TIP

When you are working with table cells, the text alignment buttons affect the placement of text or an image between the right and left edges of the cell. To affect the placement of an element relative to the top and bottom of a cell, use the top alignment, middle alignment, and bottom alignment buttons that appear in the tool bar to the right of the text alignment buttons.

13. Click on the **Toggle Preview Mode button** to see how the table places elements on the page. Notice that the headings are directly centered under the images. They will remain so, regardless of the width of the browser window.

Quitting PageMill

Once you feel satisfied with the Web pages you've created, you'll next want to exit PageMill.

1a. **Choose Quit** from the **File** menu. If any document has not been saved, an alert will appear to give you a chance to save them.

OR

1b. **Press** ⌘-**Q**. If any document has not been saved, an alert will appear giving you a chance to save them.

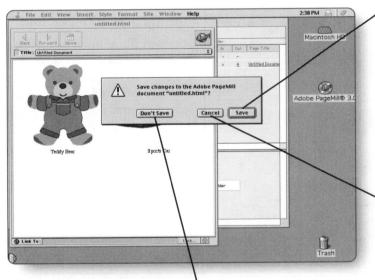

2a. **Click** on **Save** to save the unsaved documents. PageMill will save the document, and display a Save File dialog box if the file has not been named. PageMill then displays an alert asking if you want to close the site.

OR

2b. **Click** on **Cancel** to abort the quit process and continue working with PageMill.

OR

2c. **Click** on **Don't Save** to exit PageMill without saving any unsaved documents. PageMill discards the unsaved document. PageMill then displays an alert asking if you want to close the site.

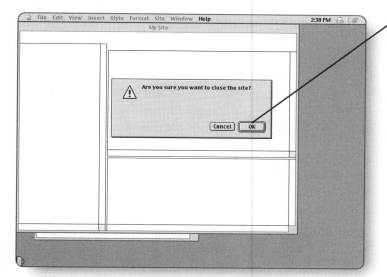

3. Click on **OK** to close the site and finish exiting PageMill.

Uploading to a Site

Once you have created Web pages, you will probably want to make them accessible to the world by transferring them to your Web space on the computer that will be *hosting* your Web site. (Transferring a file from your computer to another is known as *uploading*.) PageMill can automate the uploading for you. However, if you are using AOL to host your Web site, it's easier to work directly with the AOL software.

Uploading to EarthLink or Another ISP

If you're using EarthLink or a local ISP, you can take advantage of PageMill's automated upload capabilities. Doing so helps eliminate the need to deal with some of the details of transferring the files.

You'll need to re-launch Adobe PageMill to upload your site to your Web server.

1. Choose Open site from the open submenu in the File menu. From there you will be able to select the folder you created that contains all your html documents and images for your site.

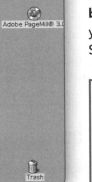

2. Click on the **Upload Site button**. If this is the first time you have uploaded files, the Site Setup dialog box will open.

TIP

If you need to access the Site Setup dialog box at a later date, you will find it listed in the Site menu.

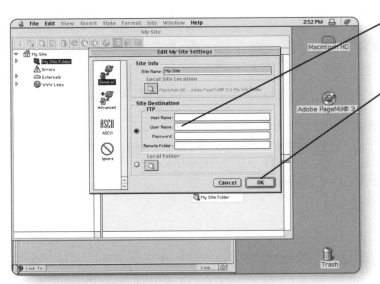

3. Type the **information** in the FTP area. You will need to get this information from your ISP.

4. Click on **OK**. If you are not connected to the Internet, PageMill will open a connection. The files will be transferred and you will see a progress bar that will keep you informed about which files are being transferred.

NOTE

Your EarthLink account comes with 6Mb of Web space. Although you use the same user name and password as for e-mail, it isn't automatic: You need to go to **www.earthlink.net/ benefits/6mb.html** and register before trying to upload pages.

Once your files are transferred, you can quit PageMill and launch a Web browser to look at your site. You will need to ask your ISP for the correct URL.

Uploading to AOL

The Web space that AOL gives you is located at keyword MY PLACE. When you get there, you can easily upload your files from your hard disk. The URL of your Web site is **members.aol.com/your_screen_name/index.html**, where your_screen_name is the screen name you are using. This URL also assumes that index.html is the first page you want a visitor to see. If not, substitute the name of your home page for index.html.

Follow these simple steps upload files to your Web space on AOL.

1. Sign on to **AOL**.

2. Press ⌘**-K**. The keyword dialog box will appear.

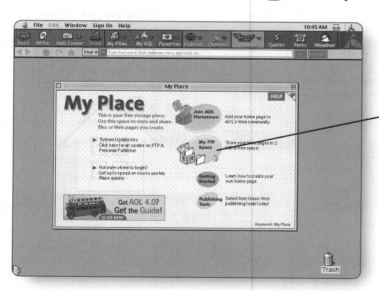

3. Type MY PLACE in the text box and **press** the **Enter key**. The MY PLACE window will appear.

4. Click on **My FTP Space** to gain access to your Web space. A listing of the files stored in your FTP space will appear.

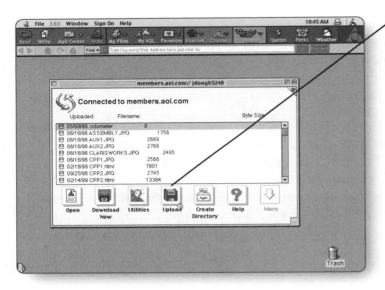

5. Click on the **Upload button** to begin the upload process. The members.aol.com dialog box will appear.

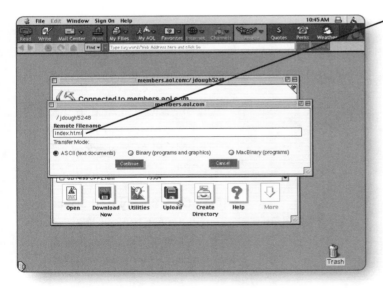

6. Type the **file name** that the file will have on the Web site in the Remote File Name text box. This does not need to be the same as the file name on your hard disk. Although AOL gives you the option of using a different name, you should type the file name exactly as it is referenced in your home page so that all your links and images will load properly when viewed from a browser. Keep in mind that file names are case sensitive (upper and lowercase letters are different).

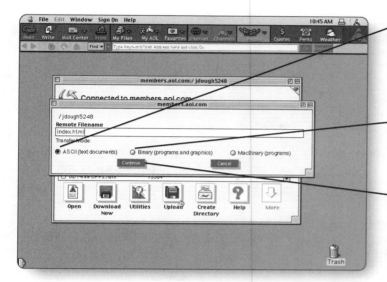

7a. Click on the **ASCII option button** if you are uploading an .html file.

OR

7b. Click on the **Binary radio button** if you are uploading a .gif or .jpeg file.

8. Click on **Continue**. The Upload File dialog box will appear.

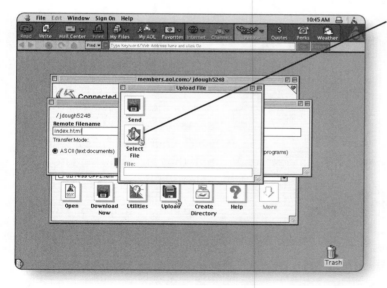

9. Click on **Select File**. An Open File dialog box will appear.

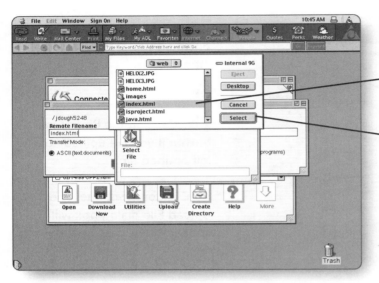

10. Locate the **file** you want to upload.

11. Click on the **file name** to select it.

12. Click on **Select**. The Open File dialog box will close and the Upload File dialog box will become active. The name of the chosen file will appear in the File text box.

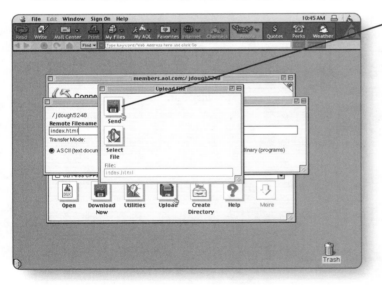

13. Click on **Send**. AOL will upload the file and close the Upload File dialog box.

Repeat steps 5 through 13 for each graphic or html file you have created and referenced in your home.html document. (You do not need to upload pages to which your page links are linked to if they have been created and uploaded by others.)

Keep in mind that if you have folders of images and documents, the file and folder structure of your Web space must match the file and folder structure on your hard disk. Otherwise, the path names in your html documents will be wrong and browsers won't be able to find your images. For example, if you created an image folder for your images, you will have to click on the Create Directory button and give it the same name as your images folder. Once that folder is created, you must double-click on it and upload all the images to that folder.

18

Sending and Receiving Faxes

Your iMac's modem can send and receive faxes, along with the help of the FAXstf software that is preinstalled on your hard disk. In this chapter, you'll learn how to:

- Set up the fax software
- "Print" a document so that it can be sent as a fax
- Send a fax
- Set up the computer to receive a fax
- View a fax that you have received

Setting Up the Fax Software

For the most part, the Faxstf software comes preconfigured for you on your iMac. Nonetheless, there are two groups of settings you may need to customize. The settings are available through the Fax Browse application.

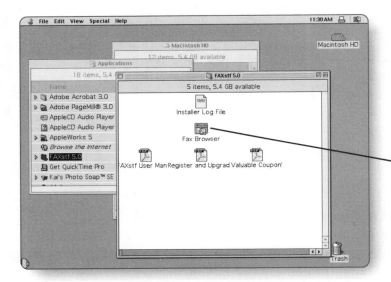

1. **Open** the **hard disk window**.

2. **Open** the **Applications folder**.

3. **Open** the **Faxstf 5.0 folder**.

4. **Double-click** on the **Fax Browser icon**. The Fax Browser will launch and its menus will appear in the menu bar. However, the Fax Browser will not open any windows.

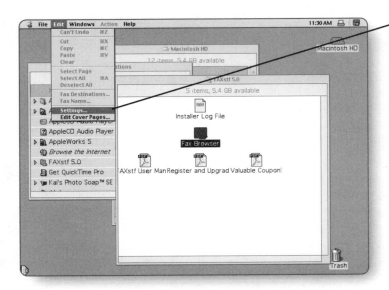

5. **Choose Settings** from the **Edit menu**. The Settings dialog box will appear. The icons in the scrolling list at the left of the dialog box are switches that change the contents of the panel at the right of the dialog box.

6. Click on the **Cover Page icon**. The Cover Page Settings panel will appear in the right of the dialog box.

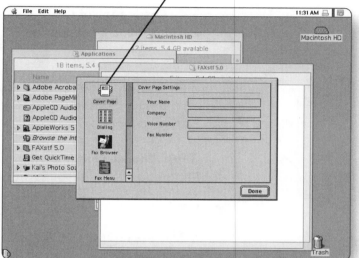

NOTE

A *cover page* is the page that is sent just before the pages of a document being faxed. Most of the time, you will want the cover page to contain your name and contact numbers.

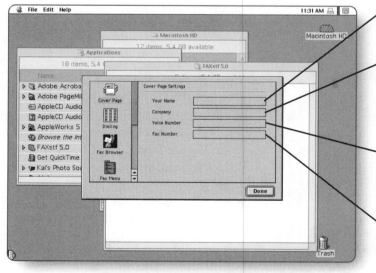

7. Type your **name** in the Your Name text box.

8. Type your **company name** in the Company text box if the fax is being sent on behalf of a business.

9. Type your **voice telephone number** in the Voice Number text box.

10. Type your **fax telephone number** in the Fax Number text box.

11. Click on the **Dialing icon**. The Dialing Settings panel will appear in the right of the dialog box.

12. Change any of the **settings** that are not correct for your situation.

13. Click on **Done** to save the settings changes and close the Settings dialog box.

14a. Choose Quit from the **File menu**.

OR

14b. Press ⌘-**Q** to exit the Fax Browser.

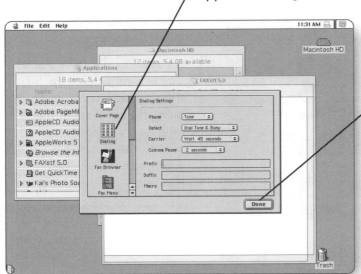

Sending a Fax

Sending a fax is very similar to printing a document on a printer. The major difference is that you have to let the fax software know the fax telephone number of the receiving fax machine.

1. Select Chooser from the **Apple** menu. The Choose dialog box will appear.

2. Click on the **FaxPrint icon** in the list of printer drivers at the left of the dialog box.

3. Click in the **Close box** to close the Chooser.

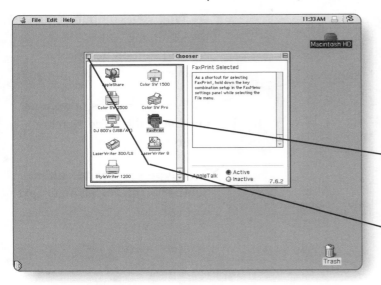

4a. **Open** the **document** you want to fax.

OR

4b. **Create** the **document** you want to fax.

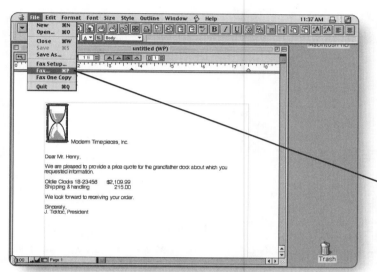

TIP

You don't need to save a document to fax it. You can therefore create and fax something that you don't intend to keep.

5. **Choose Fax...** from the **File menu.** The Fax Print dialog box will appear.

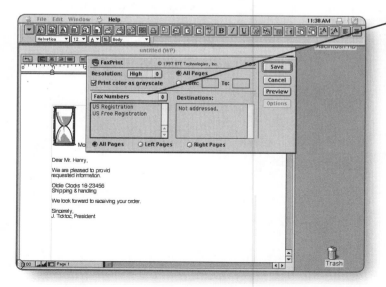

6. **Click** on **and hold** the **Fax Numbers pop-up menu** to make its options appear.

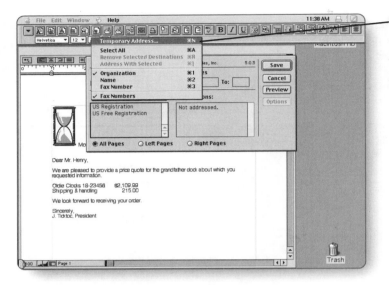

7. **Choose Temporary Address** from the pop-up menu. A fax information dialog box will appear.

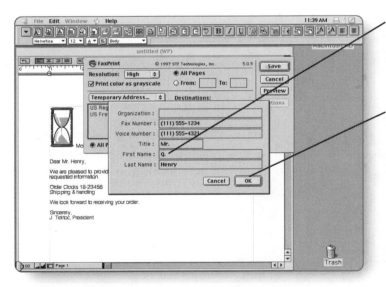

8. **Type** the **fax recipient's information**. The only value that is required is the fax telephone number.

9. **Click** on **OK**. The fax information dialog box will close and the FaxPrint dialog box will be the active window.

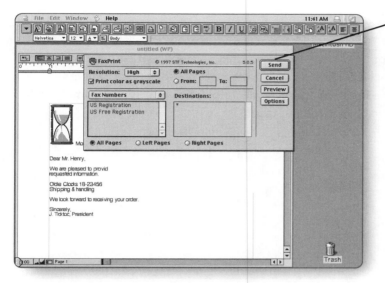

10. Click on **Send**. FaxStf will save the fax document to the hard disk and immediately attempt to send the fax. The FaxStatus window will appear.

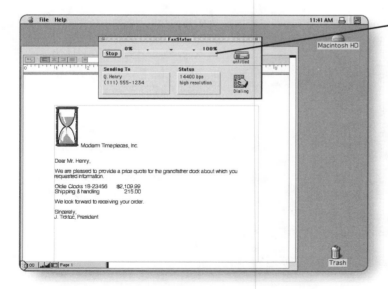

11. Monitor the **status** of the fax call in the FaxStatus window. A progress bar will move from 0% to 100% to show you how much of the fax has been sent. When the fax transmission is complete, the FaxStatus window will close.

TIP

If you change your mind about sending the fax while it is being transmitted, click on the Stop button to interrupt the transmission. The fax document will be left in the fax software's Out Box.

Receiving Faxes

You don't have to do anything except turn on your iMac to receive a fax. As long as there is a phone line connected to the iMac's modem, it will automatically answer incoming calls and save incoming faxes.

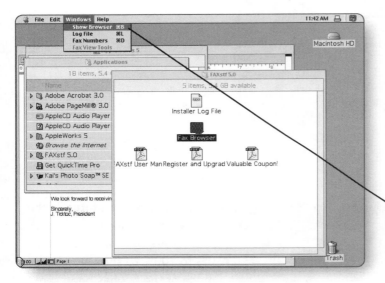

Using the Fax Browser

FAXstf's Fax Browser provides an easy way to manage faxes. To access the Fax Browser:

1. **Launch** the **Fax Browser application**.

2. **Choose Show Browser** from the **Windows menu** if the Browser window is not on the screen. The Fax Browser window will appear.

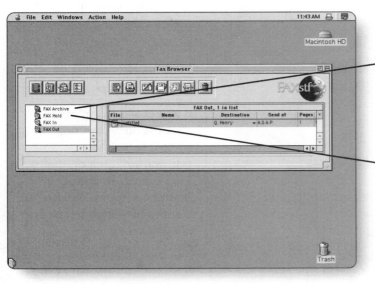

The Fax Browser organizes faxes into four categories:

- **FAX Archive**. This category contains incoming faxes that you have read and want to leave on the computer's hard disk.

- **FAX Hold**. This category contains outgoing faxes that FAXstf has been unable to send successfully. A fax might end up in this category, for example, because the recipient fax machine was busy.

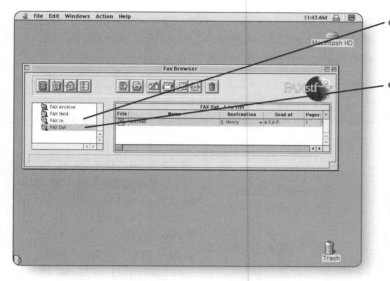

- **FAX In**. This category contains incoming faxes that you have not read.

- **FAX Out**. This category contains outgoing faxes that have not been sent.

You click on a category name to see the faxes in that category. Once you have highlighted a fax, you can do any of the following:

- **View a fax**. Select the fax you want to read and click on the View button. You can read faxes in any of the four categories.

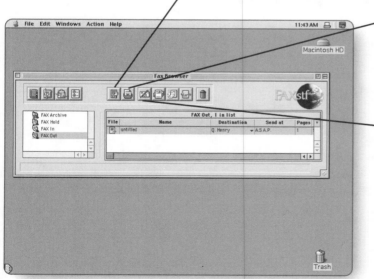

- **Print a fax**. Select the fax you want to print and click on the Print button. You can print faxes in any of the four categories.

- **Edit a fax**. Select the fax whose content you want to change and click on the Edit button. You can edit only outgoing faxes, those in the Hold or Out categories.

• **Cover page**. Select the fax for which you want to create a cover page and click on the Cover Page button. You can edit cover pages only for outgoing faxes.

• **Schedule**. Select the fax you want to schedule and click on the Schedule button. You will be able to set the time at which the fax will be sent. You can schedule only outgoing faxes.

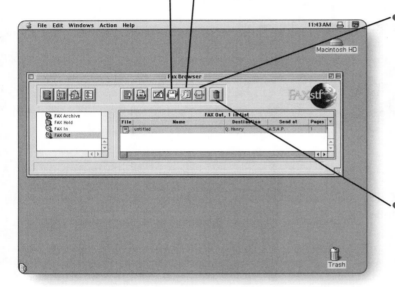

• **Send**. Select the fax you want to send and click on the Send button. The fax software will attempt to send the fax immediately. You can send only faxes that are in the Hold category or those in the Out category that are scheduled to be sent at some time in the future.

• **Delete**. Select the fax you want to delete and click on the Delete button. You can delete faxes from any category.

Part IV Review Questions

1. How do you select a local access number for connecting up with AOL? *See "Finding Local Access Numbers" in Chapter 14.*

2. How do you use hyperlinks to navigate the Web? *See "Following a Hyperlink" in Chapter 15*

3. How do you search for information on the Web? *See "Searching the Entire Web" in Chapter 15*

4. Describe the format of an Internet e-mail address? *See "Understanding E-mail Addresses" in Chapter 16*

5. What are the potential dangers of downloading an e-mail attachment from someone you do not know? *See "Handling Attachments Safely" in Chapter 16*

6. What is a Web site? *See "Understanding How a Web Site Is Organized" in Chapter 17*

7. How do you add a background image to a Web page using PageMill? *See "Adding a Background Image" in Chapter 17*

8. How do you add a hyperlink to a Web page using PageMill? *See "Adding Hyperlinks" in Chapter 17*

9. How do you send a fax from your iMac? *See "Sending a Fax" in Chapter 18*

10. What do you have to do to prepare your iMac to receive a fax? *See "Receiving Faxes" in Chapter 18*

Appendixes

A
Protecting Your iMac

You lock your doors when you leave the house and you may even turn on an alarm system. You probably have placed your iMac so that it can't be seen by someone peering in a window. That kind of security will go a long way to keep thieves from breaking into your home to steal your computer. However, that isn't all you can do to protect your iMac.

There are three other types of danger with which you should be concerned: the failure of your hard disk or other major system component; fluctuations in electrical power that can damage components; and viruses, those malicious programs that can infect a computer and destroy the contents of a hard disk. In this chapter, you'll learn how:

- Understand the importance of making backups of a hard disk and what options you have for making such copies.

- Protect your iMac from electrical problems.

- Handle virus threats.

Backing Up

A *backup* is a copy of your files that you keep somewhere safe in case the primary storage media fails—in particular, your hard disk. Although most hard disks run a long time without any problems, you should never trust that your hard disk is going to perform faultlessly forever. To be effective, you must make backup copies of your files regularly.

NOTE

How often should you backup files? That depends on how often you make changes to important files. If, for example, you are relying on Quicken as your check register—and no longer keep a manual check register—you can't afford to lose even a single entry. In this case, you should make a backup copy every time an entry is made. In contrast, backing up once a week is probably more than enough if you use your iMac primarily to access the Internet and rarely download any files or create documents.

NOTE

What should you back up? The most essential items to back up are the documents you create. If the worst should occur, you can almost always reinstall the operating system and your applications from CDs. Restoring by reinstalling from CD can take longer than restoring from a complete backup. However, backing up only your documents doesn't take as long as a complete backup and requires much less storage space.

Choosing Backup Media

The first thing is to decide what to use for backup media. The iMac doesn't come with any permanent storage other than its hard disk, so an external device is needed. The realistic choices for an iMac include the following:

- **A second hard disk**. Copying files to a second hard disk is fast and easy. The major drawback to this solution is that the size of the disk is fixed so when the backup drive fills up, it can't expand the amount of storage.

- **A Zip disk**. Zip disks are removable disks that hold 100Mb or 250Mb. Assuming that you are only backing up your documents—application programs can always be reinstalled from CD—then this is a good solution, at least initially. The disks cost about $12 and $20, respectively, and you can keep purchasing more disks as the number of files goes up. The drawback to this approach is that there comes a point where even a 250Mb disk is too small to hold a significant proportion of the files. Backup will then take a long time because you are constantly switching disks.

- **A SuperDrive disk**. The SuperDrive can read and write floppy disks (a storage capacity of only 1.44Mb) and SuperDisks (120Mb). Like the Zip disk, the SuperDisk is removable and inexpensive.

- **A tape drive**. The traditional high-capacity backup media for the Macintosh has been tape, in particular, digital audio tape (DAT). Reasonably priced tape drives have capacities from 2Gb to 24Gb. Most come with software that manage the backup process for you. There is one major stumbling block to using a tape drive on an iMac, however. At the time this book was written, there were no USB tape drives. The vast majority of tape drives use the SCSI interface, which was found on older Macintoshes. The solution is to purchase a USB to SCSI converter. The backup works and is very convenient, but it's slow.

- **CD-RW**. A CD-RW drive can read, write, and erase CDs. Each disc can store about 650Mb. Although the discs cannot be reused as many times as the preceding types of magnetic media, if you have a reasonably limited number of files that don't change daily, a CD-RW drive can be a cost-effective backup medium.

What should you do? In most cases, when people have to make a technology decision, doing nothing is a viable alternative. However, where backup is concerned, doing nothing is simply begging for disaster to strike. The Zip drive and SuperDrive's low initial prices and reasonable media costs make them good first choices as backup devices. Consider the second hard drive or tape drive options if the volume of documents grows so large that either of those become inconvenient.

Storing Backup Copies

Where should you keep backup copies? The most secure backup scheme is to keep a current backup copy in a different location from the computer. For example, if your iMac is at home, you would keep a set of backup disks or tapes in a drawer at the office. Barring that, a fireproof safe or filing cabinet is a good choice. If none of those are available, a drawer safe from magnetic interference (except next to the computer) will work.

Providing Power Protection

The voltages that travel over electric lines usually are not constant. Sometimes they are low; sometimes they are high. High voltages arrive suddenly, in spurts known as *surges*. Although low voltage (often known as a *brownout*) can cause a computer to shut down, it rarely causes any permanent damage to the equipment. In contrast, a power surge can severely damage any piece of electronic equipment connected to the power line. Power surges can also jump from electrical lines to telephone lines running next to them through your walls and destroy modems and fax machines. Just as it is foolish never to back up your hard disk, it is foolish not to provide your iMac with some type of protection against power surges.

Using a Surge Protector

The simplest, and least expensive, type of power protection for your iMac is a *surge protector*, a piece of hardware that

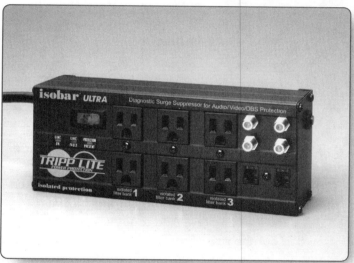

looks a great deal like a powerstrip with plug ins for four or six devices. A surge protector has one function: It isolates equipment plugged into it from power surges.

Surge protectors can cost anywhere from $10 to $50. For the most part, you get what you pay for. At the low end, is a device that will stop a surge— at least once. The surge suppression circuitry in an inexpensive surge protector is likely to be destroyed by the first powerful surge that it handles. And, because the device in all likelihood has no indicators on it to tell you if surge protection is still available, you have no way of knowing that it is no longer functional.

Photo courtesy of Tripp Lite

More expensive surge protectors provide outlets for phone lines as well as electrical equipment. They also have indicators that tell if surge protection is still in effect. In addition, many come with warranties that guarantee that if the surge protector fails and equipment is damaged, you'll be reimbursed up to limits between $25,000 and $50,000. If nothing else, a high-end surge protection provides very inexpensive insurance against power surge damage!

Choosing a Line Conditioner

A *line conditioner* combines a surge protector with brownout protection. It has a capacitor that stores a small bit of electricity. When the voltage drops below a threshold level, power is discharged from the capacitor to ensure that the equipment receives a constant voltage. A line conditioner cannot handle a total power outage, but instead is designed to handle normal power fluctuations.

Photo courtesy of Tripp Lite

Line conditioners come in various sizes, depending on the number of watts they can handle and cost between $80 and $200. To find out what size you need, check the back of each piece of equipment or the specifications in the users guide to find out the maximum wattage the hardware can draw. Add together all the numbers to find out the size of the line conditioner you need. For example, the most recent version of the iMac draws a maximum of 480 watts. Therefore, a 600 watt line conditioner would probably be big enough to handle the computer and an ink-jet printer.

Upgrading to a UPS

An *uninterruptible power supply* (UPS) provides battery backup for a computer in case of a total power outage. Most of today's UPSs also include surge suppression and line conditioning, although it is very important to read the specifications of the device to ensure that you are receiving complete power protection.

Photo courtesy of Tripp Lite

The typical UPS is a *stand-by UPS* that runs the computer off the house current until the voltage drops below what the line conditioning circuitry can handle. At that point, the UPS switches the computer to the backup battery. The switchover is so fast that computer operations are not affected. The alternative is a *full-time UPS*—one where the computer always runs directly off the battery. Such UPSs are more expensive than the stand-by products, but do eliminate any chance of problems from power fluctuations because the battery provides a constant voltage.

A UPS battery is not intended to run a computer for a long period time. It holds just enough charge (usually 5–20 minutes) for you to save files and shut down the computer. The amount of charge depends on the size of the UPS and the amount of power being drawn. UPSs are sized like line conditioners, based on the maximum number of watts they can handle.

In most cases, you plug your computer and monitor (if the monitor is a separate unit) and any external disk drives into a UPS. Other devices—in particular, printers and scanners—are protected by a surge suppressor or line conditioner. You can restart a printing or scanning job without losing anything but time, and those devices require so much more power than a computer or monitor that they would force you to purchase a much larger, and therefore more expensive UPS.

UPSs are relatively more expensive than line conditioners. Although you can purchase a 250 watt UPS for about $80—one that isn't large enough to handle an iMac—the more powerful models, such as a 500 watt unit, cost between $100 and $500. The price depends on the size of the battery, the number of electrical outlets, surge suppression and line conditioning capabilities, and the type of software included, if any. Prices vary for UPSs to handle desktop computer systems but the high end would be around a 3000 watt model for about $1500.

Making the Final Decision

What power protection should you purchase? If the power coming into your home or office is relatively constant and you're willing to take the risk of losing 15 minutes or so of work (assuming that you save work every 15 minutes), a good surge protector will certainly do the trick. However, if your power is not constant, especially if you suffer from frequent outages, you should consider either a line conditioner or a UPS for the iMac and any external disk drives you might purchase. Use a high-end surge suppressor for the rest of your equipment.

Handling the Virus Threat

Computer viruses have been around since people have been trading files between desktop computers. Every time you download a file over the Internet, there is a risk that a virus program has piggy-backed itself onto the legitimate file.

Viruses don't arise by accident. Someone must write the virus program and send it out over the Internet, either attached to an application program or e-mail message. Once a virus infects a computer, it may do something as benign as displaying a dialog box or as destructive as destroying files on the hard disk.

Because of the current predominance of the Windows operating system, the majority of new viruses created today affect Windows machines only and do not threaten a Macintosh. However, some viruses can attack an iMac and if you happen to send an infected file to someone else, the recipient's computer will become infected as well! It's therefore wise to pay attention to what you download and occasionally run virus detection software to scan your disk storage.

Practicing Safe Downloading

As you read in Chapter 16, "Using E-mail," attachments to e-mail and other files for downloading can contain viruses. You can't test for the presence of a virus before downloading a file, but you can minimize the chance of that occurring: Only download files from people or locations that you know. For example, it is fairly safe to download a file from the AOL software libraries because AOL has taken special care to scan all files for viruses and other problems. In addition, the Web sites that have been mentioned throughout this book are relatively safe.

Notice that the phrases *relatively safe* and *fairly safe* appear in the preceding two sentences. It is impossible to be totally immune to a virus threat.

Using Virus Detection Software

Virus detection software is commercial software that can scan a hard disk for the presence of viruses. At the time this book was written, three programs were available for the Macintosh, each costing less than $75: Norton AntiVirus, Virex, and Dr. Solomon's Anti-Virus.

Virus detection software works by scanning each file for the presence of a virus it recognizes. If it finds one, it removes the virus from the infected file. The software can only recognize viruses that it has been programmed to detect. When a new virus is released, the developers of the virus detection software must update the software to handle it. Although updates usually appear quickly on a software manufacturer's Web site, it still can't be fast enough to prevent everyone from being affected by the new virus.

As a result, a never-ending cycle of new viruses follows a software upgrade. In fact, a few developers of virus detection software discontinued their products because they felt that virus detection software was issuing a challenge to virus writers, goading them into writing ever more powerful and hard-to-defeat viruses.

If you do a lot of file downloading, you should purchase virus detection software. Although it's not a perfect defense against viruses, it's the best protection available.

B

Adding Peripherals

The iMac marks a major change from earlier Macintoshes in terms of what hardware is included and what ports are available. The floppy disk drive, the old standby ports for keyboard and mouse (ADB), the serial ports (for modems and printers), and ports for adding hard disks and scanners (SCSI) were eliminated. Instead, a new connection device called Universal Serial Bus (USB) is used for all of these.

The USB has several advantages over the older connections. It has the ability to add many devices to the same computer, and to plug and unplug them at any time with no worry of damaging the computer. The disadvantage is that because it is new technology, the number of devices that can be connected is somewhat limited. Also, USB is not as fast a SCSI, although it can be as fast as serial and ADB ports.

Other connections to the iMac are Ethernet (10/100BaseT); the modem; sound in and out; and, on the early (Bondi-blue) iMacs, an IrDA infrared port and an odd internal connector called the Mezzanine port. There are also two slots to add extra main memory. The iMac wasn't designed with expandability as a primary goal, but there's quite a lot you can do.

Printers

One of the first peripherals you are likely to add is a printer. Printers vary widely in the interface they use, the quality of the output, and the price. In general, the higher the print quality, the more costly the printer. Color always costs more than a black-and-white printer with the same quality.

Network (Ethernet) PostScript Laser Printers

At the high-end of the printer world are laser printers, which use a technique similar to photocopy machines to place an image on paper. Some laser printers can print in black-and-white only; others can print in color. Laser printers provide the best possible output from your iMac.

Price Range: $500–$5,000

Driver: Included with Mac OS 8

Accessories required to use with iMac: Ethernet crossover cable ($25 and up, depending on length) *or* Ethernet cable ($15 and up, depending on length) and Ethernet hub ($50).

Sample manufacturers: QMS, GCC, Hewlett-Packard, Lexmark

USB Printers

The easiest and most cost effective printers to use are those that have a USB interface. You just plug them in, install driver software, and print. The output is excellent and at the high-end of the price range, difficult to distinguish from a low-end laser printer.

Price range: $150–$500

Driver: included, or download from vendor Web site

Accessories required to use with iMac: USB cable ($10)

Sample manufacturers: UMAX, Epson, Hewlett-Packard

NOTE

When you scan a page of text, the text is not editable with a word processor or text editor because a scanner produces a graphic image. If you want to "read" the text and turn it into an editable text document, you need *optical character recognition* (OCR) software.

Scanners

A *scanner* is a device that digitizes printed matter. You can use scanners to load photographs or other documents onto your iMac's hard disk. There are two reasonable choices for an iMac scanner: a USB scanner or a SCSI scanner. The SCSI scanners tend to cost more because they provide higher resolution and require the use of a USB to SCSI adapter.

USB Scanners

Price range: $50–$300

Accessories required to use with iMac: USB cable ($10)

Sample manufacturers: UMAX, Agfa, Microtek

SCSI Scanners

Price range: $150 and up

Accessories required to use with iMac: USB to SCSI adapter ($80), USB cable ($10)

Sample manufacturers: Microtek, UMAX

NOTE

If you plan to use a joystick or gamepad, you'll want to install Game Sprockets from the iMac Install CD that came with your iMac (in the folder CD Extras:iMac Device Drivers:iMac Game Device:), or, even better, download the latest version from Apple's Web site (**http://developer .apple. com/games/ sprockets**).

Input Devices

USB has been welcomed by many Mac users because it makes a wide range of input devices—for example, keyboards, mice, trackballs, trackpads, graphics tablets, and game controllers—available at a price that's lower than that for similar ADB devices. If you don't like the keyboard or mouse that came with your iMac, you can pick up another style for a rather reasonable price. For example, at the time this book was written, a combination extended keyboard and oval mouse were available for around $50. There's even an little sock attachment called the iCatch that covers the iMac mouse to make it oval instead of round ($10).

Data Storage

One of the greatest criticisms of the iMac has been its lack of removable storage, especially the omission of a floppy disk drive. Given that you need some form of external storage for backup, adding a disk drive is something you are likely to do.

Several types of USB drives are available, including hard disks.

Floppy Drives

Floppy drives store 1.44 MB on an inexpensive disk (less than $1 per disk). Working with floppies is inexpensive and the format is compatible with the floppy drives used by most of today's computers. Having a floppy disk drive also makes it possible to install software that is supplied on a floppy disk. However, the limited storage capacity makes a floppy drive unsuitable for much else than the transfer and backup of small files.

Price range: $100–$150
Sample manufacturers: iDrives, VST , Newer Technology

SuperDisk

A SuperDisk drive can read and write 1.44 MB floppy disks as well as its own 120 MB SuperDisks. The major drawback to the SuperDisk is that the 120 MB disks can be read *only* by another SuperDisk. This is *not* a standard format adopted by a large number of vendors. It is therefore great for backup purposes and installing software from floppies, not necessarily for file exchange.

Price: $150
Sample manufacturers: Imation/Panasonic, Winstation

Zip Drives

The Zip drive uses a 100 MB or 250 MB cartridge, but cannot handle 1.44 MB floppy disks. The Zip 100 format has become a de facto industry standard and many computers come equipped with Zip drives. The Zip is therefore well suited for both backup and transferring files. It does not, however, allow you to install software from 1.44 MB floppy disks.

Price range: $150–$200

Sample manufacturers: Iomega, Microtech International

CD-RW Drives

A CD-RW drive allows you to burn your own CDs, as well as reuse CDs that were erased. Most CDs hold about 650 MB and can therefore be used for backup. You can even burn CDs that would allow your iMac to boot from them when they are placed in the internal drive.

Price range: $300–$400

Sample manufacturers: QPS, LaCie, Fantom Drives

Hard Drives

USB hard drives make it easy to expand your hard disk storage. However, they are much slower than the iMac's internal hard drive and therefore may be best suited for backup rather than day-to-day processing.

Price range: $250–$350

Sample manufacturers: LaCie, Fantom Drives

Flash Memory/ SmartMedia Readers

Many of today's digital cameras and held-held computing devices use tiny storage media known as *flash memory* (or simple, flash cards) or *SmartMedia*. The cameras and other devices were designed to connect to a computer's serial port, which of course presents a problem for the iMac. Fortunately, stand-alone USB card readers are now available.

Price range: $50–$100

Sample manufacturers: Kodak, Hewlett-Packard

Audio and Video

There are now USB peripherals that are designed for hobbyist and casual business use.

USB Video Cameras

To have a small video camera for video conferencing, Web video, or still photos for the Web, you can use a USB version that works smoothly with the iMac.

Price range: $80–$130
Sample manufacturers: Logitech, Ariston

USB Video Capture and TV Tuner

Video capture devices grab a single image from a live motion video source such as a VCR or video camera using composite or S-video, audio in and out, a TV tuner, and a TV port.

Price: $150
Sample manufacturer: Focus, Interview, Belkin

Still Cameras

Some digital cameras are beginning to appear with USB ports, eliminating the need for one of the separate storage card readers mentioned earlier in this appendix.

Price range: $400–$1100
Manufacturers: Most all major still camera manufacturers are now in this market.

USB Speakers

The iMac is equipped with stereo speakers, but if you're an audio buff, you'll probably cringe whenever you hear sound coming from them. Fortunately, you can purchase external USB speakers to provide better sound quality.

Price range: $50–$250

Sample manufacturers: Philips, Roland, Jazz

MIDI

MIDI (musical instrument digital interface) provides a means of connecting a MIDI-compatible instrument to a computer so that the computer can either capture what is played on the instrument or play music through the instrument.

Price range: $150–$500

Sample manufacturers: Emagic, Mark of the Unicorn, Midiman, Opcode

Standard Audio Input and Output

As noted earlier, the iMac includes two built-in stereo speakers with Surround Sound technology. It also contains a microphone port, two front headphone jacks, and two minijacks for CD-quality sound input and output. With a couple of minijacks to RCA stereo connectors, you can hook the iMac into a stereo system, Home Theatre system, BoomBox, and so on. Regular computer speakers will also work fine, as will an external Apple Plaintalk microphone, or Griffin's NE microphone.

Hubs

A *hub* is a piece of hardware that distributes signals between hardware devices that use the same type of connection to a computer. Both USB and Ethernet use hubs to connect multiple pieces of equipment.

USB Hubs

Your iMac can have up to 127 USB devices connected at the same time. However, devices must be attached to the iMac itself in some way, either directly or indirectly through a hub that is connected to the iMac. The iMac has two USB ports, and the keyboard is a two-port hub. Therefore, with the keyboard and mouse plugged in, you only have two ports left.

If you want to add more than two additional USB peripherals, you'll therefore need a hub. Also, some devices such as printers and scanners tend to pull quite a bit of power from the USB circuitry, and you'll run into problems getting the hardware to function properly if you don't have a powered hub. Powered hubs usually have small "brick" style power supplies. Hubs typically have 4 or 7 ports.

Price range: $40–$150

Sample manufacturers: Entrega, Micro Connectors

Ethernet Hubs

To connect more than one other device to the iMac by Ethernet, you'll need an Ethernet Hub. A 10BaseT 5- or 8-port hub can be found for under $50, and is probably large enough for a home network. Hubs that allow you to interconnect 10BaseT and 100BaseT devices (the iMac can run at either speed) will cost significantly more. Cables are also needed to go between each device and the hub, which run from $10–$25 dollars depending on length.

Price range: $30–$500

Sample manufacturers: Asanté, Farallon, Cisco, 3Com, Hewlett-Packard, IBM

NOTE

The question that remains is whether the iMac's game sprockets software will recognize all the signals, especially the unusual ones, coming from a device that uses a standard game port.

Port Adapters

Although Apple Computer would like to see everyone using USB peripherals, the truth is that there's a lot of existing hardware that people want to use that cannot be connected via USB. To provide access to these devices, you can purchase a port adapter that converts the USB signals to the signals required by some other type of hardware interface.

USB to ADB

This converter allows you to use Apple Desktop Bus peripherals, such as older Mac keyboards, mice, joysticks, and ADB "dongles" (copy protection devices required for some software to operate). Unless you already have ADB devices that you want to use, you'll probably find cheaper USB devices that do the same thing.

Price: $35

Sample manufacturer: Griffin Technology

USB to Standard Game Port

This adapter allows the use of the 15-pin game port that you might first remember from Atari games, and is still very common on various game systems and PCs. There are hundreds of joysticks, game pads, steering wheels, flight yokes, data gloves, guns, and other toys that will plug into this converter.

Price: $25

Sample Manufacturer: iMaccessories

USB-SCSI

USB to SCSI adapters allows the use of SCSI devices such as SCSI Zip drives, external hard disks, and SCSI scanners with the iMac. However, because the USB data speed is much slower than even the slowest SCSI speed, this isn't a very good solution unless you already have SCSI equipment you need to use.

Price range: $70–$80

Sample manufacturers: Microtech, Newer Technology, Second Wave

USB-serial

USB to serial adapters allow various serial devices to work with the iMac. Adapters have from one to four serial ports, and various versions have different levels of support. Generally they support serial printers for which a driver is available (such as StyleWriters), external modems, and digital cameras with serial connections. None yet available will allow the use of LocalTalk or GeoPort functions. Because not all serial devices are supported, check with the vendor to see if the product you're considering will work for your particular application.

Price range: $65–$85

Sample manufacturers: Momentum, Keyspan, Inside Out Networks, Peracom Networks

USB-parallel

Many printers require a parallel interface. You can use them with an iMac if you purchase a USB to parallel adapter. However, unlike the adapters discussed previously in this section, these adapters are closely tied to specific types of printers.

Epson and HP, for example, each provide a USB to parallel cable to work with their own printers, and include the necessary drivers for those printers. Belkin's product is very similar to Epson's, and includes Epson drivers. InfoWave's PowerPrint includes drivers for hundreds of printers, including many for which no Mac-compatible drivers exist. MacJet's Drivers provide driver software that is similar to those included with PowerPrint—you may need to purchase the drivers with one of the other cables if your printer doesn't have Macintosh drivers available.

Price range: $45–$100

Sample manufacturers: Compucable, Epson, Belkin, InfoWave, Hewlett-Packard, Entrega

C

Choosing a Communications Service Provider

If you're feeling overwhelmed by the number of choices available to you for setting up access to the Internet, you're not alone. The Internet has opened up the complex world of data communications to the average user. The following is a basic primer on the essential equipment you'll need to get connected. You'll also learn what questions to ask in order to make an informed decision on choosing a service provider.

Introducing Data Communications Components

In this chapter, "data communications" refers to anything except video or audio that travels over a network. E-mail and the Web are types of data communications.

There are four major components to a data communications connection:

- **Communications line**. You must have a communications line over which signals will travel. For most users in a private home, this will be a standard telephone line, or POTS (Plain Old Telephone Line). The data communications portion of this book will assume that you are using a POTS line.

- **Hardware**. When you use POTS for your communication line, you need some hardware to translate between signals sent by the computer and the type of signal required by the telephone line. This hardware is called a *modem*. The iMac's modem is *internal*; it is inside the system unit.

- **Software**. The computer must have software that sends data to the modem port and monitors the port for incoming data.

- **Service provider**. The typical POTS communication connection has a single user equipped with a personal computer and modem at one end, and a *service provider* with one or more large computers and many modems at the other end. A service provider that connects to the Internet is known as an *Internet service provider* (an ISP).

NOTE

There are two alternatives to POTS. One is a cable modem, where data signals travel over the same cabling used to deliver cable television service. The second is *Digital Subscriber Line* (DSL), which uses existing phone lines. With DSL, you can have both a voice call and a data communications call active at the same time.

Choosing a Communications Service Provider

There are two basic types of service providers today. ISPs allow connections to the Internet but generally do not provide online content of their own. *Information Services*, such as American Online (AOL), not only provide Internet access, but have their own content that is accessible only to their subscribers.

When choosing an ISP or information service, there are a number of things to consider:

- When your modem dials the service provider's modem, is it a local call or a toll call? If possible, you want to choose a service provider that has a local access point so you don't incur telephone line charges when you are online.

- Does it cost money to join the service? Many service providers offer free service for a short trial period to entice you to purchase their service.

- How much does it cost per month? Most service providers today allow unlimited time online for a flat monthly fee.

- How much time will I spend online? Some ISPs offer lower-cost services if you don't spend too much time online. If you'll be online a great deal, then an unlimited service is the best choice.

- Does the service provider support the Macintosh? Some ISPs provide software and technical support only for computers running Windows.

- Is the company reputable? Many small ISPs have emerged to take advantage of the explosion of Internet use. Some have gone out of business, leaving their customers stranded. It pays to look into the track record of a local ISP.

- How difficult is it to make a connection? A service provider never has as many modems as customers. Therefore, a data communications call may result in a busy signal, no matter who the provider might be. However, you should be able to get through on at least the third or fourth re-dial. If you can't, the service provider may not have enough modems to handle its subscribers.

- Do they have customer support, and can I actually speak to them? Everyone needs technical support once in a while so make sure that your service provider has support personnel available for you to speak with.

D

Adding Software

The iMac's hard disk is preloaded with a number of programs, but others can be found in the wallet of CDs that should have been included in the Accessories box of your iMac's packaging. To use them, these programs must be manually installed.

CDs are the most common method of distributing software today. To obtain free updates, visit the Web sites of software companies. In this chapter, you'll learn how to:

- Install software from a CD
- Find and download software updates via the Web

Installing a Program from a CD

For reasonably-sized programs, such as Adobe PageMill, the installer program copies all the software you need onto your hard disk. Other programs, such as the World Book Encyclopedia, install only the portion of the software package needed to access data on your hard disk. The actual encyclopedia data remain on one or more CDs because of the enormous amount of space the data would take up if loaded fully onto your hard disk. Consequently, you must have the CD in the CD-ROM drive to access and view all parts of the software.

1. **Insert** the **CD** in your iMac's CD-ROM drive. After a few seconds, the CD's icon will appear on the desktop.

NOTE

Some installations require that no other program be running except the installer. It is therefore wise to save all files and quit all programs before installing additional software.

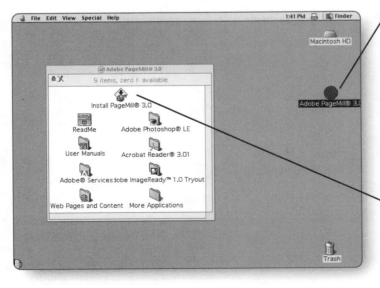

2. **Double-click** on the **CD icon**. A folder will open to display the top level of the CD's file and folder hierarchy. Generally, one of the most prominent items will be the installer program for the software, and will have the word "Install" in the file name.

3. **Double-click** on the **installer icon**. A splash screen will appear, identifying the software that you are installing.

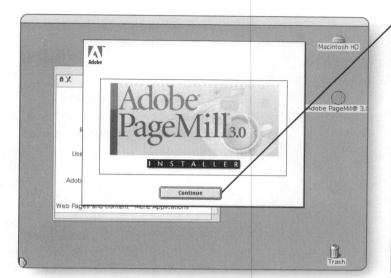

4. Click on **Continue**. The next window or windows that appear will deal with the software license.

NOTE

Exactly what software license windows appear will vary somewhat from one installer to another. What appears in this chapter is a typical example.

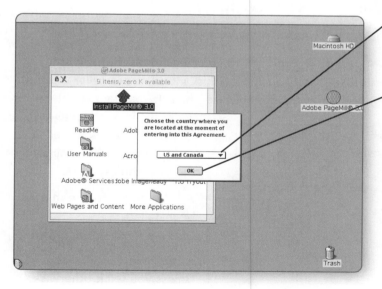

5. Choose your **country** from the pop-up menu if you're not located in the U.S. or Canada.

6. Click on **OK**. The license agreement window will appear.

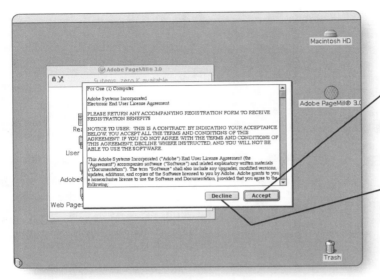

7. Read the **license agreement** to make sure the terms are acceptable.

8a. Click on **Accept** if you agree to the license agreement. The Installer window will appear.

OR

8b. Click on **Decline** if you do not agree to the license agreement. The installer program will quit and you will return to the Finder.

The Installer Window

The typical installer window includes the following:

• A pop-up window where you can choose the type of installation. If you choose Easy Install, the installer will give you the most commonly used files. If you want to select your own files, choose a Custom Install. However, in most cases the Easy Install is the best choice.

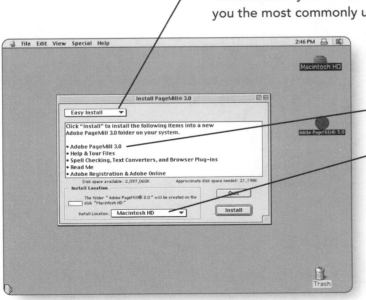

• A list of the software that will be installed.

• The location where the software will be installed. Unless you tell it otherwise, an installer will place the new software in a folder on the top level of your hard disk. (If you have more than one hard disk, it will use the one that contains the System Folder.)

Assuming that you are going to use the Easy Install, the first step in software installation is to choose the location for the software:

1. Choose Select Folder from the pop-up menu in the Install Location: list box at the bottom of the installer window. An Open File dialog box will appear.

2. Find the **folder** in which you want to install the new software. In most cases, it will be the Applications folder.

3. Click on the **folder name** in the dialog box to select it. The folder name will be highlighted.

4. Click on **Select** to choose the folder. The Open File dialog box will close and you will return to the installer window.

5. Click on **Install** to start the installation process.

A dialog box appears with a progress bar to show how the installation is progressing.

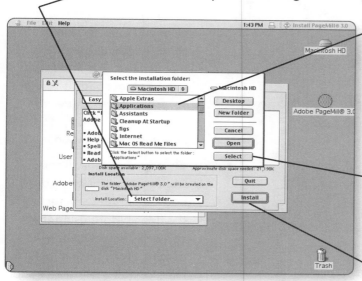

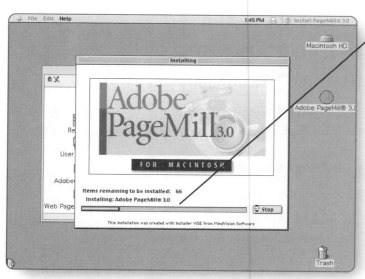

Finishing the Installation

The final step in installation may be one or more of the following, depending on how the installer was programmed:

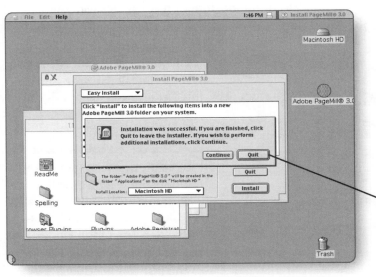

- **Registration**. Many installers allow you to register your software automatically. You fill in your information in a series of dialog boxes and the installer dials a toll-free number that sends it to the software manufacturer. Or, you can decline to do to the automatic registration.

- **Quit or Continue**. If the software you just installed does not require that you restart the iMac before using the software, you can choose to continue with further installations or quit the installer and return to the Finder.

TIP

A CD can hold a lot of data (about 640 MB). Often CDs will have demonstration versions of other programs, extra libraries of files that will work with the program, or extra documentation. It's therefore a good idea to poke around on the CD!

Downloading and Installing from the Web

There is a great deal of excellent Macintosh software available on the Web. Some good and reasonably safe sources are:

- Apple Computer (**www.apple.com/**)

- Download.com (**www.download.com/**)

- The InfoMac archive (**hyperarchive.lcs.mit.edu/HyperArchive.html**)

CAUTION

Be careful where you download software—from the Internet or even from friends and coworkers—because computer viruses may be riding along. Refer to Appendix A, "Protecting your iMac" for more on viruses. Some reputable download sites will tell you if the file has been scanned for viruses already.

Checking the Apple iMac Web Pages

The Apple Computer iMac Web pages are a great source of iMac information and software updates. To return to the site quickly, add a bookmark to your Web browser.

To visit the iMac Web pages:

1. Connect to the **Internet** if necessary. If you're using AOL as your ISP, you *must* connect to AOL before you launch a Web browser or you can use AOL's browser.

2. Launch a **Web browser**.

3. Type www.apple.com/support in the text box that holds the URL of a location you want to visit.

4. Press Enter. The Apple Support page will display.

5. Choose iMac Support from the **menu** under the **iMacs**. The iMac support page will appear.

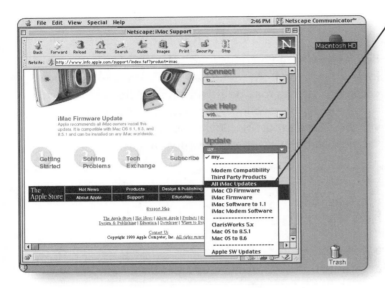

6. Choose All iMac Updates from the menu under **Updates**. A page will appear that includes a table showing the recommended updates for specific iMacs, based on when the iMac was manufactured.

7. Make a **note** of which updates apply to your iMac.

8. Click on the **Back button** to return to the iMac support page.

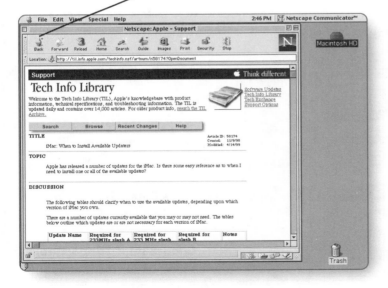

Downloading an Update File

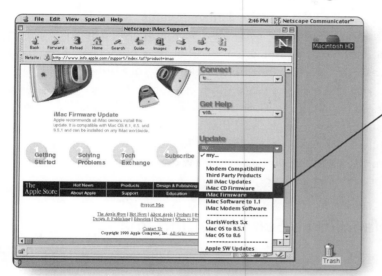

Once you have found an update file on a Web page, download that file to your iMac's hard disk. To download the file:

1. Choose an **update** recommended for your iMac from the Updates pop-up menu. A Web page will appear that explains what the update will do, how to download the update file, and how to install the update.

2. Click on the **hyperlink** for the MacBinary download. As soon as you click on the link, the download will begin or a Save dialog box will open asking you where you would like to save the file. If so, find a location and click save.

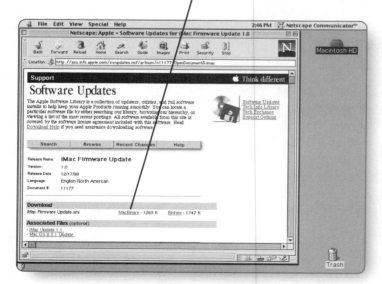

TIP

MacBinary (a program in compressed form) usually provides the smallest file for downloading and is usually a better choice than BinHex (a program translated into text characters).

3. Quit the **Web Browser** when the download is complete.

4. Sign Off from the **Internet** if necessary.

Installing an Update

The result of the download of an update is a new icon on your Desktop. The icon may be for a Stuffit archive, a *self-mounting disk image*, or some other type of archive. If the file is a Stuffit archive, then in all likelihood, your browser will extract the files and place them in a folder. (If there is only a single file, Stuffit will not put it in a folder.) If Zipit is available, your browser can also use that to extract files from a Zip archive. However, if you've downloaded a self-mounting image, you must go through a few extra steps to get to the update's installer program.

Handling a Self-Mounting Image

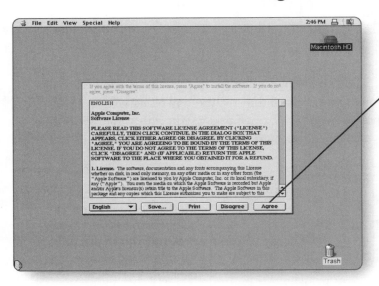

1. Double-click on the **icon** of the downloaded file. A license agreement will appear.

2. Click on **Agree**. The license agreement dialog box will disappear and a new icon in the shape of a floppy disk will appear on the Desktop.

The new floppy disk icon is a virtual floppy disk. If you double-click on its icon, a window will open, to show the contents of the disk, including an installer file.

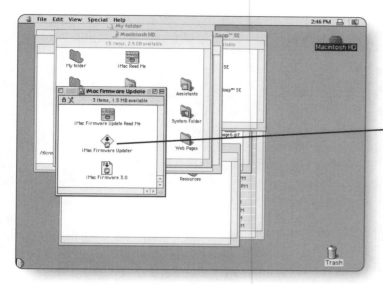

Performing the Install

1. Open the **installation folder**, if necessary, to find the installer file.

2. Double-click on the **installer or updater file**. The installer or updater will launch. In most cases, an update installs itself without any user intervention needed. When the update is completed, an alert will appear.

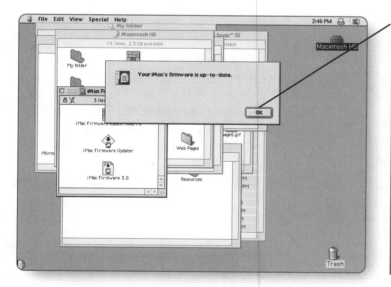

3. Click on **OK** to remove the alert.

TIP

You may want to download all the recommended update files before installing any of them because system software updates almost always require you to restart the machine for the updates to take effect.

Glossary

A

Active window. The window with which the user is currently working. Only one window can be active at a time, although an unlimited number of windows can be open.

ADB. Apple Desktop Bus. A peripheral bus that allows the use of multiple input devices such as mice, keyboards, trackballs, and so forth, used on Macintosh computers from the Mac SE until the introduction of the iMac. ADB is slower than USB and does not allow hot swapping of peripherals.

Alert. A window that appears to notify the user of some condition that must be handled right away. No further work can proceed until the alert is removed from the screen.

Alias. An icon that stands in for another file. Double-clicking on an alias will open the file or application that the alias represents rather than the alias itself.

Analog signal. A smooth, continuous waveform signal. *Contrast with* digital signal.

AOL. America Online, the largest Internet Service Provider and on-line service.

ARA. Apple Remote Access. The ARA control panel controls remote connections via dialup (or any connection that is intermittent in nature).

AppleWorks. Formerly ClarisWorks, an application that includes word processing, spreadsheet, data management, paint, draw, and communications capabilities.

Application. A file that contains application software.

Application software. Software that performs useful work for a user.

Archive. One or more files compressed together into a single file.

Arrow key. A key on the iMac keyboard with an up, down, right, or left arrow on it that moves the insertion point in a text document.

ATA. Advanced Technology Attachment. *See* IDE.

ATAPI. An extension of the IDE interface description to allow the use of CD-ROM players and tape drives.

Attachment. A file sent along with an e-mail message.

B

Background application. In a multitasking operating system, an application that is running but with which the user is not currently working.

Background printing. Printing that occurs while the user is working with another program.

Backup. A copy of files stored on a disk that is saved in case the original is damaged.

Beep sound. The sound made by the iMac's speaker when an alert appears on the screen.

Bit-mapped graphics. *See* Paint program.

Bookmark. Save the URL of a Web site so a browser can return to it quickly.

Boot. Start up a computer.

Brownout. A dip in electrical voltage that is not necessarily enough to shut down a computer.

Button. An area in a window that triggers some program action when clicked with the mouse pointer.

Byte. The basic unit of computer storage, large enough to hold one character.

C

Carrier tone. A sound of a constant frequency sent out by a modem that is modulated to carry a digital signal.

Cascading delete. The deleting of everything within a folder, including all other nested folders, when that folder is deleted.

CD-ROM. Compact Disc Read-Only Memory. An optical storage medium that uses a laser to read the contents of the disc. Standard CD-ROMs can be read from but not written to.

Central processing unit (CPU). Often known as the "brains of the computer," a CPU can perform mathematical computations and make decisions based on whether something is true or false, greater or smaller, and so on. *See* system unit.

Check box. A square that can be empty or checked to select or deselect a program option.

Click. A single press and release of the left mouse button, usually after positioning the pointer over a particular location.

Clip art. Royalty-free artwork that can be reproduced with obtaining permission from the artist.

Clipboard. An area of computer memory where information is held temporarily. Each new item saved or cut to the Clipboard replaces whatever was there before. Items can be retrieved from the Clipboard and placed elsewhere, even in an application different from the one in which it was created.

Close box. A square at the far left edge of a window's title bar on which a user clicks to close the window.

Command ⌘ key. A modifier key on the iMac keyboard that, when paired with a letter or number key, can be used as a substitute for making a menu selection.

Contextual menu. A pop-up menu that appears on the Desktop or in a program when the control key and mouse button are pressed together.

Control key. A modifier key on the iMac keyboard.

Control panel. A small program that provides configuration for the Mac OS and other software. Control panels are stored in the Control Panels folder in the System Folder and accessible through the Control Panels submenu of the Apple menu.

Control Strip. The Control Strip is a floating pallet of tiles that represent controls for volume, screen resolution, and other commonly used system settings.

Control Strip module. A single tile in the Control Strip.

Cooperative multitasking. A type of multitasking in which the operating system and application programs cooperate to determine which program has access to the CPU at any given time.

Copy. Copy the selected portion of a document to the iMac's Clipboard.

Cover page. A page that is sent at the beginning of a fax to let the recipient know who sent the fax.

CPU. Central Processing Unit. The "brains of the computer," where data are actually processed. A CPU can perform arithmetic computations and make decisions based on whether something is true or false, greater or smaller, and so on.

Cross-platform. A program or file that can be used on more than one type of computer.

Current folder. The last folder accessed by an application.

Cut. Remove the selected portion of a document and places it on the iMac's Clipboard.

Cycle. One tick of the CPU's internal clock.

D

Data communications. Using computers to exchange information.

Data management. Software that stores, organizes, and retrieves data.

Database management. A type of data management.

Default. A value or choice that software assumes a user will want to make. The most commonly chosen option from a group of options.

Default button. A button with a heavy border than can be selected by pressing the Enter key.

Demodulate. Remove the carrier tone from an analog signal to retrieve the digital signal that has been imposed on it.

Desktop. The Mac OS interface to the user, which resembles a physical desktop.

Dialog box. A window that is used to collect information necessary to perform a specific task from the user.

Digital signal. A signal made up of discrete elements such as 0s and 1s.

Digitize. Transform a paper, film, or audio image into a pattern of 0s and 1s that can be stored and manipulated on a computer.

Directory. A folder.

Document. The work that a user prepares on a computer, such as a letter or an illustration.

Document file. A file that contains the contents of a document.

Document window. Displays the contents of a document regardless of whether it is text or graphics.

Double-click. Two quick presses of the mouse button, occurring close together.

Download. Transfer a file from a remote computer to the user's computer over data communications lines.

Drag. Pull something from one location to another across the computer screen by holding down the mouse button while moving the mouse pointer.

Drag and drop. A technique in which one file is dragged and dropped (the mouse is released) on top of another.

Drawing program. A graphics program in which images are created from shapes that retain their identify as shapes.

DSL. Digital Subscriber Line. An emerging digital service where data communications signals travel on the same wires as voice telephone signals.

E

EarthLink. EarthLink/Sprint is a leading American Internet Service Provider whose software is included in the iMac package.

E-mail. Electronic mail. Message exchanges over data communications lines.

Escape (Esc) key. A key that allows the user to escape from some action when working with a program.

Ethernet. A type of networking provided with the iMac, typically used as part of a local area network. The iMac includes an Ethernet port that can use 10Base-T or 100Base-T Ethernet transmission.

Extension. A small program that adds functions to the Mac OS and is loaded into main memory when the iMac boots.

Extension conflict. A software problem that occurs when two or more extensions are incompatible with one another.

F

File. A named, self-contained element on a computer usually containing a program or document and stored permanently on a disk.

File management. A type of data management.

File name extension. Characters following the name of a file that indicate the type of file, used primarily for cross-platform files.

Find and replace. A feature of a word processor that allows the user to search for words in a document and, if desired, automatically replace them with alternate text.

Finder. The operating system program that manages the Mac OS Desktop.

Floating window. A window that appears on top of all other windows, even if it is not the active window.

Folder. A container on a disk that can hold files and other folders.

Finder window. Displays all the files and folders stored within a folder or disk icon.

Font. A design for type.

Foreground application. In a multitasking operating system, the application with which the user is currently working.

Form. A Web page that contains elements that collect information from the user.

Forward. Send an entire e-mail message that a user has received to another recipient.

Freeware. Free software.

FTP. File Transfer Protocol. An Internet protocol for transferring files between two computers.

Full-time UPS. A UPS that always runs equipment off its internal battery, totally isolating connected equipment from house current.

Function key. One of keys at the top of the iMac keyboard numbers F1 through F12 that is used as a substitute for a menu selection.

G

Gigabyte (GB). Approximately one billion bytes.

H

Handle. A square that appears in the corner or on the side of a graphics object. Dragging the handle resizes the object.

Hard copy. A paper copy of a computer document.

Hard disk. Permanent, high-capacity storage for programs and data. A hard disk retains its contents even after a computer is turned off.

Hardware. Computer equipment.

Home page. The first page that a user sees in a Web site.

Horizontal scroll bar. A scroll bar along the bottom of a window that moves the view of a document from right to left.

Host Address. A host address is a hierarchical naming system that uses names separated by periods, going from specific to general. Host names are associated with a particular IP address through the Domain Name Service.

Hot key. A key or combination of keys that initiates some action, such as hiding and showing the Control Strip.

Hot swapping. The ability to change out hardware components without shutting down the computer.

HTML. HyperText Markup Language. The basic language in which Web pages are coded. HTML is plain text, with tags offset by a set of brackets (< and >), that affect how the page will look. Files that contain HTML have names that normally end in .html or .htm.

HTTP. HyperText Transfer Protocol. An Internet protocol that is the basic method for transferring the content of Web pages across the Internet.

Hyperlink. A portion of a document that, when clicked, transfers the user to either another portion of the same document or to another document.

I

I-beam (or I-bar). A mouse pointer that looks like an I.

Icon. A small picture on a computer screen that represents some element in the computer's environment.

IDE. Integrated Drive Electronics. The name for the interface to certain hard disk drives, such as the one in the iMac. Also known as ATA.

Import. Copy the contents of one document into another.

Inactive window. A window that is open on the screen but not active.

INIT conflict. An old term for an extension conflict.

Input device. Hardware that takes data from the outside world and translates it into a form that a computer can store.

Insertion point. The place in a document where the next characters typed will appear, marked by a flashing straight line.

Integrated package. A program made up of tightly connected application modules.

Information service. A service provider that includes its own content that is accessible to subscribers.

IP. Internet Protocol. This is one of several protocols which allow communication on the Internet.

IP Address. An IP address is a set of four numbers between 0 and 255, separated by periods, such as 128.158.1.72. IP addresses are assigned from a central source.

IrDA. Infrared Data Association. IrDA is a standard created by the Infrared Data Association for communication between computing devices using infrared signals. IrDA compatible ports may be found in desktop and laptop computers, Personal Digital Assistants, some digital cameras, printers, and even some telephones.

ISP. Internet Service Provider. An organization that provides a connection for a computer to the Internet. The most typical way for the home user to connect is to dial into one of the ISP's modems from a modem. The ISP's modem then routes the transmission to the Internet.

K

Keyboard. A common input device on which a user types text.

Killer app. A program that performs some work never before done by a computer and therefore causes a significant change in an industry.

Kilobyte (K or KB). 1,024 bytes.

L

LAN. Local Area Network. A computer network that covers a small area (less than a mile radius, generally, and possibly as small as two machines sitting side by side) for relatively high speed communications.

Landscape orientation. Page orientation in which the page is wider than it is tall.

Launch. Start a program running.

Line conditioner. A piece of equipment intended to stop power surges and increase line voltages during brownouts.

M

Main memory. Temporary storage for programs and data while the computer is processing them. The contents of main memory are lost when power is removed from the computer.

Megabyte (MB). Approximately one million bytes.

Menu. A list of program options and actions from which a user can choose.

Menu bar. The strip at the top of the screen that contains the names of available menus.

Metasearch engine. A search engine that searches a collection of other search engines.

MHz. Megahertz. One million cycles per second. The unit used to measure the speed of a CPU.

MIDI. Musical Instrument Digital Interface. MIDI is the standard for computers to communicate with musical instruments.

Modal. A property of a window such that no other actions can take place in the program until the window is closed.

Modem. A hardware device that translates a computer's digital signals into analog signals that can travel over standard telephone lines.

Modifier key. A key on the iMac keyboard that, when pressed in combination with another key, changes the original meaning of the other key.

Modulate. Raise and lower the frequency of a carrier tone to impose the pattern of a digital signal on it.

Monitor. A screen for viewing the output of a computer. The iMac's monitor is built into its system unit.

Motherboard. A computer's main circuit board.

Mounted. A property of a volume where it is recognized by the Mac OS and an icon for the volume appears on the Desktop so the user can access its contents. *See also* Unmount.

Mouse. An input device that, when moved, causes a pointer on the computer screen to move.

Mouse pointer. The small pointer on the screen that moves proportionally to the movement of a mouse, track ball, trackpad, or other computer pointing device.

Multitasking. A feature of an operating system where more than one program can be running at the same time.

N

Navigation key. A key on the iMac keyboard that scrolls one page up in a document, one page down in a document, or to the beginning of the document.

Network server. A computer on a local area network or Intranet that provides shared files.

Nonmodal. A property of a window such that other actions can take place in the program while the window is open.

Non-printing character. A character that can be generated by pressing keys on the iMac keyboard but for which there is no visible symbol.

O

Object graphics. *See* Drawing program.

OCR. Optical character recognition. The process of recognizing graphics characters and translating them into editable text.

Offline. Not connected to a service provider.

Online. Connected to a service provider.

Operating system. A collection of programs that manage a computer.

Option key. A modifier key on the iMac keyboard.

Output device. A piece of hardware that takes data stored in the computer and translates into a form that a human user can understand.

P

Page. The amount of a document that will scroll each time the mouse pointer is clicked in a vertical scroll bar.

Paint program. A graphics program in which the image is made up of a pattern of very small dots.

Partition. A portion of a large hard disk that can be mounted as a separate volume.

Paste. Insert the contents of the iMac's Clipboard into the active window at the insertion point.

Path name. The path from the top of a disk directory hierarchy down to the location of a specific file.

PDF. Portable Document Format. A format, developed by Adobe Corp., that preserves the layout of a document and that can be read on any computer for which a version of Adobe Acrobat Reader exists.

Pixel. A picture element. One dot on a computer screen.

Point. The unit of measurement for the height of type. There are 72 points to the inch.

Pop-up menu. A menu whose name is one of the options in the menu and whose options appear when the mouse pointer is held down over the viewable option. Pop-up menus are typically found in dialog boxes.

Port. A connector into which external equipment is plugged. Each port is designed to work with a specific type of connection, such as USB, Ethernet, or standard telephone line.

Portrait orientation. Page orientation that is taller than it is wide.

PostScript. A computer language developed by Adobe Corp. that describes the layout of a printed page.

PostScript font. Type that is described by the outline of its characters and designed specifically for printing on a printer that uses PostScript. PostScript fonts require separate screen fonts.

POTS. Plain Old Telephone Service. Standard analog telephone service.

Power surge. A sudden increase in electrical voltage in the power entering a piece of electrical equipment.

Preferences file. A file stored in the Preferences folder in the System Folder that contains configuration options for a program.

Print file. A file in which a print job is stored.

Print job. A unit of work sent to the printer to be printed, usually made up of one document or a part of a document.

Print queue. The list of jobs waiting to be printed.

Printer. An output device that takes a document stored on a computer and copies that document to paper.

Printer driver. Software that acts as an interface between an application and a printer.

Q

Quoting. Include a portion of an e-mail message in a reply to that message.

R

Radio button. A circle that when clicked on makes a choice from a group of options (a black dot appears in its center when selected.) Radio buttons are frequently used in dialog boxes and only one radio button in a set can be selected at a time.

RAM. Random-access memory. Temporary storage for programs and data while the computer is processing them. The contents of main memory are lost when power is removed from the computer.

Replace all. A feature of a word processor where a user can replace all occurrence of words with specific replacement text.

Resolution. The amount of detail on a computer screen. The higher the resolution—the more pixels per inch—the more detailed the images.

Rollup box (Windowshade). A square at the far right of a window's title bar that causes the window to collapse to nothing but the title bar when clicked. Clicking the rollup box a second time returns the window to its original size.

ROM. Read-only memory. Permanent storage inside the system unit that contains programs that start up the computer.

S

Scroll. Move the contents of a long document so that a new part of the document is brought into view on the screen.

Scroll bar. The right side or bottom of a window that provides control over scrolling.

Scroll box. A square inside a scroll bar that can be dragged to provide large movements through a document.

SCSI. Small Computer System Interface. SCSI is a standard for communication between a computer and its peripheral devices.

Search engine. A Web site that searches the Internet based on a search term supplied by the user.

Select. Choose something for software to act upon.

Self-mounting image (SMI). A method of storing the entire contents of a floppy disk in a file on a larger disk. A disk image isn't just the contents of the floppy, but every bit of information on the floppy in the same order. When the image launches, an application program in the image fools the operating system into thinking the original floppy disk has been inserted into a "virtual" floppy drive, so that the disk contents appear on your desktop.

Service provider. An organization that provides data communications services to subscribers.

Set. A group of extensions that the Extensions Manager can enable and disable as a unit.

Shareware. Software that can be copied and used for a trial period. At the end of the trial period, payment should be made if the user intends to continue to use it.

Shift-click. Click the mouse button while holding down the Shift key on the iMac's keyboard.

SimpleText. A text editor that comes with the Mac OS.

Software. Computer programs.

Spam. Unwanted and unsolicited e-mail.

Splash screen. The initial screen a program puts up when it launches, usually a graphic showing what program it is and who made it.

Spool. Save a print job in a disk file.

Spreadsheet. The electronic equivalent of an accountant's journal. Spreadsheets manage numeric data, such as analyzing a budget. Most spreadsheet software can also draw graphs from stored data.

Spring-loaded folder. A folder that springs open when the user drags and holds an item over the folder.

Standard document window. A window with a title bar, zoom box, close box, rollup box, scroll bars, and size box.

Stand-by UPS. A UPS that runs equipment off house current until a power failure occurs, and then switches immediately to its internal battery.

Submenu. A menu whose name is an option in another menu. The submenu's options appear when the user drags the mouse pointer over the submenu's name in its parent window.

Surge. *See* Power surge.

Surge protector. A device that is intended to stop power surges before they reach electrical equipment.

System beep. The sound that is played when an alert appears on the screen.

System extensions *See* Extensions.

System software. Software that performs management tasks for the computer.

System unit. The case in which the major components of a computer are installed.

T

Terabyte. Approximately one trillion bytes.

Theme. A collection of settings for the look of the Mac OS Desktop.

Thumb. *See* Scroll box.

Thumbnail. A small image showing the contents of a graphics file.

Title bar. The strip across the top of a window that contains the window's name.

Toggle. A switch that is turned on by an action and turned off by repeating the same action.

Trash can. An icon on the Desktop into which the user drags icons for files and folders to be deleted.

Triple-click. Three quick sequential clicks of the left mouse button.

TrueType. A type of font in which characters are described by their outlines. TrueType fonts appear smoothly in any size on the screen and provide good printed output.

Typeface. A design for type.

U

Unmount. Remove a volume from the Desktop. If the volume is stored on removable storage, unmounting it will also eject it from the drive.

UPS. Uninterruptable power supply. A device that provides surge protection, line conditioning, and a backup battery in case of total power failure.

URL. Uniform Resource Locator. The standard format for identifying the location of information on the Internet.

USB. Universal Serial Bus. A peripheral bus that allows plug-and-play integration of many medium speed peripherals at the same time. The iMac has two USB ports, a USB keyboard with two more ports, and a USB mouse.

V

Vertical scroll bar. A scroll bar along the right side of a window that moves the view of a document up and down.

Virus. A malicious program that causes damage to the computer, often by erasing all or part of the hard drive.

Volatile. A property of main memory (RAM) where its contents are lost when electricity is removed.

Volume. A disk or portion of a disk that the Mac OS can mount on the Desktop.

W

Web page. A single HTML document that is part of a Web site.

Web server. A computer on which a Web site resides. Software that transfers HTML pages over the Internet.

Web site. A collection of related HTML documents presented over the Web.

Window. A container on the screen that allows the user to view something.

Windowshade. *See* Rollup box.

Word processor. A program for entering, editing, and formatting text. Many of today's word processors also can handle graphics.

Word wrap. A feature of word processors where a word that will not fit on a line is moved in its entirety down to the line below.

Z

Zoom box. A box in the top, right-hand corner of most Macintosh windows that looks like a box in a box. Clicking the zoom box once will make the window expand to fit the screen or as large as necessary to show all the window's content, whichever is smaller. Clicking the zoom box a second time returns the window to its original size.

Index